D0984692

18th & 19th CENTURY WORKS

THOEMMES

Printed in Great Britain by
Antony Rowe Ltd, Chippenham, Wiltshire

EXPLORATIO PHILOSOPHICA

Rough Notes on Modern Intellectual Science

Volume II

John Grote

THOEMMES PRESS

© Thoemmes Press 1993

Published in 1993 by
Thoemmes Press
85 Park Street
Bristol BS1 5PJ
England

2 Volumes : ISBN 1 85506 193 7

This is a reprint of the 1865 Edition

Publisher's Note

These reprints are taken from original copies of each book.
In many cases the condition of those originals is not perfect,
pages having suffered from such things as inconsistent printing pressures resulting in faint text, show-through from one
side of a leaf to the other, the filling in of some characters,
unstable, often handmade, paper and the break up of type.
The publisher has gone to great lengths to ensure the quality
of these reprints but points out that certain characteristics of
the original copies will, of necessity, be apparent in reprints
thereof.

EXPLORATIO PHILOSOPHICA

PART II

Grote

EXPLORATIO PHILOSOPHICA

PART II

BY

JOHN GROTE, B.D.

SENIOR FELLOW OF TRINITY COLLEGE
AND PROFESSOR OF MORAL PHILOSOPHY IN THE UNIVERSITY OF CAMBRIDGE

EDITED FOR THE SYNDICS OF THE PRESS

BY

JOSEPH BICKERSTETH MAYOR, M.A.

HON. FELLOW OF ST JOHN'S COLLEGE, CAMBRIDGE
HON. LITT.D. OF DUBLIN UNIVERSITY

CAMBRIDGE
AT THE UNIVERSITY PRESS
MDCCCC

Cambridge:

PRINTED BY J. AND C. F. CLAY,
AT THE UNIVERSITY PRESS.

PREFACE BY THE EDITOR.

THE First Part of the *Exploratio* appeared in 1865. In p. xxx of his Introduction the Author expresses a hope that the Second Part might be completed in a month or two. He mentions, as to be there discussed, the views of Prof. Bain, Mr Herbert Spencer (pp. 54, 70), J. D. Morell (p. xxi), Sir W. Hamilton (p. 87), and J. S. Mill (p. 166), with special reference to his *Examination of Sir W. Hamilton's Philosophy.* He also speaks of dealing more at length with the Theory of Vision (p. 40); and concludes the book (p. 258) as follows: "The next chapter (or one soon to follow) will have reference principally to Mr Mill. In the other chapters I shall follow out the scheme indicated in the Introduction and discuss the remaining works there mentioned. I may add some others to them, and I hope to finish by putting the views here given in a clearer manner than I have been able to do in the course of the 'exploration,' in consequence of the additional hold upon them which, I trust, this may have given."

Unhappily, the Second Part was still unfinished at the time of the Author's death in August 1866, the 54th year of his age. He left to his literary executor a great mass of MSS. to be published or otherwise, as, and how, he might think fit. In the exercise of the discretion thus allowed to me, I brought out the *Examination of the Utilitarian Philosophy* in 1870, explaining in the Preface my reasons for beginning with this

rather than with the Second Part of the *Exploratio*. The
reasons there stated are (1) the very unfinished condition of
the latter, (2) the fact that the Author attached more importance to his ethical than to his metaphysical writings, (3) the
probability that a larger number of readers would be found for
the easier and more popular subject.

The *Examination of the Utilitarian Philosophy* was followed
in 1876 by the *Moral Ideals*, to which allusion is made in the
Exploratio, p. vii, in the words, " I determined to put together
in an uncontroversial form what seemed to me to be the truth,
in opposition to what I thought error."

Besides these treatises the following papers were published
from time to time in the periodicals named below :

An article on Materialism (printed as chapters I and II of
Book III in the present volume). *Macmillan's Magazine*, 1867.

On a Future State. *Contemporary Review*, 1871.

Thought versus Learning. *Good Words*, Dec., 1871.

Memoir of Leslie Ellis. *Cont. Rev.*, June, 1872.

Papers on Glossology. *Journal of Philology*, 1872 and
1874.

Montaigne and Pascal. *Cont. Rev.*, July, 1877.

Imaginary Conversation between Mr Grote and Socrates.
Classical Rev., March, 1889.

A small selection of Sermons was also published in 1872 by
Messrs Deighton.

The very limited circulation attained by the three philosophical treatises gave little encouragement to publishing anything
more of the same character; but every now and then I received
letters asking what was being done about the continuation
of the *Exploratio*; and early in 1898 Mr H. W. B. Joseph,
Fellow of New College, Oxford, who had already written to me
on the subject some three years before, made another appeal,
stating that it was felt by many in Oxford that the publication
of the Second Part of the *Exploratio* would be of service to the

cause of philosophy in England, and asking whether it would be possible for the MS. to be deposited for a time in one of the Oxford libraries, with a view to its being consulted by persons approved by the Librarian. I felt that I had no right to resist an appeal of this kind, which, coming, as it did, from members of the sister University after a lapse of 35 years, I believe to be almost unprecedented in the annals of philosophy, and in answer promised Mr Joseph that, if he could let me have a list of those who felt with him in the matter, I would forward it to the Syndics of the Cambridge University Press, offering to prepare the MS. for the Press if they would make a grant towards the expense of printing. The result was (1) a letter to me signed by twenty-three Oxford Graduates, almost all of them Fellows or ex-Fellows of Colleges, in which they expressed their desire that the book might be published, and (2) a most generous offer on the part of the Cambridge Press to defray the whole cost of publication.

I proceed now to give a short account of the papers which form the material of the present volume. In the first instance I had to deal with those which were evidently intended to be included in the 'rough notes' entitled *Exploratio Philosophica*. These make up some twenty parcels, with nothing to mark their intended order, and most of them without any title or heading. After repeated perusal I was able to some extent to make out the order in which the several parcels were written, and marked them accordingly with the letters of the Greek Alphabet; though it seemed desirable in some cases to adopt a different order for the final arrangement in chapters. Thus the 1st parcel, containing 65 pages, numbered 210 to 274 (amounting to about half the same number of the printed pages), seemed like a rough draft of what had already appeared in *Exploratio, Part I*: pp. 275—315 were missing, having probably been used as copy for the same: then came pp. 316—342, marked by me (*a*), which form a kind of introduction to two parcels, marked

by me (β) and (γ). These three parcels correspond to Chapters
I, IX, X of the present volume. The parcel marked (δ), which
contains 40 pages on the Psychology of Locke, Stewart, &c., and
parcel (ε), containing 10 pages on Stewart's account of Perception, were used for Ch. II.   Parcel marked (ζ), which is headed
'À propos of Cousin's Lectures on Locke, &c.,' contained 18
pages, and constitutes the present Ch. III.   Parcel (η) contains
64 pages on Berkeley, and constitutes Ch. XII.   Parcel (θ),
containing 24 pages on Scepticism, is the present Ch. VIII.
Three parcels (ι, κ, λ), entitled 'Impression, Imagination, Idea,'
contain together 68 pages, and are now divided into Chapters
IV, V, VI, and VII.   Parcel (ν) on Sight, containing 6 pages,
is the present Ch. XI.   Parcel (π) entitled 'Aphorismi
Finales' contains 17 pages, and is printed below on pp. 325
foll.   Parcels μ, ξ, o, ρ, containing together about 30 pages,
were omitted, as adding nothing new.

A second set of papers written a little later than the above,
but dealing with the same subjects, were divided into two
parcels, one of 113 pages entitled 'Self-self and Thought-self,'
the other of 59 pages entitled 'Perception, etc.'   These now
make up Book II, to which I have given the general title
'Immediateness and Reflection,' and have divided it into eight
chapters.

A third set of papers of about the same date bore the title
'What is Materialism?'   They were divided into two parts,
containing respectively 38 and 17 pages.   These make up the
three chapters of Book III.   That which appears as the Fourth
Book was written as a comment on Mr Cope's criticism of the
view given in Grote's Plato of the argument in the Theaetetus.
The MS. consists of 58 pages, and was written, as I learn from
the Author's diary, between June 29 and July 2, 1866, that is
less than two months before his death.   It will be seen that I
have divided it into three chapters, using the Protagorean
maxim as the general heading.   Though it was probably
written without reference to the *Exploratio*, yet it contains an

allusion to Part I[1], and, I think, will be felt to be a fitting supplement to the preceding Books. Indeed, in my opinion, nothing in this volume is more characteristic of the Author, or likely to be of more value at the present time, than the remarks on the Right and Duty of Private Judgment contained in Ch. II.

The Fifth Book is taken from a series of papers headed 'Idealism and Positivism,' containing about 120 pages, which were originally intended to form an Appendix to the *Examination of the Utilitarian Philosophy*, but the Author, as is stated in *Exploratio*, p. vii, changed his mind, thinking it better 'to put together in an uncontroversial form the intellectual views on which the moral view rested.' As, however, there is much in this earlier draft which is not included in the First Part of the *Exploratio*, I have thought it well to append it to the Second Part, dividing it into three chapters. Of the 'Aphorismi Finales' I have already spoken. The 'Epilogue' was written, I fancy, before the publication of *Part I.*, and would no doubt have been considerably added to, if the Author had lived to complete *Part II.*

In reading the criticisms passed by the Author on the writings of other philosophers, it is important to remember his own account of the reasons which led him to give so much space to such criticism. "I care not in the least," he says[2], "to dispute what anyone says, except with a view of clearing up my own thoughts and those of others." "Let us suppose Mr Mill to be A, a character in a philosophical discussion, and if the actual Mr Mill has changed his views, or (which is exceedingly likely) I have misunderstood him, then let it not be supposed it is Mr Mill I am discussing with at all[3]." Again, speaking of his doubt as to the exact force of certain statements of Prof. Ferrier, he says[4], "When I say that I agree with him, I interpret him in my own way, and if anyone disputes that being his meaning, I have no care to maintain that it is.

[1] See below p. 272.   [2] p. xxiii.   [3] p. xxx.   [4] p. 69.

What I say *then* is not applicable to *him*. I have observed on the inutility of lengthened controversy as to whether a philosopher means this or that. Let us see only how what it may be thought he means, helps the truth, and suggests thought in us."

It may be well for me to take this opportunity of giving some account of the remaining MSS. left by Prof. Grote. They were arranged by him in the following groups:

I. Four volumes containing about 900 pages. The earlier part consists mainly of lectures, or notes for lectures, on Moral Philosophy and the Relation between Thought and Action. Among the most important sections are the chapters marked N (= 'Noematism'), containing about 80 pages on the subject of ' Glossology,' or the changes in the meaning of words. Part of this has been printed (as mentioned above) in the *Journal of Philology*. There is much of interest also in the section marked S, containing 60 pages on the classification of the different kinds of History; in T, containing 70 pages on Practical Ethics; in V, containing 148 pages on Ethics and Religion; and in Z, containing 200 pages on Christian Ethics, with discussions on International Law and Casuistry.

II. Consists of one volume of 270 pages, containing lectures on Morality, Society, Progress, etc.

III. Comprises three volumes of Essays and Reviews, and contains about 800 pages. The most important sections here are 263 pages on Froude's *History of England*, 82 pages on Mansel, 30 on Temple's Essay, 30 on Goldwin Smith, together with papers treating of Dante (50 pages), St Gregory on Job (25 pages), Thomas Aquinas (90 pages), Mill on Sedgwick, Whewell, Bentham, etc. What is now published under the title *Examination of the Utilitarian Philosophy* originally formed Vols. IV. and V. of this group.

IV. Comprises four volumes of about 1200 pages, bearing date 1861. It is made up of Notes, Essays and Lectures, and includes articles on Bentham (50 pages), Pascal (55 pages), Channing (40 pages), Antoninus (20), Charles Lamb (18), Forster's *Great Rebellion* (20), Comte and Buckle (130), Plato's *Gorgias* (30), Place of the Individual in History (50), Law of Honour illustrated from Beaumont and Fletcher (20), etc.

V. One volume on Moral Philosophy, containing 317 pages, (apparently a preliminary sketch of *Moral Ideals*).

Series 3[1]. Two volumes of 590 pages on Morality and the History of Moral Philosophy.

Language. One volume of 422 pages, part of which has been already printed in the articles on Glossology, and in *Good Words* under the title 'Thought versus Learning.'

The Authorized Version, tracing its changes up to the present time, 138 pages (used by Dr Scrivener).

There are a number of smaller parcels on various subjects and a quantity of notes on Philology, on Architecture, on Ruskin, etc., together with note-books innumerable, touching on all conceivable topics, from the humblest incidents of village life to the highest flights of philosophical or religious meditation : some of these might supply material for an interesting collection of miscellaneous Aphorisms. Probably, however, it will be thought that his latest ethical writings have the first claim to be printed. These are 'Honestarianism and Utilitarianism,' of 217 pages, finished June 5, 1866; 'The two Πολιτεῖαι,' of 18 pages, and other shorter papers written in the same month.

To complete the general view of Prof. Grote's literary work, I will add a list of Pamphlets and Essays printed before the publication of the First Part of the *Exploratio*.

Commemoration Sermon preached in Trinity College Chapel Dec. 15, 1849. Deighton, 1849.

---

[1] Series 1 and 2 had been incorporated in the preceding groups with an altered title.

Remarks on a Pamphlet by Mr Shilleto entitled 'Thucydides or Grote.' Deighton, 1851.

A few Words on Criticism à propos of the Saturday Review. Deighton, 1861.

Examination of some portions of Dr Lushington's judgment in the cases of the Bishop of Salisbury v. Williams, and Fendall v. Wilson. Deighton, 1862.

Old Studies and New in Cambridge Essays, 1856.

On the Dating of Ancient History in *Journal of Classical and Sacred Philology*, vol. I. pp. 52—82. Camb. 1854.

On the Origin and Meaning of Roman Names, Ib. vol. II. pp. 257—270. Camb. 1855.

A few Words on the New Education Code. Deighton, 1862.

It only remains for me to return my warmest thanks to Prof. Henry Sidgwick, who has gone through the proofs with the utmost care, and whose advice throughout has been of the greatest service to me; also to Mr H. W. B. Joseph, to whom the publication of this volume is really owing, and who has not only helped to revise the proofs, but has himself compiled the Index; lastly to the Syndics of the Cambridge University Press, who have shown, by their readiness to undertake the expenses of publication, that the name of John Grote is still not without honour in his old University.

P.S. The portrait of the Author which forms the frontispiece is a copy of a photograph taken when he was about 50 years old.

CONTENTS.

PART II.

BOOK I.

THE AUTHOR'S VIEWS COMPARED WITH THOSE OF OTHER PHILOSOPHERS.

BOOK II.

IMMEDIATENESS AND REFLECTION.

BOOK III.

WHAT IS MATERIALISM?

BOOK IV.

πάντων μέτρον ἄνθρωπος.

BOOK V.

IDEALISM AND POSITIVISM.

CORRIGENDA.

p. 3, § 3, last word, for 'this' read '*this*' followed by a colon.

p. 19, § 3, put in brackets 'and may do so, I suppose, in other books.'

p. 27, § 3, comma after 'knowledge.'

p. 152, § 1, l. 4, insert 'immediate' before 'thought.'

The notes marked G are by the Author, all the others by the Editor.

CHAPTER I.

ARISTOTLE AS THE FOUNDER OF PSYCHOLOGY.

I HAVE spoken of the treatment of philosophical subjects from the point of view of Real Logic[1], which might also be called Physical Logic or Applied Logic, in contrast to Pure or Formal Logic. The subject of this is the study of the actual advance of man in phenomenal knowledge with the view of drawing *logical* conclusions from it: *i.e.* of understanding better the action of the human mind in knowing, and applying the knowledge to good purpose.

The study of the advance of human knowledge with the view of drawing from it conclusions, not logical (*i.e.* relating to the action of the mind, or subject of knowledge), but real, or objective (*i.e.* relating to the constitution of the universe), leads to a different line of thought, to which various names might be given. The former being called Real or Physical Logic, this might be called Real or Physical Epistemology: it is the studying the nature of knowledge not in the abstract as knowledge merely, but as *man's* knowledge of an *actual universe*: and studying it, not with a view to conclusions about the knowledge only, but about the universe. Of course the limits between this and the abstract science of knowledge, the science of the human mind, and real logic, are very indefinite. But there is a branch of literature, very important of this kind, which I will now speak of.

I have mentioned more than once what I have called 'the higher philosophy[2].' I shall hereafter speak of it more. I mean

---

[1] *Expl.* pp. 153, 171 foll.   [2] *Expl.* p. 179.

by the term what represents, so far as anything represents,
that which is by many called 'ontology': that which treats, so
far as they can be philosophically treated, the great principles
of morals and the Divine Nature, and which must judge as
to the value or non-value of such doctrines as the Platonic
doctrine of ideas, &c. The real or physical epistemology which
I have spoken of covers in several respects the same ground as
this does; but does not, as I shall endeavour to show, cover it
properly.

But there is another region of thought partly corresponding
with this Real Epistemology, and partly differing from it, one
of the various regions commonly designated by the very vague
word Psychology.

Aristotle, writing on philosophical subjects, takes in his
Organon a purely logical view, a view, the developements and
applications of which I have in various ways alluded to. In his
Περὶ Ψυχῆς he takes a view which, whether as taken by him
or in various forms by a great many since, needs examination
as to the propriety and absence of confusion in it. He calls
the view 'physical' as distinguished from the views in his
Organon and Metaphysics: but by 'nature' and 'physical' he
means hardly perhaps the same thing that we should mean.

Philosophies of the Human Mind may be considered, to a
certain degree, developments of Aristotle's Psychology, and are
often called by that name. In reality, however, their point of
view is much more logical than his. They start with, if they
do not confine themselves to, the intellectual part of human
nature, and they take very little account indeed either of other
forms of sentient existence besides the human (which is looked
at rather as the type of mind in general), or of other parts of
the human being besides the mind. The consequence is, that
the subject is supposed to belong to philosophy, not to physics
as distinct from philosophy, like the Aristotelic. It is to be
observed, that the making the study belong to physics on a
merely materialistic view, which allows of no such thing as
philosophy, is quite as un-Aristotelic a view as the opposite.

The Aristotelic psychology is really the Comparative Science
of Life in the widest possible sense of the word Life, of which

therefore the science of the Human Mind, or of man's particular conscious life, constitutes a very small portion. I avoid using the word 'soul' on purpose, because the endless confused controversy about it has rendered it, like many other words, unfit for use as a philosophical term, unless with constant accompanying definition.

Psychology is therefore most simply viewed as the study of all the nature, and all the facts, of sentient and active being: and Comparative Psychology is the study of these, as they are manifested in different beings.

I said that what I called above Real Epistemology, or in other words, the science of *Human* knowledge, occupies in part the same region with Psychology. I mean this.

In our theorizing about knowledge as *Human*, one great point of necessity to be considered about it is, that man, the knowing subject, stands at one point in a chain of gradation of different kinds of knowledge, all animals, from the highest to the lowest, possessing their special manner of knowing.

Closely corresponding with this fact is another, viz. that man's knowledge is only one part of his conscious life, and in intimate relation with the other parts, just as such knowledge in other animals is in unison with their life. The whole science then of Comparative Psychology comes into intimate relation with Real Epistemology.

But again, beginning from the other side: Psychology altogether, and especially Comparative Psychology, cannot really exist without the corresponding study of the universe, in which life has existence, and to the particulars of which all the particulars of life itself have relation. The study of the circumstances and environment of life is indispensable to the study of life itself. The whole universe and the living part of it belong to each other, and form—what, in Dr Whewell's language, might be called—a great antithesis[1], the study of the one involving the study of the other.

In Human Epistemology, the antithesis between subject and object of knowledge is a portion of this greater antithesis.

[1] *Expl.* ch. xi.

The universe fits our faculties of knowledge in the same way as
the air fits our lungs, or the light our eyes. The real subject-
matter of knowledge is the relation between these two, not
either of them without the other: and this relation is looked
at not *à priori*, as in abstract epistemology, but in the manner
in which the continued advance of knowledge and experience
presents it to us ever more and more perfectly.

Psychology thus, here again, comes to coincide with the
concrete study of human knowledge.

In one point of view, the two may come to coincide in a
higher region still. Aristotle must be considered as virtually
saying, that what gives to living things their reality, what
constitutes, in other words, the thing which is known or
understood about them, when we talk of knowing them, is the
life. Livingness, where it exists, is in this way the subjective
and objective in one; it is 'knowingness' and 'knowableness'
in the particular thing, identical; existence in its character of
what thinks, and existence in its character of what may be
thought of, in one. Hence a wide region of speculation, belonging, according to the view taken, either to psychology or to real
epistemology. Is this completeness the *type* of being, and is
unity or reality without it a case where something is abortive?
Or are the two notions of existence radically different and the
particular identification only occasional or accidental? Or
what otherwise *is* the relation of the two forms? Speculations
of this kind may be said to constitute Psychology or Real
Epistemology in their most abstract character.

On the other hand Human knowledge may be looked at
from a merely phenomenalist point of view, as a portion of the
relation between one of the organized beings of the universe,
man, and his environment or circumstances. In this case the
distinctive character of the study, as the science of *knowledge*,
pretty much vanishes, and merges into a wider psychology,
treating of the relation of the different organized beings of the
universe to the universe in which they are.

Aristotle treated Psychology, or wrote of the *soul*, so to
call it for a moment, as a part of physics. That is, he started, in
discussing sensation, feeling, and thought, with a definite and

clear view of that kind which I call *phenomenalist*. His 'soul'
is life, 'livingness,' the living principle, as we see it exhibited in
the spatial universe (assumed in *this* case fitly as groundwork),
and again in its various forms and degrees, in plants, animals,
and man. He tries to get as deep as he can, so to
call it, into mind this way. I am not going to examine his
treatise: what I shall say about it for my present purpose is
this: first, what is almost superfluous to say of any work of
Aristotle's, that it is full of energy of thought, suggesting
and opening views in every direction, and scattering seeds of
after speculation: next, that it is full of what I have called
'notionalism[1],' or the realizing of logical notions: third, that
it confuses the phenomenalist and philosophical views in two
manners, which I will notice, but to a less degree than much of
later psychology.

About the 'notionalism' I shall say little, for it is the trite
and ordinary charge against Aristotelianism. I mean by it
this. The treatise is one of physics, but it is Aristotelian
physics. That is, the investigation is about the *being* or *essence*
of the soul or livingness, with full account of what speculators
had thought it to be, and much besides of like nature; and all
this in association with the Aristotelian physical views about
motion, action, and passion, which give to Aristotle's philosophy
a very different character from what I have called phenomenalism. I am half ashamed to blame Aristotle's notionalism,
because to me, just in virtue of its thoroughness, it seems better
than the later notionalism, much of which is full of contempt
for his, and is even perhaps introduced in supposed remedy of
his. For instance, in relation to his investigation of the being
or essence of the soul or livingness, what will be said by many
is that this is foolish, since being or essence is unknowable,
and we can only find out qualities and phenomena. This seems
to me a worse notionalism than his. No doubt there is in him
a confusion between the philosophical and phenomenalist views.
To assume the existence of something, which you cannot
describe, and of which each philosopher, as you show, has a

---

[1] *Expl.* pp. 73, 150.

different notion, is really a matter of logic: the assumed existence is not something unknown, but is only a logical peg on which to hang a certain number of things which you do know and can observe. Go through then with these: and Aristotle does so most admirably: he gives us the various phenomena of 'livingness' in plants, animals, man, with a vigour most wonderful, considering how little could then have been comparatively observed. All these phenomena are *realities*: *i.e.* as real as anything can be, of which at the last it has to be said, I think this is so, their reality depending upon whether I am right in thinking so. Do we get then to anything beyond such phenomenal reality? It is probable that then, as now, great importance was attached to the supposition of the existence of this livingness, or soul, in the way of a *basis* for these phenomena. This is what I do not understand: the phenomena want no basis of this kind, and if we try to give one, we really make it of the same kind as they, and come only to what I should call a very refined materialism. Aristotle says, ' the soul thinks, the soul feels, the soul acts,' when I should say, ' I think, I feel, I act:' and when I say, as above, that there is confusion of views, I mean this: that *thus* we are vainly trying to go beyond phenomenalism along the way of phenomenalism, instead of altogether changing our point of view to that of consciousness. If we say, the body feels, the eye sees, the hand handles, what we mean is something phenomenal, that the parts of the body are in a certain state, determined by, or related to, the state of things outside it. If we say, the soul feels or thinks, we really mean either to phenomenalize the soul, and to assert something the same as to that, *or* we mean to change our point of view altogether and to say, *I feel*; and when we say *this*, for all that we know, everything else vanishes. ' I feel' may be the only fact of all that we suppose: for that there *is* such a thing as body or universe, is all a part of the feeling. Only, if ' I feel' is a fact, ' I' *is*, and we *are ourselves* existent with an existence higher than phenomenal.

To a certain degree then there seems to me confusion of view in Aristotle's *notionalism*, as there is likely to be in most. But besides this, his view of sensation could not but be imperfect considering the imperfect physical knowledge of his time: the wonder is, not its imperfection, but that, with all the advance in physical knowledge, it was so long before it was improved upon.

I described two ways of his confusion, and I meant them in regard to νόησις or thought, and αἴσθησις or sense: but I will treat them together.

With real deference to the opinion of any who have more knowledge of Aristotle's physics than I have, and have given more special attention to this treatise,—keeping in mind also the very defective physical knowledge of Aristotle's time, knowledge, that is, of the actual facts of the communication between brain and nerve on the one side, and natural agents on the other—I am inclined to think that Aristotle took more clear hold of the distinction I am trying to draw, than most psychologists since. His medium, the τὸ μεταξὺ[1], seems to me to represent the physical communication: his transmission of the αἰσθητὰ εἴδη[2], (the sensible species) from the object to the soul, the τόπος εἰδῶν[3], seems to me to represent (what I have called) the communication between mind on the one side and reason or meaning in things on the other, i.e. the comprehension, conception, or forming a notion of them. I do not say this because I have any particular care to make Aristotle think the same as I do: and I am quite aware of the manner in which, since Aristotle, these two notions of his have been treated. But so far as the αἰσθητὰ εἴδη represent anything even in any way physical, passing between the object and the sense, I do not see how they will agree with the τὸ μεταξὺ: I cannot understand the consistency of the two intermediations—unless indeed one is wanted for primary qualities, the other for secondary. But I do not at all want to enter into the Aristotelian theory of perception. I shall perhaps, in commenting on later views of perception, slightly refer back to it.

His notion of the distinction between 'common and proper sensibles[4]' or qualities, as those with which we communicate on the one hand by means of the whole organization, and on the

---

[1] Περὶ Ψυχῆς II. 11, cf. Bonitz *Index*, *s.v.*
[2] *l.c.* II. 12.　　　[3] *l.c.* III. 4. 4.　　　[4] *l.c.* II. 6.

other by means of special instruments for the purpose, seems to
me a truth of sensation for all time, and to be far superior to
all later discussions on the difference between primary and
secondary qualities.

While however it appears to me thus that the notions of the
τὸ μεταξύ and the εἴδη are genuine efforts after the truth, it
may perhaps be doubted whether Aristotle's own view was
definite. 'The sense receives the sensible forms without the
matter, as the wax receives the imprint[1]'—it is difficult to say
how far this is to be regarded as mere metaphor or illustration.
Again: Aristotle apparently approves the calling of the soul
τόπος εἰδῶν, saying however that it is the soul intelligent or
thinking that is this, as distinct from the soul sensitive[2]. I
praise the application *here* of the word τόπος, where a something
thinking is mentioned, for it does not seem to me that Aristotle
meant anything spatial, and if we could form the notion of a
τόπος or 'continent[3],' what anything could be *in*, other than
space, it would be very convenient, and would save much
mistake as to 'outward' or 'external.' However, Aristotle's
notion of the several functions, as above, of the sensitive and
thinking soul is hard to get, and it may perhaps be questioned,
as I said, whether it is definite.

Beginning with a clear phenomenalist view, Aristotle does
not say much about the *thinking* soul till after discussing the
sensitive, and this is *one* reason why there is less confusion, it
seems to me, in him, than in later psychology. For when we
do come to that, we get into the difficulty. Ἡ ψυχὴ τὰ ὄντα
πώς ἐστι πάντα[4]. That is what I say. The thinking soul,
when you come to that, absorbs everything else. When, in
discussing the universe, you come to a *knowing* part of it, and
begin to discuss *knowledge*, you find you have got round to the
beginning again, or rather to a point before the beginning—
for all existence depends to us upon our knowledge of it—and
you discover yourself building the foundation high up upon
the roof. Here Aristotle, otherwise true in the main to his
present investigation as *physical*, comes really to philosophy,
and wiser than many, does not, out of place, enter upon this.
Still even the mention of it puzzles.

[1] II. 12.   [2] III. 4. 4.   [3] *Expl.* p. 10.   [4] III. p. 8.

CHAPTER II.

So much now about Aristotle. I will proceed to remark a
little upon the later 'noö-psychology[1],' if one may call it so,
as distinct from the simply phenomenalist science of physio-
psychology.

I will say first that the word which lends itself more than
any other to the confusion which I have continually spoken of
is the word 'perception,' which is the reason why, as may
perhaps have been observed, I make little use of it. Lest,
however, it should be supposed that this is because I am
afraid of it, and that the use of it really involves a truth, we
will a little examine it.

I 'perceive' a thing, in the simplest signification of the
word, means in my view no less than this : I conceive (or have
the notion of) my body or, as I should call it, *myself* phenomenally filling space in a spatial universe, and something filling
space also in *communication*[2] with it (whatever the communication may be); along with the further thought, that I am
right in having the notion of this communication, or, in other
words, that this something exists in the same manner in which
my body does. This latter is what distinguishes perception,
to the perceiver, from simple conception or imagination. Still,
it is not, necessarily, perception, unless it can be said (with
a knowledge independent of the perception), There is a stone :

---

[1] *Expl.* pp. 73, 151.   [2] *Expl.* p. 7.

for, if there is not a stone to be perceived, the perception is only supposition of perception.

It will be seen that the existence of anything which we suppose we perceive is here referred to our body: when we say a thing *is* (what I call) *phenomenally*, we mean, that it does, or can, communicate with our corporeal frame. The notion of rightness as it accompanies the notion of phenomenalism altogether,—our body, universe, and all—I have discussed already[1]. On that depends the difference between perception altogether and imagination, or a sort of imagination. On the rightness of the supposition that the thing communicates with our body, depends the distinction of the particular perception from imagination.

I said that this is the simplest notion of perception: this is what we mean when we say I perceive 'something.' If we say, 'I perceive a stone'—the more proper application of the term—we add a fresh intellectual element to the process, *i.e.* there is reference to previous knowledge, and recognition or identification. There is then not only the notion of the thing, as spatial, being in communication with our body, but there is the notion of something about the spatial thing, of the *thing* as constituted, as generic, as serving a purpose, &c., communicating with our thought. This is the principle, as I have before described[2], of notice, recognition, identification: and is the truest 'thinghood,' the most essential quality of the thing.

It will be seen then that when we talk about perception, we proceed, if we are consistent, outward and divergingly from the body to the universe—supposing, that is, ultimately or at the limit, something common between space and 'mindhood'— not inwardly and convergingly from the universe to the body and so to the mind, so far as there is meaning in doing this latter. This latter *is* the way in which we proceed in examining the corporeal communication: a great part of the language of physio-psychology will, therefore, naturally and rightly go upon it: but unfortunately a great deal of the language of noö-psychology will, by a wrong analogy, go upon it also.

[1] *Expl.* p. 13.   [2] *Expl.* pp. 37, 45.

The '*basal*' fact, or fact of facts, as I have described it[1], is variety of consciousness (or, in other words, a succession of various feelings) bound all together by the '*I-hood*' or feeling of personality. This fact developes itself into others, or is exhibitable, on certain suppositions, in relation with others. If we examine the development, or look at the fact without special supposition, completely, we are following out the course of thought or knowledge : and the study of *perception*, perception being supposed an action of the mind, must be in *this* way. On this view, the distinctive character of our consciousness, as reasonable beings, is, correspondently with the variety of our feeling, to conceive ourselves, in the way I have just described, as corporeal and forming part, as such, of a spatial universe, in communication with different portions of it, and to suppose, as I have said besides, that we are *right* in conceiving thus.

It is this conception with the feeling of rightness attached to it, which makes what we call 'consciousness': and when we conceive consciousness as different from imagination, we give significance to this notion of *rightness* in it.

Our thought and the thought of a state of things in relation to us (I would say a state of things we are *in*, if 'in' could be understood without necessary relation to space) seem to me indistinguishable. Our notion of existence and reality, or, which is the same thing, our notion of the rightness attaching to the conception, which we then call our consciousness, seems to me in substance a *trust*, which we may equally describe as a trust in our thought or a trust in things: for I look upon the two as two sides of what is the same, only that *thought* is the side towards us. The reason why what we trust is to us (at the furthest point to which we can follow it back) *our thought*, not *things*, is because we cannot escape from the position of thinking: that position is necessarily the last that we get to: we cannot realize fact *unthought*, and cannot say we trust to fact as against thought, or as testing the rightness of thought, when after all it is only fact *as thought* that we trust to. But the trusting to thought is the trusting to things as corresponding with it.

[1] *Expl.* pp. 23, 47, 57.

Taking the investigation not quite so deep, going only to the *basement* of knowledge and not to the actual hidden foundation, we have the phenomenalist view, the 'cosmocentric[1]' instead of the ' autocentric' or ' *nucentric* ' one. Here we begin with the supposition of the spatial universe existing, and ourselves with our bodies, and things existing in it. On this view, the *basal fact*[2], consciousness, is to be considered not developed, as before, but as contemporaneous with a phenomenal fact, viz. what I have called bodily communication with things, the fact of our nerves being in a particular state on the occasion of their presence in various ways. These two facts are constantly *both* called by the name of sensation. Mr Mill, we have seen, distinguishes them with great care[3], though, I think, scarcely able himself to be faithful to the distinction. Of philosophers of the last century, some may be said to have maintained the distinction universally : some to have maintained it in regard of *some* sensations, but not in regard of all : some to have entirely neglected it.

The ultra-Lockian, sensationalist, or sensualist philosophy of the last century takes, I think, no notice of the distinction, and in this it is followed by various philosophies of a different kind which adopt its language. The sensations or impressions, which are spoken of as the beginnings or constituents of knowledge, are treated as each one a particular consciousness and a particular bodily state in conjunction, without further attention to them in *this* way.

' Noö-psychology,' or the Lockian psychology, is something which, when I look at it, always fills me with a mingled admiration and bewilderment. It is a subject which has absorbed a vast amount of ingenuity and power of mind, and each philosopher struggles hard to set the confusion right, and as Stewart says of Reid, ' to strike at the root of the common theories on the subject,' and remove the perplexity. Unfortunately it has a terrible tendency to begin again. I do not know of any subject in which there seems to have been more of what I should call intellectual conscientiousness, that is, honest effort to face the difficulty, than in this : and I

[1] *Expl.* p. 11.   [2] *Expl.* p. 70.   [3] *Expl.* pp. 162, 192.

think the point which is wrong seems to have been abundantly well seen, but we cannot get hold of it, and in spite of the reforms, noö-psychology has gone on increasing in intricacy. My own view, as I have said, is that it is two subjects involved together, in regard of which our thoughts will never be clear till we distinctly separate them. I think I cannot do better than quote a long passage from Stewart's *Elements of the Philosophy of the Human Mind*[1], eminently characterized by the real effort after truth which I have spoken of, exhibiting the nature of what I have called the continued *reform* of noö-psychology, with its little result for good, and which I think will illustrate the difference between my manner of thinking and that of these psychologists. The 'difficulty' spoken of at the beginning is that of ' the intercourse between mind and matter,' and ' the influence of the will over the body.'

Singular as it may appear, Dr Reid was the first person who had courage to lay completely aside all the common hypothetical language concerning perception, and to exhibit the difficulty in all its magnitude by a plain statement of the fact. To what, then, it may be asked, does this statement amount? Merely to this, that the mind is so formed that certain impressions produced on our organs of sense by external objects, are followed by correspondent sensations, and that these sensations (which have no more resemblance to the qualities of matter than the words of a language have to the things they denote) are followed by a perception of the existence and qualities of the bodies by which the impressions are made; that all the steps of this process are equally incomprehensible; and that, for anything we can prove to the contrary, the connexion between the sensation and the perception, as well as that between the impression and the sensation, may be both arbitrary; that it is therefore by no means impossible that our sensations may be merely the occasions on which the correspondent perceptions are excited; and that, at any rate, the consideration of these sensations, which are attributes of mind, can throw no light on the manner in which we acquire our knowledge of the existence and qualities of body. From this view of the subject it follows, that it is the external objects themselves, and not any species or images of these objects, that the mind perceives; and that, although by the constitution of our nature certain sensations are rendered the constant antecedents of our perceptions, yet it is just as difficult to explain how our perceptions are obtained by their means, as it would be upon the supposition that the mind were all at once inspired with them, without any concomitant sensations whatever.

[1] *Works*, vol. II. p. 111, Hamilton's ed.

On this passage I will make a succession of remarks.

1.   The fallacy running through the whole of noö-psy-chology is this. We begin with saying 'Certain impressions are produced on our organs of sense by external objects,' and we go on to say that then, after perhaps something else also has taken place, we get 'a perception of the existence and qualities of the objects by which the sensations are made.' Now, supposing the impression and the perception different and successive, as they are here described, how can we possibly know that what we perceive is 'the existence and qualities of the objects by which the impressions are made?' In the first line we have got so far as this: the objects exist, though not as yet for us: other people perceive them probably, though we know nothing about them : next, they make impressions on our organs of sense : it is difficult to say who knows this, (for *we* as yet do not know their existence), but we will accept this account of the fact, which any physical philosopher looking on would know took place, if he saw an eye directed towards an object, viz. that light passed in various ways between them. Then, after something else which just now I need not notice, comes the perception—we perceive the existence of the object by which the impressions were made. Now what human being can know that the object, the existence of which we perceive, is the same as the object which made the impressions? Not we ourselves; for if we had known, in receiving the impressions, that it was the object made them, we should have known the existence of the object, before we are represented as having got the perception of it. Not the spectator; for he knows indeed, perhaps, what object it must have been which made the impressions on us, seeing, for instance, where our eye is directed : but what object it is which we perceive the existence of, is a matter which he cannot possibly know, being simply a matter of our consciousness. Nobody then can know it[1].

---

[1] That is, no one single person : for we might suppose (I put it in this way as it may help some persons to see what it is that is wrong) a conversation between the perceiver and the physiologist who stands by looking at him. The former might say : I imagine or conceive a great green thing with leaves—a tree in fact. The latter might say to him : Do not say you imagine or conceive such

This is no vain subtlety, but is what, if people would have considered it, might have saved worlds of writing. I have only here put into another form what I said in reference to a sentence of Mr Mill's involving the same confusion[1]; we have a thing which may equally well be described in *either* of two ways. The object which makes impressions is the same as the object the existence and qualities of which are perceived, for the simple reason that its producing impressions followed by a sensation is the same thing, if we look in one direction, as our perceiving its existence and qualities, if we look in the other.

a thing : you see or perceive it, for there *is* a tree right in front of your eyes and your eyes are open, and I know by my science that, when a tree, *e.g.* and an eye are in that relative position, light travels from the former to the latter, and there take place in the latter a variety of processes as to the light and the nerve, which I have studied carefully, and never could tell what they were for. I now see they must have something to do with that feeling which you describe as conception of a thing—but then I suppose you sometimes have that feeling *without* your eyes being open and the thing in front of you : if so, you ought to have two words, and perhaps it would be as well if you called the feeling in the one case imagination, in the other perception : only then again there is this misfortune, that you want *me* to tell you whether your feeling is imagination or perception, *i.e.* whether the thing is in front of you or not. You might, to be sure, tell that, in the case of the tree, by your legs and hands, by going and feeling, but then we cannot carry that out, for you want somebody to tell you, in the last resort, whether you have got legs and hands, or whether *that* is not all imagination.

Of course for the physiologist to say this, he must be possessed of that power of momentary forgetfulness which is an incalculable advantage for philosophical imagination and abstraction. He must forget all his conscious knowledge, and be the physiologist only. He must possess knowledge without knowing what knowledge is, so that he wonders at it and is able freely to study it when he finds it. We must suppose that it has never struck his mind that he possesses, as parent of his knowledge, the feeling *himself*, which he is here wondering at in another. It is evident that this requires a good deal of imagination, and that it does so, the noö-psychologists have very little understood. They suppose us with our clothes or environment of the external universe already on, and then proceed to put them on.

If the perceiver depends on *himself* alone, and has not the physiologist by his side to tell him *when* his conception is accompanied by impression or presence of the thing, he must have some means of determining *in himself* whether his conception is imagination or perception—in fact, more than this, of determining whether the distinction which he makes between perception and imagination is itself other than delusion. This is the question of scepticism or reality of knowledge.—G.

[1] *Expl.* p. 193.

These two ways of considering the matter will be recognized
as the two views which I have all along urged should be kept
separate: the view from consciousness and the view from
phenomena: the view of the perceiver himself, and the view
of the observer of the phenomena of impression and sensation.
And the psychology which I am speaking of stands upon two
stools in a position quite impossible to maintain.

2. I will say in a moment in what way sensation and
perception may to a certain degree be put together as two
processes: but as Stewart describes them here, they are *one*.
More accurately: Stewart's *sensation* is sensation as I have
described it, *the basal fact*. Stewart's *impression* is what I have
called the corporeal communication. Stewart's *perception* is the
sensation, looking the other way. Only when Stewart speaks,
first, of the sensation as sensation, it is left unexamined. All
the study or investigation is directed to the impression or
communication which is accompanied by the sensation. Then,
when Stewart speaks, *second*, of the perception, (or as I
should say, of the sensation or perception), *it* is to a certain
extent analyzed, and we are told *what* it is a sensation or
perception of: in other words, what, in the realm of thought
(which we are in *now*, analyzing a sensation described as
quite out of relation with matter) it results in or developes
into, viz. a perception of the existence and qualities of
bodies. The sensation in fact is of *self-hood* or *I-hood*, with
the added consciousness *either* of pleasure and pain *or* of will,
and of something conceived as occasion of the pleasure and
pain, or reaction against the will; which something, according
to the varied nature of the sensation, we conceive in various
manners, and call the whole result of our conception *body* and
its qualities. These occasions and reactions are, if we like to
use the language, the same thing as the impressions or communication: that is, the two ways of speaking are two ways of
describing the *same* thing or things: seen from within, they are
the occasions or reactions: seen from without, or studied by the
physiological anatomist, they are the impressions or communication.

It is to be remembered, that though, in studying the bodily

states, we carefully distinguish between them and the accompanying proper sensation, we must still *suppose* this latter as what, in our inward following of the bodily states, they end in, nor is there any harm, if we can, and so far as we can, in taking physiological hold (so to speak) of the sensation, or making efforts to give a physiological account of it. All that I have protested against is the refusing to admit as real what cannot have this physiological account given of it, whereas it is what is most real of anything, as seen from the point of view of highest reality and most intimate knowledge. Let us have a phenomenalist study of states of mind (so to call them) so far as we can get at them by following inwards the anatomy of our nerves and brain: this is what I have never dissented from: what I have protested against has been putting into the same class facts of matter as phenomena of a spatial universe, and feelings as feelings or consciousnesses, that is, as we know them each for himself individually, not by the road of physiological and anatomical study; whereas our feelings belong to a different and higher domain of thought, the whole existence of this universe itself being one of them.

I have mentioned this because, in the study of the impression or communication, this consciousness must be continually supposed, and because of course there is (what we may call) *local* sensitiveness of the nerves of the body, while nevertheless the sensation, as such, is all one : it is *we* that feel, not our body in this or that part of it. This being so, it is unwise to throw any hindrance in the way of such physiological investigation, so far as it can go. The phrase ' impression on the organs of sense' inevitably suggests a sort of local sensitiveness : considering Stewart's distinction of it from sensation, it ought to mean only material displacement : but we cannot help its conveying more. I have used the expression, corporeal or material communication : but of course in using these terms (and it would be the same with any), one must be prepared to accept physical and physiological research as to the nature of matter and body, and I am so most thoroughly. I do not at all mean to assert that we can draw the line of boundary, proceeding what I will call *inwards*, between feeling and material fact or phenomenon.

I do not even assert there *is* any such line. I do not say but that enquirers from the side of consciousness and enquirers from the side of phenomena might not hope ultimately to meet, like the excavators at the opposite ends of the Mont Cenis tunnel. If ever they do, our posterity will have phenomenalism, which will not, like the present, call in question our highest and nearest consciousnesses, and on the other side a sort of consciousness or knowledge, which will enable us to understand the relation between what I will call efficient and formal creation, viz. the former the generation of things, the latter the generation of ideas or knowledge. Any such possibility as this however is not my present concern.

The difficulty of drawing this line of boundary is a sort of excuse for all that philosophy which, as I said a short time since, neglects the difference between the sensation as consciousness and the sensation as communication, if only it be kept in mind that when this is so, the investigation is really what I call phenomenalist: *i.e.* that it is not in a position to dispute, from *its* point of *imperfect* hold of sensation as consciousness, anything which is borne witness to by consciousness from its own proper point of view.

I have been a little too long on a by-point, and now return to Stewart. We have three things given by him as consecutive, impression, sensation, perception, which are really, in substance, three views of the same thing: there is no consecution or sequence: all is contemporaneous. The sensation is the 'basal fact': and this may be exhibited either, from the point of view of the spatial universe, as impression on the organs of sense vanishing unfollowably into sensation or consciousness, or, from the point of view of consciousness, as thought digesting and analysing particular consciousnesses or sensations, and interpreting portions of them into what we then call qualities of body, calling at the same time our mental relation to them 'perception of them.'

3. Stewart's supposition of consecution or sequence in all this leads him into many perplexities and inconsistencies.

One of the purposes which I have proposed to myself in what I am now doing is to get a clearer and better phenomenalism

by removing philosophy which is out of place, and I think
what Stewart says about consecution here puzzles it.

Causation or production, he says, is merely a particular
form of antecedence: we need not wonder therefore at sensation
succeeding impression, however different the two: we know
about them the same that we know about any cause and effect,
and ought to be satisfied.

We find in Mr Mill's *Logic* and may do so, I suppose, in
other books how cause and effect are to be looked at from the
phenomenalist point of view [1]: something very different, it
seems to me, from what there is here in Stewart. Observe the
confusion of language: how the consecutional relation is spoken
of sometimes as production, sometimes as sequence, sometimes
as (whatever it may mean) correspondence. How inconsistent
here, where the purpose is carefully to examine the supposed
consecution, to attribute (which often is no harm) activity to
the object, and talking of its producing impressions on the
organs of sense. Then, what is the meaning of talking of all
the steps of the process as equally incomprehensible? if they
are matters of simple consecution, or of causation *as such*,
what is there to comprehend? Again, what is the meaning of
'arbitrariness' in the connexion between impression and sensation and between sensation and perception? Stewart had said, a
page or two before [2], in a manner to which I have just referred,
'It seems now to be pretty generally agreed among philosophers,
that there is no instance in which we are able to perceive a
necessary connexion between two successive events,' and he
ends a long sentence to which I refer the reader, in explanation
of his views as to 'causation,' by saying: 'and, if there are any
such (*i.e.* necessary) connexions existing, we may rest assured
that we shall never be able to discover them.' How then could
the connexions here be other than arbitrary? and what could
the sensations be, in reference to the perceptions, *more* than the
occasions of them? And then, 'from this view of the subject
—*i.e.* the view 'that our sensations are followed by a perception
of the existence and qualities of the bodies (previously called

---

[1] *Expl.* p. 222.　　　　[2] p. 96.

'objects') by which the impressions are made—it follows, that
'it is the external objects themselves, and not any species or
images of these objects, that the mind perceives': is this re-
assertion, or inference, or what?

I am afraid, however, that to understand what I have said
as to the clearness of our view of phenomena being injured by
associating with it the consideration of our manner of sensation
of them, the reader must look at the context preceding the
passage which I have quoted. It is itself too long to quote.
I would, however, slightly refer to it, because it illustrates the
general confusion of view of which I have spoken.

Stewart[1] quotes a variety of passages in which authors have
held that the mind, and that which it perceives, must be
present the one to the other; because a thing cannot act where
it is not; and, therefore, whether it is the object that affects
the mind, or the mind that, in perceiving, acts upon the object,
they must be together. Hence, Stewart says, philosophers
have been driven to the unsatisfactory alternative of saying,
either that the actual object perceived was at the nerves or
sensorium, and that we did not perceive the things themselves,
or that the mind, in perceiving, was present all over space
wherever there was an object perceived. Stewart says, there is
no occasion for this supposed presence, and that we are not
entitled to say that a thing cannot act where it is not. What
I say is, that if we are speaking of thought, the associating it
with locality has no meaning[2]: it is not, 'I am here, and I
think I see a candle before me,' but 'I think that I am here,
and that I see a candle before me': the thought is not
comprehended in the space, but comprehends it as an object
with the other objects: as thought, it is *unlocal*: the thought
may be in some 'continent[3],' to use the language which I have
used, but this is not *space*, for the space is *in* the thought.
Now it will be seen that all the speculators whom Stewart here
quotes, are obliged to 'unlocalize' (or 'delocalize') *something*.
One set do so to the *object*: 'the sun,' they say, 'which our mind
perceives is not in far off space, but is in our sensorium.' An

---

[1] *l.c.* p. 99 foll.   [2] *Expl.* pp. 88, 117.   [3] *Expl.* p. 10.

opposite set do so to the mind: 'the mind,' they say, 'when it perceives what is distant from the body, is not where the body is, but present with the distant object.' Observe this: the mind, capable of locality, is yet not where the body is. I think Stewart is right in saying that, when we speak of *the mind* acting, or anything acting upon the mind, we are in no relation to locality, and are not at all entitled to say, that a thing cannot act where it is not: but on account of the imperious necessity of all this philosophy to co-ordinate, as I have called it, thought and phenomenal action, he cannot say this without adding, 'Even in regard of mechanical action, we cannot understand the action of a body, *where it is:* the communication of motion by impulse to a thing in contact with it is a phenomenon as inexplicable really as any communication we may suppose between two things separated the one from the other by a vacuum.' Now this was not what we wanted. It is what I alluded to as puzzling phenomenalism by philo- sophy, in order that we may be able to account phenomenally for what does not need to be so accounted for. It is in analogy with a line of argument not uncommon now in the higher philosophy, which calls upon us to digest difficulty because there is difficulty even in what we have hitherto thought easiest. The communication of motion by impulse is one of the simplest of phenomena, however difficult may be its ulterior explanation. The question as to the acting, or being acted on, of mind, is, Can it be brought into relation with the order of things of which this communication of motion by impulse is a leading phenomenon ? To say that we do not understand this latter, and that therefore we may say what we please of the former, is not to the purpose.

Is not the simplest way of settling all this to say, that thought, as thought, has no place ? On what conceivable prin- ciples, or by what logic, can it ever be settled whether the object is in the brain, or in the mind away from the body at the object, or whether they act one on the other afar off,—a thing which, we are told, we need not wonder at, because we cannot understand how a bat acts upon a cricket-ball near ?

Let us then gain first a clear view of the phenomenal state

of things, dismissing all talk of *qualities* and all logical words, and all supposition of *objects* operating or acting, or mind acting (*now*), or anything acting which we do not know physically to move or stir something else. We have then the sun by means of light '*en rapport*' with our brain, and we know that there is a consciousness accompanying this relation, which consciousness however we do not, because we cannot, follow. Here is the region to which all our notions of space, distance, mechanical action, belong, and in which we may trust to them.

But if we want to analyze our consciousness we come to a different region. Then let us freely use our logical terms, our language about the mind acting and being acted on, let us talk of subject and object, notions and ideas, but let us not *localize, i.e.* phenomenally realize them. There are no qualities in the world of space, no notions or ideas in it, not properly *objects*, not properly *colours:* we can fix no *locality* for these, nor need we.

The use or necessity of all this logical language arises from—what we may variously call—either the absence of any fixed point to fasten our knowledge on, *or* the incompleteness of our knowledge, such incompleteness necessarily involving a certain amount of wrongness, or in other ways. This logical language is the language of *learners*: it is supposition to be gradually replaced by knowledge of fact, but still to go on in our process of learning *more* fact: it is the centering, by the aid of which we build our arches of knowledge one after another: it has only relation to the building: when we are dealing with what is *built*, the actual knowledge, we must have it out of the way. Qualities of bodies, or of matter, or of the universe are not realities of any kind: and the bodies, or matter, or the universe, are not realities when we speak of them as constituting the substratum of the qualities: they are realities as compositions of a variety of material or phenomenal elements: and similarly 'qualities' is a term by which for particular purposes, we designate these various elements, and such things. It is here that popular or common language continually betrays us: not that it is *its* fault that it does so, as philosophers one after the other, in a manner very wearying to my patience, have reiterated; but *ours*. Popular language is the language, as all our thought is the thought, of learners: a complete philosophical language at any stage of knowledge short of complete, say the present, would be a hindrance to advance: we do not want our language to fit any particular stage of our knowledge, because then it would not fit the next: we should be like growing boys in an old dress, cribbed, confined, embarrassed, not knowing what to do with ourselves. All this logical and common language is an elastic dress of our thought, which will fit any particular state of knowledge, if we use it properly. There is no harm in our using the term 'colour' *now*, in respect to any particular body, though we know it to be exceedingly different from what people, Aristotle for instance, thought was the case, when they talked and reasoned about colour long ago. In the same way we may talk of secondary qualities, and this 'colour' as one of them, and may find it very convenient to do so. But it is only convenient on the condition of our not (what I may call) *mis-realizing* them. It is merely unmeaning to discuss whether colour is in the brain, or in the object, or where it is, as if it was something which we knew must be somewhere. Let us convert every such apparent problem as this into the real problem or problems, viz. what are the physical circumstances of our brain and of the thing which we consider we see and of the interval between them, as to light, on the occasion of the seeing? and so, if we like, for the philosophical problem also, what are the circumstances of consciousness which make us say that out of all the field of view, we see *that* thing?

The use of this logical language is for the purpose of keeping up a relation, if I may so speak, between the two manners of thought, that of consciousness and that of phenomenalism: or, which is the same thing, between the two views of knowledge which I mentioned[1], that of judgment and that of acquaintance. The phenomenalist says, with some reason, Away with *qualities*—let me have *things*. Let me see and think of the white object as it *is*, namely as a mass of matter

---

[1] *Expl.* pp. 60, 122, 148.

of a certain chemical constitution, one feature [of which is to reflect white light to my organ of vision][1].

The knowing things in the *two* ways which I have described, viz. with knowledge of acquaintance and knowledge of judgment, is the knowing them in the first case *substantively* or substantially, in the second *adjectively* or predicatively. For a complete phenomenalism, if we may so speak, there are no *adjectives* and no adjectival substantives, like whiteness, hardness: the realities of the world are *things* of different sorts, elements (*e.g.* fluids, minerals, &c.) and compositions of these again with definite shape, which are what we commonly call things, and so on. Besides these *things* of course there are *movements*, which are the (physical) reason for *verbs*, and various facts in this way happen about the things. What we express by adjectives is facts about the things (Mr Mill has treated this well). When we say a thing is blue, what we mean is that it absorbs all the light but the blue, and transmits the blue light. But this is what we come to find out about it, and as we have come to find out this, we shall perhaps come to find out more of the fact, so that this our present view will be absorbed in a wider and, so far, truer one. In the mean time we began with describing this fact, when altogether vaguely conceived, by saying, 'the thing is blue': now that it is pretty clearly conceived we continue to call it blue, and have not thought it necessary to alter our language and say, 'Blue is just the colour which we ought *not* to call the thing, because the blue rays *leave* the thing, and it is just the rays which are not blue which remain in it, and form a part of it.' Yet it is clear that, when people first called the thing *blue*, they thought it was the blue light, or as they would say colour, that was *in* the thing. *We* may explain the calling the thing blue by saying, this represents our sensation, the communication between the thing and us: but this was not so to the people who first made the language, nor is it to the mass of people who use the language now.

Advancing physical knowledge thus converts all the qualities

[1] The clause in brackets is added by the editor.

which are what we express by adjectives, into things and facts expressed by substantives and verbs—blue colour for instance is luminous undulation of such and such an amount or rapidity— and this is what we call coming to the knowledge of things: as in fact it is.

But the manner of our gaining our knowledge, as I have several times said, is by the *union* of the contact or communication which, so far as it is able to become knowledge, is knowledge of *acquaintance*, and generates phenomenalism, *and* the *judgment* or *thought* which is knowledge proper. (In calling this *union*, I guard myself: its nature I have explained.) For a complete *judgment* of the universe we have one initiatory *substantive*, and all our proceeding is by adjectives or predicates of it: for substantives predicated of a subject are *pro tanto* adjectives. It is this way of viewing knowledge which led to Aristotle's arrangement of categories, as I said in beginning to speak of Mr Mill's book[1]: it is this way again which has led philosophers and psychologists, in speaking of our sensation and perception, to describe the object of it, not generally as *things*, but as primary, secondary, &c. *qualities* of the initiatory thing, the *subject* of which all our after phenomenal knowledge is the great predicate, matter, body, or whatever we call it.

As I have said before, this *matter*[2] or *body* is not something mysterious and unknown, but is known in so far as we know its qualities, and otherwise there is nothing to know: it is assumption only for the purpose of after knowledge.

Knowledge proceeds, as language shows us, by the way of acquaintance and judgment, or notice and predication, or realization and description, or by whatever other pairs of names we like to use for the conjunct processes, the one supplying us with subjects or substantives, the other with adjectives or descriptive terms.

We mentally construct the universe by imagining space, and furnishing it in the same manner with what we call matter, like and in communication with our body, arranged in units or portions which we call things: and then by hanging on to

---

[1] *Expl.* pp. 151, 160.   [2] *Expl.* pp. 147, 176, 186 foll.

these things notions or thoughts about them, which we call
their qualities.   If we want to suppose, for these qualities, an
existence like that of the things, we have to analyze them and
translate them, into things and facts.   But when we simply
express the quality substantively, as hardness, whiteness, we
are expressing no *phenomenal* existence; that is, we are
expressing what is still in the form of a thought of ours *about*
things, and though what we call *things* may be really no more
at the bottom than this, yet they are, as I have expressed it,
deposited, crystallized, become part of the abstraction which
we call phenomenalism, or phenomenal reality.   We may make
the other so if we like it: the notion *colour* is very readily
translated into the phenomenal facts which are concerned with
light, and then we at once see the spatial relations.

But I am getting to much too great a length and depth
on this subject, and quite leaving the passage of Stewart which
I began with examining.   I will just finish with an illustration
which will give me occasion also to speak of the circumstances
under which the notions of 'sensation' and 'perception' may
legitimately be put together.

Suppose the object of thought is a plough.

We perceive then, in Stewart's language, its existence and
qualities.   These 'qualities' are the primary, secondary, &c.
which have been abundantly discussed.

I do not at all quarrel with the manner of expression.   The
question is, How are we to realize it?   Or in other words,
What does it exactly mean?

The logical 'mis-realization' which I have condemned is
this: the supposition that 'the thing in itself,' 'the plough in
itself,' the *substratum*, is something unknown and unknowable;
that body, matter, or whatever we call it (which *has* the
qualities which we then *besides* perceive) is something similarly
unknowable; in other words, that we do not know the meaning
of existence, while nevertheless in Stewart's words we perceive
existence.   This is the first portion of the logical mis-realization: corresponding with this is the second, that the qualities
are realities, and realities which *are* known: that hardness,

redness (if the plough is red) and other such adjectival
substantives, represent things. The reasons for my noting
this latter, which as thus barely put is alien from our present
ways of thinking, are two: first because the former, which, as
we have seen, prevails extensively in our present way of
thinking, really goes hand in hand with it: next, because,
though in this broad way we do not take the qualities for
realities, yet it seems to me (from observation and experience
both) that the language about 'qualities' introduces much
difficulty, when one begins to think *what* we see or perceive,
and even confusion, when we come to specify and classify the
qualities. However, I do not complain of the language, so
long as we can keep it clear of confusion.

We may *realize*, it seems to me, or conceive reality, in two
ways, and also in a certain way mixed of the two: but not in
the psychological way.

The first gives us what I have called phenomenal reality.
For this we take knowledge as Stewart first describes it, viz. as
impression (my 'communication') followed by sensation, un-
examinable further. The impression, Stewart says, is produced
by 'external objects.' Keeping up the metaphor of 'impression'
(for which may be substituted the more exact 'corporeal
communication') what does 'object' (or objects) mean here?
As it is what *impresses* (or corporeally communicates), it
means carbon, oxygen, &c. (constituents of wood), the constituents of iron, whatever they may be, light (causing
colour)—all these in a shape which we can in such and such
a manner handle. Now *here* comes the point. Phenomenalism,
as I have said, is a manner in which we can *hold* knowledge, but
not a manner in which we can *get* it. Supposing our knowledge
complete, it might be considered as much a phenomenon or
fact about the plough, that it turns up the ground, or is
meant to turn up the ground, or however we describe it, as
that it is of wood and iron, its colour red, and its shape
whatever it might be. And it is this its purpose, meaning,
use, which makes it a plough, *i.e.* which makes us call it a
plough. It is a plough, *i.e.* the thing which it is, in virtue of
its doing this, or being meant or intended to do this, not in

virtue of its being wood and iron and in colour red. When
then we *realize* according to the abstraction which I have
called phenomenalism, we have as the most important or
highest facts (facts, that is, which most make things things)
certain facts which in their own nature we need not dissociate
from the rest of phenomena, but which only *half* belong to
phenomenalism, because we cannot give that full account of
them, phenomenally, which we could wish : because, though
we can conceive phenomenal knowledge of them, we *get* our
knowledge of them another way.

The second way of realizing gives us 'philosophical reality,'
as I have called it,—the highest and most comprehensive
reality, viz. right thought about what we think of. In this we
take knowledge, as Stewart in the second account describes it,
omitting his confusion between it and the first, which I have
noticed, and bearing in mind, as I have also noticed, how this
language about qualities is for a particular purpose, which
must not mislead us : we have not impression or communication,
but *perception* as I lately described it, or consciousness as I
described it before.

In this, what things are *substantially*, or we might say
materially, is not an object of our thought : they *are* what they
do, what is done to them, what they are meant or made for,
what they are of use for, what they remind us of, what we
think about them in fact, with the important addition which
we make to our thought, viz. that we have reason in thinking
so. This is, in philosophic language, the conceiving things,
the forming notions of them, and the notion is the thing. As
Dido 'concipit flammas,' begins to feel love, so we 'conceive
things,' begin to feel or think them, and they are things. In
this way of realizing, the plough *is* the thing which turns up
the ground, or which is made and meant for that purpose : this
is its existence, and so far from being unknowable, it is the
first and main thing known about it : the thing in itself is that
which we begin with. Stewart, in speaking of his perception,
puts things in their right order ; 'a perception of the existence
and qualities' : the 'existence' here as realized, not being
a logical substratum of the qualities, but the most real and

actual being of the thing, that which makes us call it a plough, and to which all the 'qualities,' hardness, colour, &c. are comparatively accidental.

If we now make the same supposition as we did in the case of phenomenalism, assuming the completeness of our knowledge from the other point of view:—*i.e.* that we thought rightly, and judged correctly, about whatever could be thought of, without any corporeal communication with anything,—we come then to something which, as contrasted with phenomenalism, is (in my mind) the highest fact, and the true account of knowledge : but still which is not, any more than phenomenalism, knowledge as we learn it, attain to it, and have it. We should then understand all that communicates with our frame, and the manner of communication, and our frame itself, not as now, by particular sensations accompanying the particular communications, but as a Creator of the whole might have fore-understood his work, or as a bystander able to enter into all.

As it is, we are in the position of beings, one portion of whose thought is of ourselves as communicating with some particular portion, or portions, of what we consider a spatial universe ; while at the same time we are able to see, *both* that it is a portion, not all, of our thought about ourselves, and *also* that the portion of this universe which we communicate with is but a small portion of it : that is, our thought expands itself beyond, and comprehends, both our experience on the whole, and the sum of our particular experiences. And with all this, we are not knowers, but learners : we may be said really to know nothing, in so far as incompleteness is in a sense falsity, and more especially incompleteness in a case such as ours, where on every side we are freshly learning. My difference with those who talk of an 'unknowable' is this, that though we may *know* nothing, we are *learners* of everything.

Our process of learning, or advancing in knowledge, is, as I have at various times said, by the double manner of acquaintance and thought, communication and thought, or in whatever way we like to characterize them : not that we gain one portion of our knowledge in one way, and one portion in another, but that we gain all our knowledge, and each portion of it, by the mixture of the two. Either would be *knowing*, the one more thorough knowing than the other: the mixture of the two is learning: it is because we cannot in ourselves dissever the two that we seem to *know* nothing: but this is only because in regard of everything we are in a better position —the position of *learners*.

Hence, if we take care how we use the words, there is no harm in saying that those parts of knowledge which, as I have just described, have *least* the character of phenomenalism are objects of perception, and that those parts of knowledge which, in the same way, have least the character of thought are objects of sensation: and in fact, this represents to a certain degree the way of our *learning*, of our coming to the knowledge of one and the other sort of objects. But we must remember, that according to the way we look, all knowledge is perception, or all knowledge is sensation: we really perceive equally the purpose, the shape, and the colour of the plough: or, the other way, the colour, the shape, and the purpose of the plough equally impress us or communicate with us, at different points of the scale of our intellectual organization. These two manners of knowing represent two methods of learning, and though, in a manner, we learn *each* point of our knowledge by the two methods combined, still at a higher point in the scale there enters more of the one method, lower down in the scale there enters more of the other: and therefore, if we do it with care, we may describe the objects at the higher part of the scale as learnt by way of thought or perception, those at the lower as learnt by way of feeling or sensation.

This is one way of using the terms sensation and perception, and if they are so used, it might be said that every act of observation or apprehension was divisible into three parts, the lower or chemical[1] sensation of secondary qualities, the upper or mechanical sensation of primary qualities, and the perception of the 'thinghood' of the thing. We might even suppose, phenomenally, a succession or order of time in this: that the colour of the plough struck our eyes first, its shape our eyes

---

[1] *Expl.* pp. 39, 106.

II.] MILL AND STEWART. 31

and thought second, its purpose our thought last. Here we have something like the succession which Stewart describes: but if we suppose this, as *phenomenally* we may, we have to remember that it is not phenomenally only that we get our knowledge, and that if it happens on the particular occasion that our other manner of learning, *thought*, is the more energetic,—then the order of time will go the other way. When *this* is the order of succession, the term we ordinarily use is *noticing* things. What makes us think first about the plough and look at it may be the brightness of its colour, as we have just seen: or it may be our asking ourselves, or wondering, what it is meant for and how it is used, and then we begin with perception.

In reality however there is *not* a succession of time, though there is no harm in our supposing it: the whole act is one, and instantaneous.

The above use of 'perception' is not the same as the following. The *basal* fact, as I have called it, the sensation or consciousness, is triply divisible into the feeling of *I-hood*, the feeling of pleasure and pain or of will, and the feeling, with interpretation, of *occasion* of this latter feeling: this latter may be separated from the rest of the sensation as the intellectual part of it, and called 'perception.' This is Sir William Hamilton's use of the term when he gives his law, that sensation and perception vary inversely the one as the other. The use is perfectly legitimate, if only it be remembered that the perception is a *part* of the sensation in a broader view of this latter, and that the *other* part of the sensation, in so far as it gives us knowledge, is intellectual or involves perception: we perceive ourselves or know our own existence as well as that of the occasions of our sensation.

All the fact of the universe may be put in the form of *qualities*, if we like so to put it. It would probably *now* be more advantageous if the old logical language were discontinued, and if instead of qualities of bodies we talked of 'facts of the universe.' But it is only a difference of language upon which I do not think much depends, except that it might save a little perplexity of students, some *mis-realism* of logicians, and would put some controversies, like that of the enumeration and classification of these qualities, on a better footing. The distinction between primary and secondary qualities, broadly represents a difference in our sensations which will always continue one.

CHAPTER III.

WHAT IS KNOWLEDGE? HOW ANSWERED BY LOCKE, COUSIN, BERKELEY, DESCARTES.

KNOWLEDGE is the congruence between thought and things, this congruence being looked at from the side of thought—not that the word *congruence* can here be much understood, and the investigation of the nature of knowledge is in a great degree an effort to understand it.

Thought or conception may be considered the genus of which vain imagination and knowledge are the two species: imagination in itself being considered a common, or possibly common, character. How are we specifically to define knowledge, or which is the same thing, to know it from vain imagination?

I am inclined to say—Knowledge is conviction justifying itself in a manner which really justifies it not only to itself, but universally or to all possible intelligence.

Philosophers generally take one of two lines: either that

(1) Knowledge is a conviction (*i.e.* conception involving persuasion or strong belief) justifying itself by a reference of itself to things, or by its conformity with them.

(2) Knowledge is such a conviction justifying itself by its simple existence, which is *felt* to be necessary so far as *itself* is concerned, and *considered* to be necessary universally.

The justification of knowledge by its conformity with *things* is what cannot take place in regard of the first or fundamental portions of knowledge, for of course it supposes a preliminary knowledge of things, in order for the comparison of professed knowledge with them, which first knowledge is not susceptible of being justified in this manner. All attempted examination of knowledge therefore on this principle must involve some other principle on which to deal with the rudiments or great features of knowledge: if it proceeds as if it did not, it becomes what I have called 'mis-psychology'[1]: i.e. it stultifies itself at the beginning by a vast unauthorized assumption. And not only so, but by failing to take account of the great underlying portions of knowledge, it lowers and too much limits the notion of *reality* or of things, excluding from it much of what seems, to me at least, the most real.

Still it is evident that there is much reason in the view of these philosophers, that knowledge must have other evidence to justify itself as knowledge beyond its own simple assertion, or in other words, that knowledge has something else involved in it beyond what belongs to mere thought. Whether we can help thinking a thing or not, it is not knowledge *because* we cannot help thinking it, or in virtue of our being unable to think otherwise: we mean by knowledge something which has *fact* corresponding with it, fact beyond the fact of its existence, as thought, in us. When put therefore in its most general form, M. Cousin's polemic against Locke for his description of real knowledge as depending on the conformity of ideas with external things or their archetypes, is not correct, though there is much that is correct in it. As it is, in arguing against innate ideas, Locke satisfies himself with endeavouring to maintain, that in point of fact, there are no ideas which are sufficiently early, identical, and universal in all men to deserve the name. He might have gone further and said, Even if there were such innate ideas, they would not be means of real knowledge to me, unless I could understand that they had fact corresponding with them, beyond the fact of their own existence as ideas. On what ground do you assert that, because I cannot help believing that God exists, he actually does exist? Descartes went deeper than Locke. 'I, the thinker, exist, is a fact, as much as that the

---

[1] *Expl.* p. IX.

thought exists as thought': this is what I understand him at bottom to say, and I think he is right. It is not that my existence is an innate idea of mine, from the existence of which as innate idea I conclude there is fact corresponding to it, but it is that, as a fact, whether I think of it and know it or not, my existence is a fact pre-conditioning my thought, or necessarily existing previously to my thought, in order for such thought to be possible. Here we have a fact, which we might venture to speak of as known previously to knowledge, or known independently of any knowledge of things. There is no unreason in justifying knowledge by seeing whether or not it is conformable with this.

When Descartes goes on from our own existence to that of God, what he really does is to suppose a non-ego or '*besides-self*,' and to suppose this, not as an unknown reality, but as an ideal or ground of all things. And here too, I believe, he is right in the main. I do not look just now at the theological aspect of the question, whether he conceives the nature of God rightly or not: but what I understand as at the bottom of his view is this, that the fact of our existence, as thinking, involves the fact of the existence of a state of things *in* which we think, and *of* which we and our thinking are a part: and since our type or specimen of existence in this state of things is ourselves thinking, we conceive the state of things to be the result of thought, and call the thinking Being, God. The point here is, that, without particularizing to the extent to which Descartes does, we have here too a fact as to which there is no unreason in justifying knowledge by its conformity with it. This non-ego or rather *circum-ego*, that to which we belong, or of which we are a part, or in obedience to which we think, is itself a part of ourselves, and is a fact therefore corresponding with the thinking: and since the knowledge of this does not need justification, other knowledge may fairly be justified by it.

When therefore Descartes speaks so much as he does about God's not deceiving us, he is really, though in special and individual language, dealing with the roots of knowledge in a manner which most philosophers after him have neglected. God, says Descartes in effect, is the Author of fact as well as of mind; and since he has made us to think that there exists fact corresponding to the manner in which we cannot help thinking, we may be sure he would not deceive us; and therefore such fact does exist. It seems to me obvious, that all that is called 'intuitivism' involves as a basis, not indeed necessarily this, or anything in words like it, but something which in substance is of the same kind. Any universal and inevitable thought of the human race and of each man (say that two straight lines will not enclose a space) is called true, not in virtue of its being such an universal and inevitable thought (supposing it to be so), but because we believe that a thought of this character would not exist without there being reason in fact for its existing: and it is this supposition of the previous existence of fact in conformity with the thought, and supplying one portion of the reason for the existence of the thought, which makes us call the thought, not imagination, but knowledge. Where Hume says, in effect, that what we call knowledge is thought in conformity with *human custom*, Cousin, blaming Locke for saying that knowledge is thought ('ideas') in conformity with *fact*, says in effect that knowledge is thought in conformity with *human nature*. Both of these are characters of knowledge, but the Lockian seems to me the more important and intimate of the two, and the latter only to be a real character of knowledge in so far as it is virtually included in the other. What security have we that our humanly natural thought is not a sort of generically private or individual imagination (as in fact some relativists go far to think it), except our feeling that we with our thinking are a part of a constituted, harmonious, self-consistent, God-created universe?

Descartes' view may be said to include Berkeley's, involving all that Berkeley has said on the question of the existence of material things, only that Descartes goes much deeper and wider, and is so far more correct. In spite of the evident sincerity of Descartes, I am not sure how far we are able to gather his real feeling, on account of the constraint under which he, as well as many other philosophers, wrote, and which then could hardly be avoided. But still to me, there appears to be in him what I should call a seriousness, that is a freedom from affectation and from desire of paradox, a thinking of truth alone, which exists perhaps equally in Locke, but does not seem similarly to belong to Berkeley and Hume. Nobody doubts whether Locke, and whether Descartes at the bottom, is in earnest. They both of them probe things to the depth to which their line will go: Berkeley and Hume do not care to do so. Hume is content to leave knowledge as customary thought, without any care to examine the nature of this custom. In the same way Berkeley sees no difficulty, and nothing requiring further probing, in the consideration that two notions, both of which may fairly be called natural, in so far as actual human thought indicates human nature—the vulgar notion, namely, of the independent existence of the external world as we perceive it, and the philosophic notion of the independent existence of an unknown substance underlying what we properly perceive—that these two apparently natural notions are prejudices only and not correct; while what is correct is something which the natural, habitual, actual thought of men certainly does not realize at all, viz. that our thought as to what we call the external world is a quasi-inspiration of the Deity.

I am not disputing Berkeley's being to a great extent right, which I believe him to be: my point only is, that he leaves the question where no philosopher has a right to leave it. There exists really, says Berkeley, only spirit, the Infinite Spirit and our finite spirits: and what distinguishes that portion of our thought which is knowledge from that which is not, is that the former is the suggestion to us of the Infinite Spirit.

Now it is very hard to say what the natural, or habitual, or actual, thought of man as to the existence of the external world is, and I doubt whether any philosopher (certainly not Berkeley) has been even consistent with himself in his attempts to describe it. But whatever it *is*, it seems to me anyhow that it is *not* any thought or supposition of this Divine suggestion, whether this latter is the fact or not: so far as it is the fact, it is only afterwards that it is thought or known to be so. Human thought then is quietly left by Berkeley in the position, if we may so speak, of habitually misunderstanding itself, or taking itself for what it is not: or to use language more

like Berkeley's own, and that of Descartes also, Berkeley sees
nothing remarkable in the Divine suggestion being the fact as
to our minds, but not marking itself to them as the fact (except
long afterwards and as a philosophical discovery); so that we
almost inevitably take it for something else, viz. for a supposed
reality in things: that is, in fact, it *results* to us in illusion.
This may perhaps be so: if we conceive the matter in the
latter form, we undoubtedly, in spite of our dependence on the
Infinite Mind, mistake in many things, and might possibly do
so in fundamental things. If we conceive the matter in the
first-mentioned form, that human thought habitually misunderstands itself, we may say, Well, perhaps it does: and so we
come to a sort of 'regulativism': our habitual or inevitable
thought then, though free from illusion so far as it serves to
guide our corporeal action, is illusion above this point, *i.e.* it
represents to us something about which we cannot help thinking
in a way in which nevertheless we know (by philosophy or
otherwise) we ought not to think.   Or on the other hand we
may say, we ought to think that the material world exists
independently, because it is our nature so to think, and yet we
ought not to think so, because the fact is otherwise.

Berkeley, satisfied with bringing vigorously out the contrast
between human habitual thought (or prejudice) and the real
fact or truth, leaves the matter here: but Descartes is not
satisfied to do so.   Were it simply so, he says, this would be a
deceiving of man by God. If God has made me to think, and
not to be able to help thinking, that the material world exists
independently of my perceiving it, and in the same way and
for the same reason, independently of anyone's perceiving it,
then it does so exist, or God is deceiving me.   Descartes is
certainly right in not leaving human thought as Berkeley does,
but sounding deeper, though the theological language is not a
necessary part of the view here taken. The thing may be put
thus: rightness or correctness is one and the same for all
knowledge, low or high, rudimentary or far advanced: if we
know anything, whatever it is, *i.e.* think about it correctly, that
step of knowledge is good for all possible progress of knowledge,
and true in the face of the universe. We may come to find that

our supposed past knowledge was wrong, or we may come to
find it absorbed and taken up in more expanded knowledge:
but we shall not come to find that knowledge itself is something different from what it was when we began to know, in
such a way that what was once good knowledge is now good no
longer. Nothing is more possible (in fact I have no doubt but
that it is true) than that all our real knowledge is Divine
suggestion, a sort of mediate inspiration. But if we think (or
apparently know), as a part of our process of knowing, that the
mediation of this suggestion is what we call external things,
having a reality of their own, independent of the perception of
them, then the Divine suggestion is in fact equivalent to what
we understand by *creation*, as Descartes regarded it. As I
have said, what exactly we do think as to this is hard to say:
but we certainly do *not* think that the relation of what we call
material things to something which is not material, is at all
analogous to the relation which the words of a language bear
to what they signify. Things are *themselves*, or they are
nothing: if they are God's words to us, as there is no harm in
considering them, they are this in virtue of their being things,
and we come most to enter into the meaning of them as God's
words by the most thoroughly considering them as things, in
the sense in which our mind or nature leads us to view things.
On the other hand if, and so far as, our view of reality as
a Divine suggestion, or our view of things as dependent for
their reality on being perceived, leads us to alter our view of
them as *things* (upon which view we talk with others and act),
to that extent it is wrong. But where the thought of such
Divine suggestion leaves our view of things unaltered, there
is no paradox, no supplantation of one view by another,
no point in saying, that what the vulgar have conceived as
things, the wise conceives as a language, *i.e.* as signs of
things. Berkeley's favourite metaphor of language is here
singularly unhappy. Though there is no harm in calling the
external world a language of God to us, there is no *good* in
doing so, if we stop where Berkeley stops, for it is a language
entirely unknown to us. We have the letters and words, and
are told they are signs: but how are we to find out of what?

We perversely think the letters and words the things, and then we are told they are not so, but we are not told what it is of which they are signs, so that we are left without things at all, only with a language telling us nothing. Berkeley was led probably to this error, as I suppose it will be allowed to be, by his Theory of Vision, where the metaphor of language had a little more reason in it than it has here, though still not much.

In speaking of Descartes being right at the bottom, I mean expressly to imply that I do not think he is right as he proceeds.

If we really wish to do what Descartes wished to do, *i.e.* make ourselves infants in knowledge in order to have our knowledge thoroughly tested and put in a better method, we have got to strip ourselves of more than our actual knowledge of any kind: we have got to unlearn or unthink our manner of thinking: and this is what of course is hardly possible. Descartes was mathematically trained and minded. His notion of certainty was what we may call a sort of geometrical intuition of fact in a particular form, and seen reason for its being in that form—the coup d'œil or comprehension of demonstration and conclusion in one—so as at once to exclude contrary supposition. This was the manner in which he had been in the habit of looking on certainty—demonstration, but demonstration lost in a manner and absorbed in the mental view, in the now intuitive force of the thing understood to be known. It was from this habitual conception of certainty, it is to be supposed, that he drew his notion of clear and distinct ideas. We are certain of a thing, he says, when we have a clear and distinct idea of it. The language follows servilely on the sense of sight, in spite of Descartes' constant care to distinguish mental intuition from quasi-visual imagination. By 'clear' he means with plenty of light upon the idea, so that it is not dim or obscure: by 'distinct' he means standing out in bold relief, so that there is no difficulty in distinguishing one idea from other ideas, and no confusing it with them.

I mentioned a short time since the peculiar character, in the point of view of knowledge, of the fact of our own existence as thinking, perhaps also of the existence of the ideal, God or the universe, on which we depend. If the word consciousness is to be used, we should have been wise to use it only in relation to the former of these facts, applying it only to that self-know-ledge, so to speak, or rather self-presence, self-companionship, carrying ourself *with* our thought, which is involved in thinking, and is quite independent of anything which we think, of any object of thought, even of our own distinctly contem-plated selves. Both Descartes however, *without* using the word consciousness, and a whole line of philosophers after him, using it, proceed in substance differently. He joined with the 'Cogito ergo sum' a conclusion of as much philosophic bearing as that, but not equally true, viz. 'I judge this conclusion to be true only because I clearly see it to be so : therefore clear mental sight is the test of truth.' Here we have the gate opened to the endless misuse of the term consciousness, or similar terms, on the part of the line of philosophers of whom I have spoken : here we have Descartes' scepticism resulting in a bold individualist dogmatism. In Descartes' mathe-matical intuitions, it had not been the clear mental sight, but the demonstration which it, so to speak, looked through, which had been the real condition of the truth : and the clear mental sight had only been the frame of mind which the demonstration was calculated to produce, but which, or some-thing undistinguishable from it, might exist without the demonstration, being *then* really *deceptive.* In Descartes' notion of clear mental sight being the test of truth, there is involved an exceedingly abstract form of that same error which, in its gross and concrete form, makes mis-psychology. In order to be sure that what we mentally see is not hallucination on our part, what we want to be made certain of is that there is something to see (or rather to be seen); and any amount of clearness or distinctness in our view will not alter the possibility of halluci-nation unless we are made certain of this. That this is not mere words, is evident from the applications which have been made, and which even Descartes himself made, of his own view in this particular. If what we seem to see with the greatest clearness and distinctness generally turns out to be reality, it is so because reality possesses a quality which makes it thus present itself, in a manner different from what is not reality; and it is this quality which we should try to find. Otherwise the saying that what we see clearly must be true, is merely a laying claim to the privilege of dispensation from proof.

CHAPTER IV.

MILL AND LOCKE ON OUR KNOWLEDGE OF THE EXTERNAL WORLD.

LET us compare for a moment Mr Mill's view with that of Locke.

When our senses are conversant with external objects, says Locke, we receive from them passively simple ideas, as of smells, tastes, colours, also of space, magnitude, form. (This is pure sensation or impression.) These we actively put together (we may say by imagination) into complex ideas, viz. 'modes,' which in point of fact are thoughts about external objects, not purporting to have any such objects actually corresponding to them; ideas of the relation of one idea or object to another; and ideas of substances, the formation of which ideas is really the reproduction or re-creation, by the mind and as idea, of those external objects with which the senses were supposed at first conversant.

It is not my purpose now to dwell on the *circularity*[1] of this, which is what I have several times noticed as the bad psychology. I am to compare the view with that of Mr Mill.

We have, says Mr Mill (in place of the unmeaning or doubtful account of what takes place, with which Locke begins), however arising and whencesoever derived, particular sensations, which we describe as seeing something bright, *e.g.* a colour, hearing a voice, smelling a perfume, &c. Sensation is followed by imagination, which suggests possibilities of the presence

[1] *Expl.* 162.

of the past sensations in every variety of combination: hence-forward our actual sensation is always accompanied by a vast amount of imagination of this possibility of it: it is this possibility of sensation by us which we mean, when we speak of the universe, things, external objects,—more or less *concretifying* it.

It will be seen that, where Locke speaks of the previous independent existence of external objects, and of two processes or facts, first the conversance of our senses with these, and then the reception by us of ideas, Mr Mill speaks of no such previous independent existence, and only of one process or fact, our sensation or impression.

Both he and Locke may be considered to say (putting the matter a little exaggeratedly for the moment, for better under-standing) that we passively experience particular sensations, and then at their suggestion actively create by imagination what we call the external world or universe : for our idea of the universe is the sum or mass of our ideas of substances.

Locke must be conceived, I suppose, to make two bases of reality : a real substance of things, which we cannot reach, though we think we do, reaching in reality their qualities only, (so that in this view we have an idea of things, which is true but inadequate), and next a ground of sensation, viz. his 'objects with which the senses are conversant.' From these objects or this ground proceed, with passiveness on our part, our simple ideas. In them there can be no deception, since there is simple passiveness. The ideas by hypothesis come from the objects, and in their coming from the objects is all the truth they are capable of: unless indeed we suppose the objects inclined to deceive us, in which case we have the further guarantee, that the Deity who made them would not allow them to do so.

Locke says thus in effect, that the universe of things, as we conceive things in virtue of our complex ideas of substances, is what Mr Mill calls a mass of possibilities of sensation, what Locke calls a collection of powers to produce in us certain sensations: we superadd to these from ourselves the half-illusory, or at least ill-understood, idea of substance, as with

Mr Mill we do that of reality. But sensation is a different
thing with Locke and with Mr Mill. While both assume it as
fact, it has with the former, illogically, two characters, the
necessary union of which in any real fact he does not even
attempt to show: viz. the character of being a special feeling
or consciousness in us, and the character on the other side of
proceeding from actually existing objects. Mr Mill, more
logically, treats sensation as being on the whole defined and
determined by the former character. Only, with Mr Mill, there
is no certainty that the sensations which suggest our conceptions of things are any way derived from things: so that we are
cut off from things altogether: all may be imagination. Locke
will have his sensations derived from things: but the wrong
logic in this is so flagrant, that even *he* is several times obliged
to speak the language of Berkeley.

Locke's view of human impression must be taken to be,
that somehow or other we are aware, to start with, of the
existence, both sensible and substantial, of external things;
since in the case of the sensation which supplies us with the
first simple idea, we are aware that there is an actually existing
external thing from which it comes; and since, when the mind
begins to be active and to form complex ideas or ideas of *things*
with various properties, it is the supposed *substance* of the
thing, which we endeavour to make out however unsuccessfully,
and short of the idea of which we have not an adequate idea
of the thing. Though however we are thus supposed to know
at the beginning that there are things sensibly and substantially existing, how far do we really know the things beyond
our knowledge of this fact about the things? Locke's answer,
in respect of the substance or supposed true reality of the
things is, that we know it most inadequately, or it might be
said not at all. In respect of their *sensible* reality, or such
reality as may be conceived involved in their being occasions
of sensations, his answer, I should think, must be odd. Surely
we must know not only the fact of the existence of the things,
but the things themselves in that process which is described as
'our senses being conversant with external objects': but we
have to begin again with the reception, first, from the objects,

of simple ideas, from which we go on, next, to the putting the
simple ideas together and the mental making of the objects, as
if they did not exist, and had not, by the hypothesis, been
acting upon us all the time. This conversion of what is really
one process into two by looking at it from the two ends is what
I have all along condemned as the bad psychology[1]. Locke
would, I suppose, answer, that we have a sort of knowledge
of the objects from the beginning, and then, superadded to this,
the gradual knowledge of growing experience or the reception
of ideas from things, and of such imagination, or formation
of ideas about things, as can justify itself in any way to be
right and truth.

This sort of double view of knowledge seems to me
right or wrong according to the way in which we take it.
It is little different from Sir William Hamilton's consciousness of matter. We are prepared, so to speak, for the first
particular sensation which we actually experience, by the
knowledge that there are external objects from which the
sensations come, or may come. Unless we have the previous
knowledge that there are such objects, what possibly can make
us in the first instance think that the sensation, which is itself
but a feeling, comes from them? But what is the nature of
this knowledge or preparedness? Is it a first gigantic general
experience, rendering possible all following particular experience? If it is, the word 'experience' must not carry in it
the notion of 'experience as fact,' 'experience of a thing as
fact,' for that means the reference of something to understood
existing fact, and here there is nothing to refer to. Experience
is part of a course, and here there is nothing precedent.
Experience is knowledge by trial, with a conceivable alternative: and here there is neither trial nor conceivable alternative.
Experience therefore must mean here only change of feeling,
mental experience, possibly therefore imagination only, if we
conceive that, without an understood cause *ab extra*, a supposition or conception can be nothing more than mere imagination.
The knowledge then of there being external objects would be

[1] *Expl.* 73, 192.

a sort of *notio princeps,* not caused by the external objects. Locke would have to say, our mental history is first that of a purely mental experience suggesting to us that there is fact independent of us, and *then* of an experience at once mental and (so to speak) *experimental,* by which we come gradually to know all the particulars of the fact thus anticipated.

Otherwise the knowledge which Locke supposes us to have of the existence of objects, or of an external world, must be a gigantic innate idea: and in expelling from the mind one kind of innate ideas, he only introduces an opposite.

So far as we can divest Locke's view of the bad psychology, and still call it *his* view, he seems to me (and the same as to the *substantial* reality of things), to be right or wrong according as we understand him.   The substance or 'thinghood¹' of a thing I look upon as a reality, or as a notion with important meaning, but I look upon it as involved in the qualities of the thing, not as distinct from them and underlying them.   For the sake of convenience we assume as underlying the things a supposed substance, which is the *logical* subject when the thing is spoken of, and which really is the supposition of the sum of the qualities of the thing, known and unknown, with the added notion of relative importance among them.   Against this stands the view, whether in scholastic or quasi-Kantian form, of there being a substantial reality of the thing independent of its qualities or phenomena, which is the thing in itself, what we know to exist, but can form no conception of.   To which of these views of substance does Locke incline?

The kind of previous knowledge of external things which he must suppose in us is an idea of their sensible and substantial reality together.   The senses are conversant with external objects, *i.e.* not merely with the external universe, but with individualized portions of it.   This, in the mis-psychological interpretation, is really that we know in fact more, before we begin to learn, than we ever can afterwards succeed in learning. Divesting the view as far as possible of the mis-psychology, we must consider the first knowledge a sort of obscure sketch or

¹ *Expl.* pp. 106, 123, &c.

anticipation of what is to come afterwards. Supposing we had
no eyelids, but our eyes were always open like our ears, and
that our waking to sight was the gradual *distinctifying* of
itself by the prospect before them ; we should see the whole
field of view in the first look as well as in the hundredth. In
a similar manner our knowledge is in a sense always the same :
it is virtually contained in our intelligence, and might be
predicted from that: and what might be predicted from the
study of our particular intelligence and constitution by an
outsider, it is reasonable to suppose that we from within our
intelligence might anticipate by an obscure consciousness. The
eye in a way sees, though it sees nothing, the ear in a way
hears, though it hears nothing : and so our intelligence, in its
looking and listening, before knowledge is actually presented
to it, may be said, in its particular faculties and the disposition
to use them, to forecast its after knowledge. This, as I
understand it, is one of the points of Kantism : our mind is
ready for the knowledge that is coming: it is furnished, and
we can describe its furniture, but its furniture is only applicable
to that knowledge, and we misapply it if we try to apply it
otherwise. We have got, for instance, in our minds space, *i.e.*
the disposition to spatial conception, as a frame of the universe
that is coming, so that we have a sort of anticipation of it, and
yet this anticipation is nothing in itself, nothing except as
applied to what it is meant to be applied to. Locke, in that
previous *knowledge* (so to call it) that there are things and an
universe, which he implies to exist before there are separate
and distinct ideas of the things, may mean a kind of anticipation,
something like the Kantian spatial thought. This is correct,
at least in so far as that the supposing our knowledge to come
item by item, particular by particular, *is* one way of putting
the fact, which requires to be supplemented by something
further, viz. the consideration, what it is in us and in the
universe that makes our knowledge come in this succession,
history, and order. If we choose to rest in this latter as the
ultimate fact that we can arrive at, well and good : only the
proceeding is arbitrary on our part. If we say, the succession
has been what it is, because our mind and the universe have

been what they are, then, in so far as we know in any degree what our mind is, and what sort of relation it bears to the universe, we know what is coming. Each thought of ours has, in a way, our whole mind and the whole universe in it: it would not be what it is, unless they were what they are.

So much then (rather desultorily) for Locke's notion of the *meaning* of human impression, and my notion of the value of it, supposing it to be to the effect that he describes. As to his own notion of the *value* of it, he speaks, as a wrong psychologist, with a double voice, knowing the existence of things himself, while he discusses how we come to know them; or, which is the same thing, he knows that impressions come from existing objects, and therefore of course are true and valuable; while with regard to substances, his view is that we know they exist, and we know we cannot reach them, so that human impression is *not* valuable.

CHAPTER V.

HUME ON THE ORIGIN OF IDEAS. IMPRESSION AND IMAGINATION.

I AM going, in the present chapter, to use the three words impression[1], imagination, idea, in a peculiar and technical sense, which I shall carefully define in the case of each, and to which I do not know that I shall adhere in other chapters, but which seems to me of importance in reference to the question I am *now* about to discuss.

I am not going to criticize in detail the passage which I give below from Hume's *Inquiry concerning the Human Understanding*[2], but I have thought it convenient to quote it all, for two reasons: first because Hume exactly defines the term 'impression' here in the sense in which I shall use it in this chapter, with one most important qualification, which I proceed to mention under the second reason, viz. because I want the reader to watch for the beginning of the mixture of incongruous notions, or what I have called the bad psychology.

1. Everyone will readily allow that there is a considerable difference between the perceptions of the mind, when a man feels the pain of excessive heat, or the pleasure of moderate warmth ; and when he afterwards recalls to his memory this sensation, or anticipates it by his imagination. These faculties may mimic or copy the perceptions of the senses ; but they never can entirely reach the force and vivacity of the original sentiment. The utmost we say of them, even when they operate with the greatest vigour, is that they represent their object in so lively a

---

[1] See later view in Book II. on Immediateness and Reflection.

[2] Section II., *On the Origin of Ideas.*

manner, that we could almost say we feel or see it : but except the mind
be disordered by disease or madness, they never can arrive at such a
pitch of vivacity, as to render these perceptions altogether undistinguishable...

2.   We may observe a like distinction to run through all the other
perceptions of the mind. A man in a fit of anger is actuated in a very
different manner from one who only thinks of that emotion. If you tell
me that any person is in love, I easily understand your meaning and form
a just conception of his situation ; but never can mistake that conception
for the real disorders and agitations of the passion. When we reflect on
our past sentiments and affections, our thought is a faithful mirror and
copies its objects truly ; but the colours which it employs are faint and
dull, in comparison of those in which our original perceptions were
clothed. It requires no nice discernment or metaphysical head to mark
the distinction between them.

3.   Here therefore we may divide all the perceptions of the mind into
two classes or species, which are distinguished by their different degrees of
force and vivacity. The less forcible and lively are commonly denomi-
nated 'thoughts' or 'ideas.' The other species want a name in our
language and in most others ; I suppose, because it was not requisite for
any but philosophical purposes to rank them under a general term or
appellation. Let us therefore use a little freedom and call them ' Impressions' ; employing that word in a sense somewhat different from the
usual. By the term 'impression,' then, I mean all our more lively
perceptions, when we hear or see or feel or love or hate or desire or will.
And impressions are distinguished from ideas, which are the less lively
perceptions of which we are conscious when we reflect on any of these
sensations or movements above described.

4.   Nothing, at first view, may seem more unbounded than the thought
of man ; which not only escapes all human power and authority, but is
not even restrained within the limits of nature and reality. To form
monsters and join incongruous shapes and appearances, costs the imagination no more trouble than to conceive the most natural and familiar
objects. And while the body is confined to one planet, along which it
creeps with pain and difficulty, the thought can in an instant transport us
into the most distant regions of the universe, or even beyond the universe
into the unbounded chaos where nature is supposed to lie in total confusion. What never was seen or heard of may yet be conceived ; nor is
any thing beyond the power of thought, except what implies an absolute
contradiction.

5.   But though our thought seems to possess this unbounded liberty,
we shall find upon a nearer examination, that it is really confined within
very narrow limits, and that all this creative power of the mind amounts
to no more than the faculty of compounding, transposing, augmenting, or
diminishing the materials afforded us by the senses and experience.

When we think of a golden mountain, we only join two consistent ideas, gold and mountain, with which we were formerly acquainted. A virtuous horse we can conceive; because from our own feeling we can conceive virtue; and this we may unite to the figure and shape of a horse, which is an animal familiar to us. In short all the materials of thinking are derived either from our outward or inward sentiments: the mixture and composition of these belongs alone to the mind or will: or to express myself in philosophical language, all our ideas or more feeble perceptions are copies of our impressions or more lively ones.

In this passage the bad psychology hints itself obscurely in the last sentence but one of the third paragraph, and shows itself fully in the first sentence of the fifth. The former I will requote. as it is the most important in the passage.

By the term 'impression' I mean all our more lively perceptions, when we hear or see or feel or love or desire or will.

The reader will observe, that the word perception is used in a very wide application, pretty much for what we should call 'feeling': the being in a fit of anger and in love are called in the second paragraph perceptions of the mind. Some of these perceptions, which are more lively than others, are called by Hume 'impressions,' and he gives a specimen list of them: by memory or imagination these perceptions, or copies of them, may recur to the mind in a less lively form: then he gives them the name of 'ideas.'

If the reader will look carefully at Hume's list, he will see that he must for the present discard, from the meaning of 'impression,' the notion of there being something independent of us impressing us. There *may* be: but the word 'impression,' as here used does not involve it. There is undoubtedly an object, a content, of the impression: but the important point is, that the existence of this is given us by the impression, and is not independent of it.

For the word 'impression,' as Hume uses it here, it is more common in modern philosophy to use the word 'presentation.' When we speak of love and hate being 'presentations,' it is of course clear that the word 'presentation' can contain no more notion of something independent presented to the mind, than the word impression does of something impressing it.

Hume's definition of 'impressions' must be considered to finish with the first clause of the sentence, for it is clear that he does not mean that, if we hear obscurely or desire feebly, it is not an impression. But it is clear also, that the more or less of liveliness is not a sufficient distinction between an 'impression,' such as 'seeing' or 'desiring,' and what Hume calls an idea, namely, the imagination of a prospect or the remembrance that we have desired. The 'liveliness' has a peculiar or specific character about it. And this character is well suggested to us by the term 'presentation,' though I do not use that term, because I think it dangerously suggestive of error also. Where there is an impression, it is a part of the impression that there is an object of it present to us in some way (we shall see more soon about this term 'present') or in some special communication or relation with us. So far as it is hard, as it is, to realise the meaning of 'object' in this view applied to 'desire,' 'will,' &c., I think this only shows that the term 'impression' (or 'presentation') is not very happily applied to them.

The impressions which I am going to discuss are the intellectual impressions, of which Hume has mentioned two, 'seeing,' and 'hearing'; and that the reader may understand how I differ from him, and from what I have called the bad psychology, I will ask him to observe the difference of his proceeding and mine.

Many, when they read the list which Hume has given, will say, 'What is the meaning of putting thus seeing and hearing by the side of loving and hating?' When we see, we see with eyes an actually present object, as we hear with ears an actually sounding sound: but when we love, the object of our love may be here or anywhere: he or she is only *mentally* an object of it: again the particular impression of love to a person is only a part of our whole feeling or impression, which includes his existence, his being what we think him to be, &c. though at this moment he may be dead for all we know, or may not really possess those qualities for which we loved him. This is something very different from seeing and hearing things before us.

Hume would answer, or ought to answer, You must re-

member that we are dealing with these things simply as
'impressions,' *i.e.* as feelings of the mind, each with its own
particular sort of liveliness: we will observe these different
sorts, but you must remember that they are each one a feeling
of the mind, and only that. Just as you say that your friend's
existence, and his being what you think him to be, are parts of
your whole impression of love to him : so, when we are talking
of impressions, the fact of your having eyes (or a body) at all,
and the fact of the independent existence of an object for you
to see, are parts (along with the special impression that you
this moment see it) of the whole impression which you call
seeing, or of ideas derived from former impressions: you cannot
really go beyond impression. If you are not *now* beginning
to be persuaded that you have eyes, there *was* a time when
you began it; this, and the belief that there are objects for
you to see, are parts of your persuasion; as in the other case
that your friend is alive and virtuous. I will say nothing now
about the possible erroneousness.

So Hume ought to have answered, and so perhaps he would :
but his manner of proceeding is not distinct. When, in the
first sentence of the fifth paragraph, we read that, 'this creative
power of the mind amounts to no more than the faculty of
compounding, transposing, augmenting, or diminishing the
materials afforded us by the senses and experience...all the
materials of thinking are derived from our outward or inward
sentiment,' we see the entrance of that which I call the wrong
psychology. Suppose that in these impressions the mind is
not creative or capricious: we want then to determine what
are the laws and limitations of it : but we travel away from the
notion of impressions when we suppose these laws and limitations to be something outward, materials afforded us by our
senses. The mind certainly does what in the first instance
seems like 'creating'; for conceiving, beginning to feel[1], *is*
mental origination or creation. What I call the bad psychology
is the introducing here the notion about the materials, which is
incongruous. When the eye, *e.g.* (using *this* language) first
affords us materials, this very fact, which we *thus* describe, we

[1] Compare above p. 28.

may *also* describe as an impression, or the mind creating, in whatever way it does create. It is therefore absurd to say, as Hume does here, that the creative power of the mind is only the faculty of compounding, &c. these materials.

The reader will find however Hume's main line of thought clear in this respect, and I have quoted this first chapter because I should like him to continue reading the others: I shall presently discuss the account which Hume gives in them of the nature and value of the belief attending our intellectual impressions or presentations.

What Hume, in the passage which I have quoted, calls 'ideas,' I shall call 'imaginations,' because I shall have to use the word 'idea' for that which is common both to the 'impressions' and to (my) 'imaginations,' which in fact is the sense in which it is commonly used by philosophers of the last century, Hume's use being a particular limitation of it. It will therefore express occasionally either or both of the others, and we shall have occasion for its doing so.

I have then at this moment an *impression* of a scene, whatever it may be, as actually before me; the objects in it tangible and what I call both real and really present. I have perhaps at this same moment, consistently with the above, an *imagination* of a former impression, say an imagination of the Roman Forum, vividly before my mind's eye, but accompanied with the feeling that it is not actually before me, and that the objects in it, though tangible, are not tangible by me now, though real, are not really present. And I have an idea of either or both, of the trees on the one hand, which appear to be at this moment before me, and on the other hand of the ruins in the Forum, which I remember having seen, and repicture to myself now.

We are now examining the consciousness or feeling, and we call *that* an *impression* where we have the feeling (a feeling quite unmistakeable for any other) that the objects are actually and tangibly before us; and *that* an *imagination* where the feeling is the opposite of this, viz. that the objects are not actually before us but that something else is, or would be, if we were under any impression at all.

All our actual states of intellectual feeling are mixtures of impression and imagination as thus described. Each fresh particular impression is added on to a mass of remembered and digested impression, which would come under the above definition of imagination. Similarly each imagination is formed upon the surface of a mass of impression, which is what gives to it its character of imagination. I call the mental picture which I form of the Roman Forum an imagination, because I am under the impression that I am sitting in my own house in England, looking out upon trees and whatever it may be— *not* the Forum. Our conscious being is a vast mass of continuous sensation or impression, to which new impressions and imaginations are every moment added or out of which they grow, in the same way as our advancing knowledge is a vast mass of continuous mental vision or imagination, to which new impressions and imaginations affix themselves. But at present where there is fresh impression, I shall call the whole 'impression,' though there is so much involved which is more properly imagination, and the same for imagination the other way. For imagination is only old impression, and impression would be entirely barren without imagination.

CHAPTER VI.

MEANING AND VALUE OF IMPRESSIONS. LOCKE AND HUME DEPRECIATE IMPRESSION.

THE two questions of all-important philosophical interest in regard of impression, are what is its *meaning* and *value*, and what is its genesis or history.

Impression is the present and lively thought of our own corporeal reality, of the reality of an universe of things which may communicate with it, and of the actual communication of some of them with it at the moment.

I ought to have put, before 'our own corporeal reality' 'what we call,' or after it, '*i.e.* what we consider such,' in order to make the reader fully realise that all thus thought of is given us only in the impression (or *has* been in a previous impression); that it is not something previously thought of, or in any way known or named by us, with which impression, as soon as it arises, is compared, or to which it is referred.

From this point of view a very useful glance may be taken over the confused battle about 'innate ideas.' Locke says, with reason, you must not suppose anything in us antecedent to impression: *i.e.* you must not suppose that we know about things (*i.e.* future or possible things) that they must have a cause, that there must be room for them to be, *i.e.* space or whatever else it may be: we think nothing about things or about anything, till we begin to have 'impression,' *i.e.* to think about them as existing before us, and about ourselves as existing in the middle of them: and as soon as we do this, we judge of

them according as we find them. But the important error
here, the root of what I have called the bad psychology, is this :
that, while Locke rightly urges that whatever might possibly
claim to be innate idea, such as the notion of cause, space, time,
or unity, does not begin till *impression* does, and is in fact a part
of it, he forgets that the notion of any reality of things at
all, and of our own corporeal reality, is equally a part of the
impression : he says in effect, ' of course our sight of the thing
is not a chimera, for the thing was there before we saw it, for
us to see when we began to see anything.' In reality, the bad
psychologists enter upon their investigation of the history of
our successive impressions (which, put together, we call the
universe as we know it) with an innate idea on the concrete
side, far worse than the innate ideas which they attack on the
abstract side, viz., an idea, or in fact knowledge, of what is
about to impress us—the very thing which we are supposed
to be going to find out. It is plain that Locke has from the
first the notion, that the universe, as it affects our senses, is
waiting to be known by us. There is no harm at all in this
notion in its right place, only we may with equal reason say,
that our mind, with its special or appointed manner of acting,
is waiting to know the universe : and it is the law of this
manner of acting which might be called innate or preliminary
idea. Locke, while he disallows any anticipation of the universe
to be known, arising from knowledge what must be its abstract
qualities (so to speak), all along supposes us able to talk about
these objects as existing, and to examine how, thus existing
before us as they do, it comes about that we get the ideas of
them—and much beside of a similar nature.

As it is—whatever may have been the case as to the
' pre-impressional,' the waiting, whether of our minds to grasp
the universe, or of it to be noticed by us—for *us* the universe,
and to a certain extent our very self, begins with impression.
I keep here to the use of 'impression' for *intellectual* impression,
as I have explained it, and in that case, it is with impression
that begins our corporeal or phenomenal self,—what the Germans
would call ' the empirical I.' So far as we can use our mind
to find the truth, the question whether we exist corporeally, and

the question whether the universe exists (which are really one),
are questions, or a question, simply of the meaning and value
of our impression. The impression, so far as we are concerned,
seems to stand by itself, with apparently nothing to compare it
with, so as to form any judgment about it: since reality, if we
wish to compare it with that, is for us only a part of *it*, is known
to us only through *it*, is *not* reality (so far as *we* can know), if
our impression has *not* value and trustworthiness.

Still, the question of the meaning and the value of our
impression is the great question of all philosophy, and we
must make what we can of it. We cannot, I think, in our
consideration separate meaning and value, but I shall try to
be as clear about them as I can.

Philosophers, in speaking of what I have called the *value* of
our impression, have naturally taken one of the following lines:
they have either set themselves to justify and commend it: or
they have taken it as fact, giving, in one way or another, some
sort of general account of it and of how it comes about: or
they have depreciated it, and considered that, so far as we can
form a notion of the highest or proper truth, impression does
not give it us, but is, more or less, prejudice and error.

We have, in whatever way, the notion of *knowledge*, and we
distinguish, from thought which is not knowledge, thought
which is true or correct, as being a right judgment about the
object of our thought. When we thus judge, it is *the truth*
which we judge about the thing or object: or if we like rather
to apply the term to the object, it is *the truth* about things
which, when we know, we know.

The question as to the value of impression is simply, Is it
knowledge? And subordinate to this are the questions, Can
we really have any other notion of knowledge than as such
impression? Can we test the value of impression, and is there
any standard to judge it by? and others of similar import.

Imagination, impression, knowledge (whether the same or
different) are all modes or kinds of thought. Imagination is
thinking in one way, impression in another, knowledge, if it
is different from impression, in a third. Imagination is picturing
the object with the feeling of its *not* being present, impression

with the feeling of its *being* present, (to speak shortly). Imagination is wrong, is a sort of counter-hallucination or reverse illusion, if, while we think the object not present, it really is present: we may fancy a thing a dream or a mental image, and it may be the real object before our eyes,—something like Leontes gazing on the supposed statue of Hermione. This, which I call wrong imagination, looking at things from the point of view of thought, would not be imagination, but impression, if we looked at them the other way: and therefore it might be described as impression mistaken for imagination—the real for the non-real. Similarly, impression is wrong—is genuine hallucination or illusion—if, when we think the object present, it is not so. As before, I call this wrong impression: it may be also described, according to the language which I just used, as imagination mistaken for impression.

Wrong imagination we need not speak of: but it is quite clear that we are perpetually liable to wrong impression, or to the supposition that there is impression, when there is only imagination. The way in which we guard against this, or test and correct particular impressions, is by the continual bringing of different impressions into conjunction: and the final standard or short and summary formula of our different processes of correction—our test, as I have on a former occasion called it[1], of phenomenal truth—is double: true or right impression is that upon which we can, with result, *act*, or put forth our being, it being consistent with itself, true for every portion of our corporeal being, uncontradicted, and uncontradictable, by any other true or right impression, which contradiction would render our acting impossible: and next, true or right impression is that upon which we can count as being true or right for other intelligences as well as for our own, what we feel that others sympathize with us in, what is not merely individual.

The most constant occasion occurring to us for testing impression is in the case of sight. There is a visible picture

---

[1] *Expl.* 12, 13.

continually before us when it is day and our eyes are open: and this picture is *impression* to us, not imagination (in which there might be picture scarcely less definite and vivid) mainly in virtue of these two things—that we might act upon it, *i.e.* put out our hand and grasp the orange before us, and that others will share with us in it, that if we say to our companion, Look at that orange, he will understand what we mean.

Still, this visible picture, though it is impression, is what, independently or in the necessary absence of the above means of testing it, might be wrong impression, or in the other way of language, though it appears to us impression, might be only imagination: and it is *this* fact in the main which suggests to us that something similar might be the case with regard to our whole mass of impression. So it was with Berkeley. It is not what we see, he said, which is real, but what we touch, and what we see is only a suggestive of this. The next step was immediate—How do we know that what we touch is more real than what we see, and that it too may not be only a suggestive of something? If we want *touch* to test our seeing, and to make us certain that the visible picture is impression, can we, without anything to test it by, rely upon our impression and rest in that, and make certain that it is, as we think it, knowledge?

Is then the whole mass of our impression (*i.e.* all our thought that there is a local or spatial universe with things or objects in it, among which we have our place, and which we really see and hear) actually or conceivably illusion, *i.e.* are the universe and its objects one thing, while we take them for another, unreal, while we take them for real?

This is a question which is almost certain to be mistaken at the outset, when looked at superficially. I do not mean to ask, is our impression visual illusion (which is what I suppose the Hindoos mean by Maya) *i.e.* is it a wrong impression correctible by other impression, or, in the other language, is it only imagination or mental picturing, while we think it impression? This is what Dr Johnson must have supposed Berkeley to mean (*i.e.* he must have supposed him to have meant no more in his so-called Idealism than he did in his

Theory of Vision), when he gave as a corrective of Berkeleianism the simple process of touch—kicking the table. But a few minutes' thought will get us beyond superficialness like this. If we mean, in any reasonable sense, that our impression altogether is, or may be, anything which can be called 'illusion,'— to put the thing roughly, that while we think there is a real external world, there really is not—we must mean by illusion a something, of which we may take the suggestion from the relation of sight to touch, but which we must carry much further in its application. What is simply seen may be illusion: we cannot tell whether it is so or not, till it is touched: this is because, as I have previously explained, what we mean here by 'touch[1]' is a great mass of impression both more intimate to us than sight and more general, and to which we refer and (in a manner) subordinate sight, which otherwise is isolated and partial. Were there no other sense but sight, sight or supposed sight could not under any circumstances be illusion, with any significance of the term: we should have nothing then to test sight by, or compare it with, but itself. As it is, as compared with the whole mass of our corporeal sensation or impression, sight is in a manner accidental[2] (not but that our notion of the universe is materially modified, or even determined, by its existence): but still there is no sight in the dark, there are some people without sight, we might readily conceive our body without eyes: but we always touch, every one touches, our body must touch and be touched.

Now then does there exist, beyond impression, any conception of knowledge which may stand to our whole impression in the same, or something like the same, relation in which visual impression, or what we think such, stands to tactual impression, or the great mass of our impression, by which we test the visual? If there is, then, just as visual impression is wrong impression (or only imagination thought to be impression) if it will not answer the touch, so the whole tactual impression, or whole mass of impression which is taken to be knowledge, is wrong knowledge, or not real knowledge but only

---

[1] *Expl.* 7, 20, 32.   [2] *Expl.* 28.

something in the garb of knowledge, unless it will answer this higher knowledge, come into relation with it, be found to have meaning in it, bear the application of it and the being tested by it.

I do not at this moment assert anything about the existence or non-existence of such higher knowledge: I only say that it is *here* that belongs the question of the existence of an external world, or, in other words, the question of the illusiveness of our impression: we are not under illusion if it is unreal, unless we suppose it otherwise: but we are under illusion if we think it real, while it is not so. Only this illusion is *tactual* illusion, such as I have been endeavouring to explain, not visual—a thing which people, I think, find it hard to see. This illusoriness of the universe (supposing it to exist) neither would, nor does, any more hinder the objects in it being tangible, solid, substantial, than visual illusoriness would hinder their being bright-coloured. The question is, whether tangibility and solidity are our ideal of reality? We will not let visual reality stand, fair-seeming as it is: are we to rest in tactual reality (*i.e.* in *general* impressional reality), or may we go beyond *that* also?

Both those who justify, and those who condemn, on the score of truthfulness, our impression, must be conceived to go beyond the tactual or impressional reality, and to have an ideal of truth, of some kind, independent of it. Between these two, we may rest in the impressional reality, as a fact, and consider that that is all our notion of reality and all we can have: we then put aside all considerations of what I have called the *value* of our impression, and only speculate, if we do speculate, on what I have called the *meaning* of it.

Those who, in one way or another, condemn or depreciate our impressional view, as knowledge, or on the score of its truthfulness, have sometimes been called *sceptics*, and at other times, by the equally half-meant and little understood terms, *mystics* and *idealists*. The point which marks them all, however called, is, that they must have an ideal (however derived) of what knowledge, as knowledge, is, or, in other words, of what actual knowledge ought to be, to which they refer such impressional knowledge or quasi-knowledge as we have, and find it wanting.

I will proceed to speak of the manner of thinking of one or two of the philosophers who, as I have expressed it, depreciate impression as knowledge. It is carefully to be kept in mind that these philosophers may very likely, in another point of view, *exalt* impressional knowledge or, as they will call it, experience, *i.e.* they will say it is the best knowledge we have, it is all we have to go upon, it is *our* knowledge. It is not of this that I am now to speak, but of their view of the goodness of the quality of this our knowledge, if we are to call it knowledge.

Again, on each occasion of speaking of the value attributed by a philosopher to impression, I shall have to speak also of the *meaning,* as I have called it, which he attributes to our impression, *i.e.* what view (he considers) people have, man has, of the manner of existence of the supposed objects of our sensal knowledge, or, as it is frequently expressed, of the external world and the laws or relations of it. 'What do people think about what they call the external world?' is the question as to *meaning* of impression. 'Is what they think about it right?' or is what they think about it (as compared with some ideal which we have of what they *might* think), in manner and kind, poor, defective, unworthy, perhaps mistaken and illusory? or is what they think about it simply what we must rest in as a matter of fact, it being all the idea which we can have of knowledge, and there being nothing to compare it with—so that to speak of it as right or wrong, sufficient or defective, valuable or worthless, is unmeaning?

These are what we may call the three questions, or the three alternatives of the question, as to the *value* of impression ; those who answer the second question in the affirmative are those whom I have described as depreciating its value: and I will proceed to speak of the sentiments of one of them, the same by whom I have illustrated the term 'impression' and whom I have already in this chapter largely referred to— Hume.

According to Hume, our entire mass of impression, or 'our experience,' is made up of a number of customary conjunctions of *particular* impressions. These customary conjunctions lead us to the expectation, that when one of the impressions arises, it will be followed by the others, but they do not do this simply and directly, but through the intervention of an impression or thought which is chimerical or at least superfluous or un-meaning—viz. that the (supposed) object of the one impression is what we call the *cause* of the (supposed) object of the other, the effect. Thus we *think* we have before us a universe of causes and effects, of action and production, while the whole *fact* is a mental or inward *custom*, which our particular impressions have, of conjoining themselves in this or that particular manner.

There is what seems to me an omission in Hume's view above, making it incomplete from *his own* point of view, arising from what I have called the wrong psychology,—an omission in which Hume has been followed by many others. Previous to the supposition that we have before us an universe of causes and effects, we must have the supposition that we have before us an universe of *things*: we must realize, or 'mis-realize,' particular impressions into things, before we realize, or mis-realize, the customary conjunctions of the impressions in our minds into causation, action, and production. But Hume, as we said at the beginning, does not keep his notion of impression clear, or rather, may be said to define it *doubly*, without any attempt to show that there is any reality or fact of which *both* his characters or definitions are predicable, so that they do or will go together. He describes impression,—a term which is to apply to love and hate as well as to sight and hearing—as a peculiar feeling on our part, differing from a mere *idea* (thought or imagination) in its special vividness; but he also, as he goes on, uses it as if he meant by it the impression, so to call it, which things make upon our corporeal senses, though in order to mean this he must assume the existence of the external world with its objects, as people commonly speak of it, which is not a pre-assumption before, but a result from, and part of, his previous definition of impression. And yet it is evident that, exactly in the same way as cause and effect have (if it be so) no existence, except in so far as we give these

names to the conjunction of our impressions, so things have
(if it be so) no existence, except in so far as we give this name
to our impressions themselves.   We interpret (if we so like to
call it) the conjunctions of our impressions into cause and effect,
exactly in the same way in which we interpret our impressions
into things—whether rightly, wrongly, or merely *actually*, we
shall shortly consider.

CHAPTER VII.

COMPARISON BETWEEN MILL AND HUME AS TO OUR KNOWLEDGE OF THE EXTERNAL WORLD.

I PROPOSE here to give an account, as well as I can, of Mr Mill's view in his lately published work on Sir William Hamilton's philosophy, in order to compare it with that of Hume above.

With Mr Mill, the great and fundamental fact is, 'sensation' —'impression' as I have called it above. It is a main point with Mr Mill to make out that what I may call self-recognition, or feeling of ourselves *as* feeling or as impressed, is something acquired or 'adventitious': it is not conveyed in the mere notion of sensation or impression, neither of course, in his view, is the feeling of an object, or of something impressing, so conveyed. The sensation or impression itself is the primary fact: we say ' there is sensation,' without in the first instance considering that it is anybody's sensation or that it is sensation of any thing. This comes afterwards. At first, sensation is in a manner *in* us, but not yet felt as sensation *by* us. And the next great point with Mr Mill is what I have slightly alluded to, that a vast mass of what I have called *our whole impression, i.e.* our intellectual feeling at any moment, is imagination. In speaking of Hume just now, I admitted, as account of *his* ' idea ' (*my* ' imagination ') that it was remembered impression: but Mr Mill is far more true to fact in drawing attention to the great mass of antici-pated and generally imagined impression or sensation, which goes with any particular sensation, and which, we may say, is always more or less in our minds. It is the '*objectivization*' or '*concretification*' of this great mass of anticipated or possible sensation or supposed possibility of sensation, which, in Mr Mill's view, is what we mean by an external world. The *fact* being the existence of sensation or impression, what we come to *think* (our secondary or supervening impression) is, that, though at each moment sensation is only particular, yet there is possibility of an infinite mass of such sensation—possibility on the one side as capacity of feeling (from which imagined possibility we form the notion of what we call ourselves, as the *sentient*), possibility on the other side as susceptibility of being felt (from which we form the notion of what we call the objective or external world, as the '*sentible*'). What we do come to think in general (what, in my language, is the *meaning* of our impression) about the external world, I do not think Mr Mill pronounces very definitely. He seems to consider first that our notion, for instance, of the reality of Chimborazo is simply an imagination that, if we were transported so many miles in such and such a direction, we should have the visual sensation of whiteness and vast conical figure, followed by the tactual or locomotive sensation of so much effort in mounting—that is, an imagination of the possibility of these sensations for us, if we choose to satisfy the requisite conditions: but afterwards he seems to consider that the abstract possibility thus thought of is mentally *concretified* into something which is what we call the external world or things: but of this again.

I think what Mr Mill says will not stand, in this way.

Even our knowledge of our own existence, says Mr Mill, is acquired, is posterior to sensation or impression. Sensation or impression therefore, as such, is independent of it, is *to us* in the first instance 'unindividual.' This sensation or impression involves, as Mr Mill truly says, the vast mass of imagination which he describes. But since sensation thus, as a fact in itself, does not involve either self-recognition or recognition of an object, the imagination of what Mr Mill calls possibilities of sensation is simply the imagination of the possibility, so to speak, of there being sensation, as a bare fact, in the manner just described. It is not imagination of a sentient (or sensitive) and a 'sentible.' The certainly existent fact, upon which all rests, is, in Mr Mill's view, the existence of sensation, which fact does not till afterwards break itself up into two members, *perceivingness* and *perceivedness*—sentience and sentibility : and even when it does so, this division is an imagination, compared with the objective certainty of the fact of *sensation* itself. What Mr Mill does, is to add to the actual and concrete fact of sensation or impression, the abstract atmosphere, so to call it, of the possibility, or the possible existence, of sensation or impression, an Aristotelian δύναμις or bare capability inhering in nothing, and to me a piece of what I have before called notionalism[1]. It seems to me a very vain proceeding to suppose a central reality of actual sensation or impression, and around this a wide semi-reality (shall we call it ?) of possibility of such. This abstract fact of the possibility of there being sensation must surely depend upon some actual fact in the entire universe, and, even if we cannot properly apprehend this latter fact, we had better *suppose* it than employ our thoughts in that region of abstractions. The supposition made, in one way or another, by ordinary human impression about it, is that there actually exists something sentient—ourselves : and something sentible or perceivable, which, *as* perceived, we call the external world.

In Mr Mill's view, the collection or sum of possibilities of sensation will not describe the external world, or the universe, as we perceive it and as distinct from ourselves, but will only describe existence in general, our own involved with that of other things. Suppose sensation developed into notice of the external universe on the one side, and self-recognition on the other : then we want a word to express these different *sides* of sensation or impression. Call the first the objective side, the second the subjective : *then* Mr Mill may with some reason say the external world (or what we call so) is the sum of the possibilities of objective sensation, and our own being of the possibilities of subjective sensation. This subjective sensation is only another view of what I call sentience or perceivingness : and in so far as

[1] *Expl.* pp. XIII, 147.

we conceive it as something distinct from objective sensation, supervening upon sensation as a whole, and not necessarily involved in sensation from the first, and a part of the notion of it,—it is a wrong view.   Let us therefore call by the name of sensation (as Mr Mill does, with more truth than logical consistency) the objective sensation only : we then have the external world reasonably, if not rightly, defined, the sum of possibilities of sensation (*i.e.* not *now* of there being sensation, but of our having sensation), we might say, the mass of senti-bility or perceivability.   Only what is the use or purpose of this abstract manner of speaking of it ?   How is it better to speak of the universe as made up of two things so disparate as 'myself' and 'perceivableness,' than to speak of it as 'consisting of things or real existences, of which I am one.'

Human impression consists, I conceive, in the main as to this, in the supposition of a substratum to this perceivableness, or in the notion that, where there is possibility of sensation, there must be reason for the possibility, there must be a something *making* the sensation possible : we are thus *prepared*, in my view, for the notion of real objective existence : and this notion *itself*, in a manner which I have described, I think is a reflex or projection from ourselves[1].

In reality, however, there is something more to be said than this.   Mr Mill in another place rightly distinguishes sensation, as simple consciousness or feeling, from sensation as conversation or communication (through eyes and ears known to exist) with objects not perhaps themselves hitherto known, but parts of a known universe of things.   Now which does sensation mean here?   Does it mean the simple feeling or consciousness, what Hume and I have called 'impression'?   But 'possibilities of this feeling or consciousness'—'possible *occasions* of it,' we will say for greater clearness—give us no description of the external world, though they may, in a sort of way, of existence in general.   If, conceiving the feeling simply as *feeling* thus, we are to set ourselves to imagine possible occasions for it or causes of it, we might imagine or suppose all

[1] *Expl.* 48, 51.

sorts of occasions quite different from those which, in point of fact, we always *do* come to imagine and suppose, viz. that we have what we call eyes and ears, and that there are certain things, which we call external objects, which communicate with these. If, however, we conceive the feeling not simply as feeling, but as communication through eyes, ears, &c. with external objects, then we are too late to give an account of the external world, for we are in the middle of it already: it will not do to say that the external world is the collection of possibilities of images on the retina and vibrations of the tympanum, for these very things themselves are part of it. If we mean by sensation, feeling, Mr Mill's description is too wide : if we mean communication, it is too narrow.

This is in substance the same thing as what I have previously said, that the position taken by Mr Mill seems to me to spoil phenomenalism without sufficiently rising to philosophy. The external world, on Mr Mill's view, is made either too much of, or too little of, according to his meaning of 'sensation.' The external world is not so much as the (supposed) sum of possible occasions of thought; if we suppose the latter (the occasions of thought) to be no more than the former (the external world), we preclude all philosophy. But the external world is more than the (supposed) sum of possible occasions of sensive communication : it is as real, as primary and early a fact, as *that* is, and exists as much as *that* does. The external world, together with other things which we believe, conceive, or think of, waits or hangs upon our *whole* thought, and we may and must examine the nature of our conception of such a world in reference to this whole thought : but the external world does not wait or hang upon our seeing hearing, touch : it is as real as these. If seeing, hearing, touching, are active verbs with objects (*i.e.* if we see *anything*, hear *anything*, &c.), then there is an external world as real as the seeing and hearing, which is not sufficiently described by calling it the sum of possibilities or possible occasions of such seeing, hearing, &c. If seeing, hearing, touching, are viewed as modes of consciousness or feeling only, and are thus neuter verbs, not involving in them of necessity

any object beyond the sight or feeling itself—if they mean,
we feel what we call seeingly[1], we have an impression of ourselves with what we call eyes and ears in the middle of what
we call a lighted scene with sounds sounding here and there
about it—then we are giving too wide a definition of the
external world in saying that it is the sum of possibility of our
thinking in this manner. What we call the external world, in
any ordinary use of the term, is the *result* to us of our thinking
in this manner, and it is carrying the word beyond all definite
meaning to describe it as what gives possibility or occasion, or
as the condition of our thinking so. For instance, we can as
little *disprove*, as Berkeley can *prove*, that our thought of this
kind is (for so we may really put his view) an immediate
inspiration of the Deity. There is meaning in considering that
thought thus originated might result to us, rightly or wrongly,
in the notion of an external world, but there is no meaning in
defining 'external world' as the possibility, or the fact of its
being possible, that we can have such thought. We can form
no notion of such possibility: the thing might be possible,
whether in the Berkeleian way mentioned above or perhaps in
a thousand other ways: to call this indefinite possibility by
the name 'external world' is unmeaning.

In reality, for Mr Mill's definition to be in any degree not
only reasonable, but right, it ought to stand, that the external
world is the sum of the possibilities, or possible occasions which
we imagine or suppose, of our sensation as feeling, according to
the ordinary course of human imagination or supposition in
these matters, the history, as I call it, of human impression.

Mr Mill has probably, through his distinctness of thought,
got nearer than almost any Englishman to freedom from the
old Lockian mis-psychology: but I question whether his use
of the word 'sensation' here is *really* free from it, and I think
it possible that he may scarcely wish it to be, for fear lest
what he calls 'experience' may be called by others mere
'imagination.'

The application of the term *experience* to the earlier

---

[1] For this adverbial mode of expression compare *Expl.* 4, 87, 108.

processes of mind, as Mr Mill applies it, requires careful
watching, for two reasons: viz. to see how far the applier of
it invests it, in its new application, with associations and
suggestions which belong to it only properly in its old: next,
to see whether it carries with it any misleading suggestion in
this way of mis-psychology. We may describe what I call
'the history of human impression,' as 'the history of human
experience': but we must deal with the word experience here
exactly as we dealt with the word 'sensation.' If the nature
of the existence of the external world is at all under discussion,
or if, *e.g.* it is said that we learn that existence by 'experience,'
then 'experience' must mean mental experience simply, in
a somewhat similar way to the way in which it has been used
by religious writers. A man, says Mr Mill, each man, knows
nothing intuitively, but goes through a course of experience.
This experience is of certain very definite and peculiar feelings,
in the first instance called sensations, and then of the feeling
of impulse to expand or supplement them by wide-ranging
thought or imagination, making us fancy the first feelings
under all sorts of circumstances: what we call the external
world is a sort of summary conception of the whole possible
variety of such circumstances. When, in *this* view, it is said
that we know things by experience and not by intuition, all
that is or ought to be meant is, that we have a mental
experience or history, that we do not bring our knowledge into
the world with us. To any person who has pleasure in using
the word 'imagination' depreciatingly, this mental experience
is as liable to be called by that name as any individual
intuition is. But when the word 'experience' is used about
it, it is very likely that, in order to obviate this liability, the
term is made to carry with it, at the cost of mis-psychological
error, associations which it should not. Experience, as above, is
a thread or course of successive *change of feeling*; which is quite
a different thing from experience as acquaintance with anything
as *matter of fact, i.e.* from knowledge by actual communication
and trial, as opposed to knowledge (or supposed knowledge) by
thought and speculation. In the old Lockian psychology, the
two characters of the notion 'experience' fused very well into

one: experience of the external world (which world, we of course all know, exists and which our senses are conversant with) was at once a course of mental history and a course of communication with what was allowed to be fact. But with better notions of this psychology, the word 'experience,' like 'sensation,' splits into two. In experience as mental history, we are not brought into communication with any allowed fact beyond ourselves: there is nothing therefore, except what there may be in the feeling itself, to distinguish it from imagination. It is the same with Mr Mill's use of the word 'acquired.' The knowledge of the external world, he says, is not intuitive, but 'acquired.' 'Acquired' means got from somewhere. Acquired from whence? Where is there anything it can come from? What test have we that it is not invention and imagination of our own? These words 'experience' (thus used), 'acquired,' &c. all belong to the old psychology, which took for granted the external world and had therefore something for us to be acquainted with and to get our ideas from: but the notion of experience of *there being* an external world, and acquisition of the knowledge that there is such, is like taking the tortoise or elephant out of the world to support it, without thinking what is to support *him*.

It may aid clearness if I try to say as distinctly as I can in what I agree with Mr Mill's views and in what differ from them.

I will begin with quoting a passage from Locke (*Essay*, Book 2, § 3).

Our senses conversant about particular sensible objects do convey into the mind several distinct perceptions of things, according to those various ways wherein those objects do affect them: and thus we come to those ideas we have of yellow, white, heat...and all those which we call sensible qualities: which when I say the senses convey into the mind, I mean, they from external objects convey into the mind what produces there those perceptions[1].

This passage exhibits rather pointedly the bad psychology.

---

[1] The text has no exact reference, but I gather that the above is the quotation intended, from the marginal note ('"conversant with external objects," Locke, beginning').

In reality, the conversance of our senses with external objects and the formation by our mind of the ideas of the objects are the same thing looked at from one end of the process and from the other. Mr Mill as I have said, has gone nearer than most to the recognition of this. In his Logic, as we saw, he treats our knowledge as what Locke here would call 'the conversance of our senses with external objects,' as e.g. the sight of things, and repudiates the necessity of saying anything about *ideas* of things, considering this as something quite superfluous. In his Examination of Sir W. Hamilton, he treats our knowledge from the other side, the subjective, as the formation of ideas, the having sensations, however it may be described: and instead of 'conversance with external objects,' we have conception of occasions, conditions, circumstances of the above ideas or sensations, which become external objects to us (whatever we may mean by external objects) *because* the mind so looks at them.

Now Mr Mill is in my view quite right in putting into two books, or two lines of consideration, what Locke and the wrong psychologists put into one. Where I differ from him is as follows.

When I said that the formation of ideas or having sensations on the one side, was the same thing as the conversance or communication between the senses and external objects on the other, I was not quite accurate. They *are* the same thing to the whole extent of the latter, but the former is more extensive than the latter, begins earlier and runs further back than it. Previous to the possibility of the notion of conversance of our senses with the external world, we must have, and we do have, the great and cardinal idea or sensation of *our having senses,* which is the same as the notion of the existence of an external world, and the same also as the notion of our being corporeal. *This* portion of the subjective, or, as I have formerly called it, philosophical, line of thought is *outside,* previous to, independent of, the phenomenalist line of thought or investigation of the knowledge of the external world by means of our senses, though *otherwise* they are the same thought moving different ways.

When we are firmly lodged in thought upon the ground

that we are corporeal with senses, and that there is a world external or independent of us and yet of which we are a part, a world which makes known its various features to us through the variety of our senses—*then* we may talk with full meaning of *experience* of things, or knowledge by actual trial, which knowledge there is no fear of confounding with imagination or illusion : and so we may talk of *acquiring* this experience and knowledge, and be quite certain that it is a real gain.   And to the extent to which the two lines of thought, which I mentioned above, are what we may call 'counter-coincident' (*i.e.* the same thought moving in opposite directions), we may use such terms as experience in speaking of the formation of ideas, as well as of objects becoming known to us, without variation of meaning.   But it is not so when we speak of the formation of ideas in that antecedent region where it has nothing in the other line of thought to correspond with it. Experience is then undistinguishable from imagination, acquisition from intuition or mere, perhaps arbitrary, conception, unless we can find some means of distinction in the manner of the thought itself.   The force of a notion being non-intuitive is that it comes in some way or other *ab extra*, or stands in a necessary relation with the *extra* : its posteriority in date is only of importance as it bears witness to this.   Hence it is contrary to all reason to call the notion of an 'extra' itself one of experience or acquisition, unless we mean, as I have said, simple *mental* experience.   If there is such a thing as in-tuition—a word which is not a word of my use—*this* must be intuitive.

Mr Mill then is really an intuitionist, or in fact 'imagi-nationist' under the form of applying back the terms of our later processes of knowledge to our primary and rudimental processes : in the 'imaginationism,' taken by itself, I agree with him : in the language in which he attempts to clothe it, of course I differ.

In my view, our notion of the external world is a vast tactual or corporeal imagination (using 'imagination' here to express what, so far as the term goes, *may* be real, or may not be, *may* be truth, or may be illusion) having without all doubt,

its own truth, of tangibility etc., but, in so far as it may claim
to be anything more than this, and to satisfy any higher notions
of truth or reality which we may have, requiring to justify itself
and to be corrected by such higher notions, in the same way as
the visual imagination or scene is by *it*. Tangibility, (by which
I here mean the utmost amount of simply *corporeal* sentibility)
is very far from exhausting my notion of reality. *Things* are to
me something more than clouds, and *thinghood* is more than
sapid, odoriferous, coloured, shape and magnitude: and as our
touch and movement put body and solidity into the visual
scene, so we want our thought, activity, and self-consciousness
to put soul and meaning into the tactual or simply corporeal
conception of the universe, or else this latter is to us an
imagination only, or if we take it for more than an imagination,
an illusion, a shell, or superficial representation, which ought
to have a meaning, a soul, an interior, but has not.

CHAPTER VIII.

ON PHILOSOPHICAL SCEPTICISM.

THE term 'scepticism' is one which I am not very fond of seeing used, because I think in various ways it creates prejudice, and hinders justness of thought. It is used by Mr Buckle, it would almost appear with the view of giving unnecessary offence, to express that examination of the claims of whatever professes to be authoritative and true, which *is* as valuable as he describes it to be, and which is consistent with abundant readiness to believe after such examination. It is used very much by the school of psychology of which I have been speaking[1]. The notion of obviating or avoiding it has guided many late philosophical speculations. But we should try to present very clearly to our minds what it is we want to avoid or obviate.

Am I 'sceptical' in saying that, after all, the phenomenal world, or the existence of all that with which we communicate by our body or our senses, is a *thought*, *i.e.* that the question Whether it exists, is the same as the question Whether we say or think *rightly* when we say or think it exists,—in other words, that our thought, in this very ultimate and lofty region, has or is susceptible of *some* character analogous in some respects to what we call rightness or correctness of thought in the lower and commoner applications of it? The question, so far as there is any question, in reference to this is,—to what, in this high region, are we to refer rightness or correctness of thought?

---

[1] That is, by Hamilton and the Scotch psychologists.

what is the ultimate test of truth ? I say nothing of the value of speculations of this kind : I only say, that I am unable to see with what significance it is called, if it is called, scepticism. The true antidote against what I call scepticism is a firm hold of the Cartesian 'cogito,' the fact of facts in my view. Allow to the universe, with which we corporeally communicate, the fullest phenomenal existence: what is the harm in the supposition that we know its existence less intimately than we know our own ? that we know it, so far as we know it, as the supposed occasion of many portions of our consciousness, or, in Sir William Hamilton's language, *mediately* ?

It appears to me that all the supposed odiousness and terrors of the notion of *scepticism*, as applied to any consideration of this kind, arise from the false and confused view which belongs, as I have described, to the psychology of Locke and others. The term 'scepticism,' understood by none, is bandied about, and one supposed form of it is refuted, as by Berkeley, by a view then perhaps characterized as more sceptical still. The psychology I am speaking of begins with assuming, as the groundwork and frame of all, the phenomenal world as existing, and then says, we must describe our consciousness in such a manner that we shall necessarily *see* this world to exist in the same way as that in which it is thus gratuitously assumed as existing, or else we are sceptics. Is not this a thorough confusion ? If we are certain that things exist in the manner in which we thus began with assuming they do, so certain that we may assume their existence as the basis of truth, and that it is scepticism to doubt it—what good is done, what additional certainty is gained, by the proving that we are conscious of their existence, or that it is a part of our consciousness ? We have assumed their existence long ago, and everything that we have said has gone on the supposition of it. If we are not conscious of their existence, at worst it is a misfortune to us, a defect of our understanding, upon which nothing depends as to the things, for that *they* are existent we supposed at the first.

I do not see by what possibility we can ever escape from such scepticism (if so we are to call it) as is implied in saying

that, in the first instance or last resort, phenomenal existence
is a supposition or imagination on our part,—we will hope a
right one. 'Sir William Hamilton' says an admirable ex-
positor of his doctrine, Professor Fraser, whom I quote because
he has added a clearness which did not always exist, and has
put the view in a convenient form, 'maintains that certain of
the qualities of matter are the direct objects of a mysterious
insight, and thus that the mind is conscious of material as well
as of mental qualities[1]': and by this view he is said to get rid
of 'a refined or egoistical idealism,' on which we can never 'get
beyond the succession of our own thoughts and feelings, while
even this self-knowledge itself is illusory[2].' But after all, is it
not *our* insight? How can we tell it is *right*? How can we
tell it is *insight*, and not mere imagination? Is there not an
entire confusion of view here, and in the supposition that this
is any security against scepticism? Does it not amount to
saying, We know in some by-way—*how*, I cannot conceive, but
(say) by testimony—that there is an universe of things, and
now we want to make, what we *call*, our knowledge, the nature
of which we are investigating, fall in with this independent
knowledge of the things, and confirm its testimony to their
existence: so we will describe this latter knowledge as 'the
having a mysterious insight into them,' and thus prevent the
scepticism which there would be, if, knowing somehow or
other that we *ought* to know them, we yet cannot find out
that we *do*?

The insight is known to be insight, not mere imagination,
because it is supposed to be into the fact, and yet the fact
is only known to be fact by means of the insight—is the logic
good?

Just the same thing must, I think, be said on the notion of
Sir William Hamilton's which Professor Fraser describes as 'a
consciousness of certain qualities of matter.' The whole point
of the term 'consciousness' is the reference to *ourselves*: when
we speak of the evidence of consciousness being what cannot
be gainsaid, it is because consciousness is what Mr Fraser terms

---

[1] Fraser, *Essays in Philosophy*, p. 94.   [2] *ib.* p. 93.

'egoistical,' concerned only with what we are proper judges of. We are conscious indeed of a non-ego, as what I have called the occasion of sensation, as fitting to our mind, on the principle of what I have called 'counter-notion'[1]: but the supposition of consciousness going beyond ourselves is merely altering the signification of the word, and making it no longer what we can necessarily trust to. I will not say whether 'a consciousness of the qualities of matter' *would be* a going beyond ourselves: all I say is, if it does *not* go beyond ourselves, it does Sir William Hamilton no good and does not obviate the egoism, and if it *does* go beyond ourselves it is no longer consciousness in the sense of what cannot possibly be gainsaid.

The question however *now* is whether this insight, or consciousness, is the only, or the best remedy against scepticism. I do not understand how this is so at all. If we are certain that the universe does exist, why so much effort to prove that we have an insight into, or consciousness of, its existence, and how is its existence the better or the more certain for our having this? If we are not certain that it does exist, how is it any help against scepticism to establish that by means of some sort of insight or consciousness we *are* so certain, when, by the very supposition we are making, we confess that perhaps after all it does *not* exist? If we do not know that things exist, what is the harm of doubting their existence, or why should it be called scepticism? If we *do* know that they exist, what is the use of making certainty more certain?

It will be said, In thus upholding an extravagant idealism, removing from things all basis of reality, at the same time that, for actual and particular knowledge, you recognise phenomena alone as what phenomenalists call 'experience,' do you not fall into that very scepticism of Hume, which later Scotch psychology and even Kantism has never been able to take its eyes off from?

The word 'idealism' is as random in application as 'scepticism,' and therefore we had better not go in any way by the application of *that*.

---

[1] *Expl.* p. 23.

The differences between my view and that of Hume seem to be in substance two: and they are tolerably vital.

One is, that in my view (which is here the Cartesian) the great fact of facts is thinking, *cogitantia*, not, as in his, *cogitatio*, thought. The difference is, that the first does not vanish as we pursue it, though the second may. *Cogitatio*, Humian impressions, Lockian ideas, supposing all resolvable into that, may after all be supposed to be a phenomenon, and then what is there but phenomenon? How do we know that anything exists, even ourselves? This I understand as the Humian scepticism. In reality, it seems to me to be all immediately involved in the assumption from which it starts. It assumes that we have no basis of truth, but must be sceptics, unless we can get at some *fact* independent of our knowing it, on which then our knowledge follows, as what I have called a sort of accident[1]. Hume says, Try: and see whether the ultimate fact of all, knowledge itself, is other than a phenomenon. There exist—we can predicate of them no *where*, *when*, *how*, or anything but existence— *impressions*: one such impression is that *we* exist, another is that the *universe* exists: but the impressions themselves are only phenomena or a phenomenon: there is no such thing as knowledge.

Against this I assert that the fact of facts is not *cogitatio*, thought, impression, but *cogitantia*, 'thinkingness,'[2] mind (if we like to use this last word in a very vague application): and thinkingness cannot be a phenomenon, for the very meaning of the word phenomenon is what seems to it. In using the term phenomenon, and predicating it of something which nevertheless we say is the furthest fact which we can get to, we are really contradicting ourselves, for we are predicating the existence of something in virtue of which the phenomenon is phenomenon. And *cogitantia* involves the supposition of I, self, personality, as a part of the thinkingness. I do not mean that it involves it with any particularity, or tells us much about it: that is a further question: only sufficiently to negative the supposition, that even our own existence is a matter of mere seeming.

---

[1] *Expl.* 10, 16.   [2] *Expl.* p. 140.

I do not want to disguise the difficulty of all this, nor mean now to go into the question, what is the test of rightness of thought[1], or what is the meaning of that limitation of it which we have the notion of, when we speak of its being according to fact and truth, and which makes us difference it from visionary imagination. Humian scepticism is not even egoism, but is phenomenalism enthroned even above that: I have been only wanting now to describe my first difference from it.

My other difference is on the subject of what I call phenomenalism, *i.e.* on the notion of our knowledge of the spatial universe, in regard to which I think in a manner exactly opposite to the Humian.

The point of the Humian notion of experience, which is only one way of expressing the mis-phenomenalist or positivist view, is the isolatedness of particular parts of our knowledge, or as I should prefer to call it, its fragmentary character, which I have already slightly alluded to, and described as making to me a view inexpressibly dreary[2].

What I have urged, different from this, is that the phenomenalist is *one* view of nature, partial, what I have called an 'abstraction[3],' a view which we may very well take, if we like it, when we are supposed to have already got our knowledge and to be theorizing about it: but it does not represent the manner in which we get our knowledge, or in which we should get any knowledge at all[4]. It is in this respect like the description of abstraction itself, considered as a faculty. We compare two things together, see what they have in common, attend to this alone for certain purposes, or abstract it, and describe the things as so far resembling or of one kind. But in reality the whole process of knowledge of resemblances and kinds takes place by means of *generalization, i.e.* is the development, by fresh knowledge and self-correction, of the notion of *generic* identity from that of singular or particular identity, or the changing the notion of *singularness* (that to which proper names apply) into that of *individualness*, subordination to a

----

[1] *Expl.* p. 12.   [2] *Expl.* p. 15.
[3] *Expl.* 2, 30.   [4] *Expl.* 45 foll.

genus, upon which all our language and thought depends.
Knowledge *gained* in this way may be *described*, and in its
higher portions augmented by, and according to, what we
call 'abstraction.' So as to phenomenalism. There is no
harm in describing knowledge as man's actual acquaintance
with nature, so far as it goes, which is the point of the notion of
experience. It is in this view itself an irregular, partly accidental
fact, acquaintance with one fact of nature and not with another,
the acquaintance having nothing to do with any relation
between them. But man came to his knowledge by the process
of thinking about nature, and imagining all sorts of relations
between the facts. This is the *cogitantia* or thinkingness which
I spoke of, and which is the great fact: the actual communication with nature or experience of it represents a part of this,
but only a part, and is a subordinate fact.

Professor Fraser seems to put together, as belonging to one
manner of thought, an egoist scepticism—or the supposition
that all that we call our knowledge is possibly only a vain
imagination, since we have no means of testing the truth of it,
taken on the whole, and no means even of knowing that one
man's thought, *as* thought or consciousness, is the same as
another's—and an experiential and phenomenalist scepticism,
or the supposition that all that we call our knowledge is certain
isolated and fragmentary bits of chance experience, giving us
no entire views, and nothing satisfactory to the intelligence.
The two views seem to me not at all connected. The Humian
scepticism, such as it is, belongs to the latter: the description
of knowledge, on this view, does not even go so far as to allow
it to be, in the last resort, *our* impression. The egoist view, as
against this, is a step away from scepticism. *There* we have at
least an immediate and real knowledge of what relates to ourselves, and proceed by means of this to knowledge, or interpret
this into knowledge of fact independent of us. The view, so far
as it is scepticism, must be so in virtue of the supposition, that
then it is only what relates to ourselves we are really certain of:
the rest may be mere imagination. Sir William Hamilton
seems to aim at making the actual world of matter almost
what I might call a part of ourselves by calling our knowledge

of it consciousness. I do not particularly quarrel with the use of the word consciousness for all our knowledge; and think that possibly it might be useful against that *localization*[1] of the mind, when we are speaking from the point of view of knowledge or consciousness, which falsifies so much psychology. In my view we are quite as conscious of the sun as we are of the image on the retina, or of anything in our bodies unaccompanied either with will or with pleasure and pain. We may mean, by consciousness of anything beyond ourselves, either the interpretations of the will and of pleasure and pain, on particular occasions, or we may mean the whole fabric of knowledge into which these develope : but whatever we mean, as soon as we speak of consciousness of anything beyond ourselves, we have lost all value of the word consciousness. It seems to me the same thing as if I should use the above expression, 'I am conscious of the sun,' (meaning that my knowledge of it is really a mental presence at it in virtue of the communication, through the intervention of light, between the matter of which it is composed and my body or sensive frame) as constituting a claim to be believed if I should go on to assert that the sun consisted of fire, or of water, or what not. I am conscious of just what I know, and of no more. And so it is as to the external world in general.

I go on now to the problem of the egoist scepticism which consists, as I understand it, in the asking ourselves the question, How do I know but that all I *think* I know is mere imagination on my part, possibly ungrounded ? The answer will probably be, I can only know this by hanging it on to *fact* of some kind : showing it to be *true*, and showing it to be in conformity with fact, are the same thing. But what fact ? When we are speaking of it as a whole, it is no use showing it to be in conformity with phenomenal fact, *i.e.* with the facts of the universe as I understand them : of course it is *this*, because this is but *it* : the notion of truth being conformity of this kind with fact, may do for particulars, so far as we can apply it, but not for knowledge as a whole. The value of the

---

[1] *Expl.* 88, 97.

supposition that the phenomenal universe exists is the thing in question: it is no use supposing then that its existence, the very thing in question, is the fact by which the supposition is to be tried. But is not *this* Sir William Hamilton's conception of the problem ?

The problem is this. The existence of the material or phenomenal world *may* be disputed, for, as a matter of fact, it *has* been disputed. Is this disputability and disputation wrong, and can we fix the certainty of its existence on grounds indisputable ? It is to be observed, that we have no right *à priori* to assume that great interests are involved in the proving it indisputable: the destruction of such scepticism as there may be in the matter, will be effected not by the proving the indisputability, but by the discovery of the truth on the subject, whether it be the indisputability or the opposite. The philosophers whom I am now speaking of never seem exactly to understand their position, whether they are philosophers or doctrinal teachers. They waver between the position, 'The existence of things is an undoubted fact—it is a misfortune that you doubt it—we will show that you ought not to do so'— and the position, 'So far as the existence of things is disputable—and it is disputable, if it is ever with any reason disputed—it is *not* an undoubted fact, and you are right, or quite at liberty, to doubt it. We will endeavour to show however that it *is* indisputable, and that there has *not* been reason in the disputing it.'

The position of Dr Reid and of any philosopher like him, who speaks of common sense or of anything of that kind, is I suppose the former. They offer us, in various ways, a reason why we *should* believe the thing, in the fact that we *do*,—as if *our* position were this, We know (how ?) the thing is so, and we want to believe it, but we cannot succeed in doing this. *They* say, It is common sense to believe it: you cannot help doing so: everybody does. *We* say, We do not want persuasion to believe it, but we want to know that we are doing right in believing it,—how does your common sense ensure this ?

I cannot see that in substance Sir William Hamilton alters the view of the problem from this.

If we propose to ourselves the problem at all,—and the doing so is not of *my* suggestion, for I make no assertion as to its solubility, and in this non-assertion, if anywhere, must be the scepticism—what we must find is, something known to be existent with a higher knowledge or more indisputable certainty than that with which we know the phenomenal world to be existent, and then an indisputable identity of this latter existence with the former, or dependence of the one on the other. *I* should say, we are certain of the existence of the phenomenal world in so far as we recognize *mind* in it—mind, the type and test of all existence to us.

Egoist scepticism consists in denying objective value to what we call our consciousness, not in denying objective reality, so far as consciousness can give such, to the phenomenal world. To suppose consciousness to give us our own reality *immediately*[1], and that of the phenomenal world *mediately*, is no scepticism : on this I have spoken. Supposing consciousness *did* give us the second in the same manner as the first all that would result would be that we might be driven from egoist (or mis-Cartesian) scepticism to Humian. That is, this would be read by some thus, that the first is given us in the same manner as the second, and that therefore our knowledge of our own existence is only phenomenal,—similar to the knowledge we have of the existence of a horse or a dog. It is I suppose some supposition of this kind which makes such typical metaphysics as Sir William Hamilton's not unacceptable to phenomenalists. Sir William Hamilton would put the external world, as a thought, on a level with the thought of ourselves. Mr Mill would put the thought of ourselves, as a phenomenon, on a level with the fact of the spatial existence of anything (whatever we like). Against both I maintain egoism, not however I hope sceptical, viz. that we *know* ourselves to exist, and *believe* the spatial universe and our corporeal selves as a portion of it to exist also; and that if we are to show that the second of these mental operations is equally valid with the first, which I do not the least deny, it must not be by the process of saying that they are the same.

[1] *Expl.* 118 foll.

Perhaps the present researches about Plato may tell us something about this scepticism, the problem and difficulty of which, so far as I understand, Plato *did* see—but I will not touch on this.

In my view, there lies at the root of all knowledge the question what knowledge is, and what is its relation with that which, if there is an absolute region, may perhaps be its great ' co-notion,' existence, but which to us, is a derived, and therefore so far a subordinate, notion. Here is the region in which we may discuss about scepticism, if the term has any meaning in this rare atmosphere: below this, I accept the notion or notions of existence fully, as I understand them given to us—thinking-existence, consciousness—thought-existence, phenomena. If there is anything *above* what I thus call phenomena, which nevertheless we can think about and may think as existent, it must be in virtue of its associating itself with our *thinkingness* by a sort of sympathy, if I may use the term, by means of which we communicate with that higher existence, just as by our special intellectual and sensive organization we communicate with phenomena. If we know God otherwise than through phenomena, it is by sympathy or communication with his thought. If we have a notion of ideals of action above phenomena, it must be on account of the association of them with our thinkingness, our liberty, our activity—with our *thinking,* as distinct from the results of our thought.

I mention this here however only to say, that the way to avoid what *I* should call scepticism is to give their full value to the two notions of existence which I have described, without puzzling the former with phenomenalism, or the latter with metaphysics. It is no argument against the former that we cannot fit it into our phenomenalist speculations, nor does it signify to the latter how we think it: there is no need to puzzle it (as I should say) by notions of its being relative only, and a sort of dress of an unknowable corpus or substratum. What we know it as, or hope some time possibly to know it as, is all that it *is.* It *is* oxygen, hydrogen, chemical elements, light, heat, and much more, occupying room and position in indefinite space, the parts moved about by various forces, arranged in such a way as to make various kinds of things and even of semi-thinking beings, and all acting together and interacting in such a way as to make us talk of law, order, system; while with just as much reason we might go on to talk of purpose, meaning, principle, and still on, till we put the supposed whole together and call it universe, forming our notion of a whole of it after *some* analogy with our notion of particular systems, arrangements, organisms. Such is the thing or things, not which we *have to* understand (except so far as we are always going on learning) according to the perverse idea of the Lockian psychology; but which we *have come* to understand as thing or things, and our having come thus to understand them is *their being*, the reason why we call them thing or things. We have indeed come to understand them, in a considerable degree, by means of notions, and therefore by the employment of terms, very different from those given above as what we have found. We have thought and talked, and very likely with great utility, about substances, qualities, and much besides. But these are only logical notions, what the mind forms or uses in the *process* of coming to the knowledge by which we describe the universe : they belong to what I have called a different world from the above constituents of the universe : they are creatures of the mind in quite a different sense from that in which the others are—temporary or mediate creatures. Supposing we knew all these con-stituents (so to call them) of the universe, there is nothing more to know in *this* direction, not even though we were omnipotent in intellect and possessed of every variety of sensive organization that any creature has had or ever can have : the unknown and supposedly unknowable substratum is what we have been knowing and learning all the time by learning its qualities, and as we learn them, calling them by the names of the above constituents.

But may we not be wrong in thinking that these *are* the constituents of the universe? there is certainly a reality in-dependent of our thought, because we may think wrongly and call things by wrong names.

No doubt: and the wrongness may be particular or general:

meaning by particular anything short of general. We may
wrongly apprehend any physical fact in comparison with the
rest: or we may wrongly apprehend what physical fact *means*.
The latter belongs to the whole question which I have now
been treating of: the former is what good phenomenalist logic
is intended to prevent. I have before alluded to the tests of
phenomenalist truth[1]: when we conceive the universe as we do
conceive it, and are persuaded we are right in doing so, we
mean, that, for instance, if there was to be another deluge
without a Noah, and with a destruction of all record of the
past, and the human race had to begin life again, it would
think about the universe in substance as we think about it, and
call things by corresponding names; that again, in a manner
which Mr Mill has admirably illustrated, our knowledge will
answer for action, or we can *predict*: we mean perhaps other
things, whether the same in substance as, or similar to, these.
But we do not need a reference to any independent fact
which we can test our knowledge by. This is the mistaken
Lockian psychology again, and I *believe*, the whole mystery
of Sir William Hamilton's unknowable substratum. When
Locke says, an idea is right if it agrees with the thing,
what purpose is served by the language? For what is the
thing to us except the idea which we have of it, or, in other
words, except what we conceive it to be, and what then is the
meaning of the rightness of the idea of the thing being something to be tested and examined? If we can know the facts in
any independent way, so as to be able to test the notions which
we form of them by the facts themselves, what is the good of
forming the notions, if the facts are already known? This
Janus-faced knowledge, which is no knowledge, I have already
in some degree spoken of. As I have said the mystery of the
unknowable substratum seems to me to be here. The fact is
considered to be unembraceable by the notion, because it has
got to be kept free from the notion in order to serve to test the
notion by, after the extraordinary process which I have just
tried to describe.

I think however I have said enough about this.

---

[1] *Expl.* 12.

CHAPTER IX.

MR HERBERT SPENCER.

MR Herbert Spencer's book[1] contains what seems to me on the whole a more correct account of the process of perception and understanding than any other I know, and it contains what at least is a most admirable account of the progress of life and of its environment. But for all this, I cannot see that his philosophic system, or the main line of his argument, is any other than what we may call a new form of that doctrine of a sort of pre-established harmony[2] between intelligence and things, which is, in fact, almost the only doctrine possible when we assume them both independently.

In spite of all Mr H. Spencer's clearness of view as to the error of what I have called the wrong psychology, I think it must be said that his view is the same as that of Locke with a wider application[3]. He investigates not how man, but how

---

[1] *Principles of Psychology*, ed. 1, 1855, ed. 2, 1870.

[2] *Expl.* 100.

[3] Mr Spencer is perfectly aware of the difficulty of his position and most correctly sees the wrong psychology in others.
But for himself?

He says, p. 322: All phenomena of intelligence are changes of states of consciousness.

One state of consciousness which invariably exists is that we are 'an organism placed in the midst of objects.'

Hence we may say, calling it 'a fact,' that we are so.

We cannot become conscious except through the changes produced in us by these objects.

Only through changes can *it* (the organism) be made conscious of objects, and only out of changes can be constructed its knowledge of them.

intelligence, comes by the ideas of things, (to use the Lockian
phrase): in his own phrase, how consciousness, as a part of life,
becomes historically (or in the course of experience) what we
find it now in man and in animals: and he describes with great
care the nature and properties of such consciousness: he es-
tablishes satisfactorily, in his own view, that in whatever
degree or manner it exists there is always a correspondence
between it and—what *I* should call—external things and
facts,—what *he* calls,—co-existences and sequences. This is
all that we can mean by *truth*, and as consciousness advances
in the great universal progress of life which Mr Spencer
conceives, it tells us ever more and more of truth.   Still I
cannot see that the difficulty of the wrong psychology is
even *here* avoided. That difficulty arises from the fact, that
I, the thinker, am on one side only of the antithesis between
thoughts and things, between consciousness on the one side
and environment, or the universe, on the other, and cannot
put myself on both sides. Things correspond with consciousness, and consciousness with things: but how are we
to know that this correspondence is not identity, and that
we mean by 'things' something more than consciousness?
Mr Spencer meets this by assuming in the first instance,
as the definition or universal character of *the true*, that it is
that of which we cannot conceive the contrary, and then saying,
that the belief in the independent existence of sensible things
is a belief which has this character, and therefore that what is
thus believed (viz. the existence of the things), may be assumed
from the first as fact. The difficulty surely here is the same as
in Locke, viz., how far, when this is assumed to begin with, we

Are there not here *two* stages

(1) the consciousness which knows (or by what we know) that we are an
organism placed in the midst of objects, and

(2) the 'organismal' consciousness which knows the objects by means of
the changes they produce in it?

And if so, our cognitions of 'the primary properties of things' (p. 66) are
subjectively 'preorganismal,' *i.e.* are anterior to, or contemporaneous with, not
posterior to, our perception or knowledge of things by means of our organism,
or as organized beings. *G.*

can be said to have a *bonâ fide* account of the genesis of knowledge. If this is supposed to be an innate idea, a primary
intuition, a supposition which is a necessary condition for the
existence of *any* knowledge, well and good: then *its* genesis is
no matter of investigation as a part of history or experience,
and *its* consideration, and that of any kindred intuitions, if
there are such, must belong to a branch of philosophy in which
this will not help us. But in reality, to the eyes of philosophy,
if this cardinal thought, supposition, imagination or cognition
(whatever it is) is left out, because preliminarily assumed,
the evolution of mental experience is of small consequence.
Mr Spencer's account of the growing correspondence between
life and consciousness on the one side, and the things and
facts of the universe on the other is, under all circumstances,
full of physical and physiological interest: but its main philosophical interest must arise from the supposition of its being
a sketch of the way in which we, intelligent beings, viewed as
having one continuous history, have (in Mr Bain's language[1])
'come to think' as we have of the universe, or of the state of
things to which we understand ourselves to belong, as a whole,
in regard to its existence and relation to us. Can it be said to
possess such a philosophical interest? Is it, more than that of
Locke, a genuine and *bonâ fide* history of our thought? In
Mr Spencer's language, there is an indissoluble cohesion between the notion which we express by the term 'independent
existence,' and the notion, 'objects of our perception.' This
cohesion has been brought about in the course of intelligential
experience; so that now intelligence cannot think otherwise:
it is a law of intelligence: the manner of its bringing about
has been that *fact* independent of intelligence has gradually,
so to speak, impressed itself upon intelligence: external co-
existences and sequences have first existed, and then this
cohesion corresponding with them has in course of experience
come to exist. Is there not here the same *circularity* that I
supposed in Locke? the same in fact which, in its more
flagrant forms, Mr Spencer is so well aware of and so jealous

[1] See quotation in *Expl.* p. xliii.

of? We assume the cohesion as giving us truth (such truth as we can have any notion of) in virtue of its being such cohesion. It seems to me that what Mr Spencer wants to make out is, that though it is assumed in the first instance as giving truth, because we cannot help thinking thus, yet its real and proper claim to be truth is that it is in correspondence with fact, which he then proceeds, by his sketch of intelligential history or experience, to show. It is because its claim to be truth is in his view *this*, not properly the *former* (as I understand) that he is able to consider that all knowledge, not excepting these first and fundamental notions, is derived from experience. But ought he not to see that the truth in the *second* case (such truth as there is) is derived from, and dependent on, that in the first? Unless we knew first by intuition (so to speak) that there *were* things or fact, a deduction of the way in which fact by degrees impresses itself on intelligence is moonshine: all its value depends upon the truth of the intuition. If we are afterwards able to prove that fact impresses itself upon intelligence, so that intelligence in supposing the existence of fact is not merely imagining, we must not on this account say that our knowledge of the existence of fact is due to this (so-called) experience. We had it from intuition before we could even conceive the possibility of the experience.

Mr Spencer's opening chapters may be considered an expansion of Locke's 'when our senses are conversant with external objects,' and then he traces, as Locke does, but in a wider field, how intelligence becomes possessed of (or by) its ideas or consciousnesses. Simplicity, then complexity, then simplicity, of a kind, again, may be said to be the law of them: the first simplicity followed by variation ('differentiation' in his phrase), expansion, growth, &c., and then again by 'integration' (association, composition, the construction of wholes, unities, things) becoming simple again. The difference between Locke and Mr Spencer is that with the latter all is a process: activity of the mind is not much a part of his consideration: and thus, while the wholes or notions of things and their relations, formed according to Locke by individuals, are thought of chiefly as to whether they are true or false,

conformable or not with things, the same with Mr Spencer
formed by intelligence are looked at (as Locke looks on his
simple ideas) as true by hypothesis. I think then, that in
spite of the care with which he lays down the position
which he wishes to take, Mr Spencer is still not able to escape
the kind of 'circularity' which belongs to all that I have
called the wrong psychology. His proceeding is a very bold
application of the positivist or historical method, in this way:
truth *to us* is, with him, what I have ventured[1] to call
'incounterconceivableness': this incounterconceivableness of
certain things to us is a fact of our present nature, a fact
which has had a historical origin: it has been worked in us by
a long generic experience. But let us examine the nature of
this 'experience,' and see if there is not in it that ambiguity
which belongs to it in the writing of almost all those who
make much of the word. Let us compare a smaller experience.
We, as a race, we will say, have learnt now by experience,
i.e. by observation of things and thought about them, that the
earth turns round the sun and not the sun round the earth.
When we use this language, we are speaking on the assumption
that things exist (*i.e.* that we corporeally exist with an external
world around us, which I have called the phenomenalist assumption), and speaking on this assumption, we say that we
have found out by experience *about* the things the fact which
I have just mentioned. The value, necessity, meaning of this
assumption, are questions not of the physicist but of the
philosopher. Philosophers may discuss, as they do, whether
this which I have called an assumption is properly so called,
or whether it is a consciousness, or whether it is a mere
imagination, or what it is: the experience which I have spoken
of remains unaffected by all this. The physicist enters upon
his investigations at a later stage: 'Say as you will,' is his
language, 'about these *things* or *reality*, say we are conscious
of it, or we systematically dream it, or assume it in order to
act and live—that is *your* affair—*I* say, that whatever may be
the fact as to the *whole* nature of this reality, what we find out

---

[1] Cf. *Expl.* 218.

as to the particulars of it, and come to be perfectly certain of, are such things as the above-mentioned. *I* the physicist, call it finding out, and consider the *particular* or *subordinate* truth, which is all that I am concerned with, to depend upon actual experience of, *i.e.* communication with, observation of, the things themselves. You may put this into what language you please, call it consistency of assumption, system of dream, cohesion of consciousness—however described, it is true in its own region, and I claim no more.'

The 'experience' then of the physicist holds true and good, whatever we may think of the nature of reality in general: but the vast generic experience, or history of intelligence, of Mr Spencer, does not. Berkleianism does not interfere the least with Newtonianism: nor would a doctrine like that of Boscovich that all that we call matter is really some kind of force. 'The sun' and 'the earth' would each have their meaning, though we might think with the philosophical speculator that, as to their *true* nature, they were quasi-inspirations in our mind, or with the physical speculator, that they were properly vast agglomerations of force. True experience of things may change its language or verbal exhibition indefinitely without losing its truth. But this cannot be said of Mr Spencer's experience of the formation of thought itself from things. 'Unrealize' (more properly 'derealize') the things, and we have not a change of language, but a vanishing of everything. Not only all our actual thought, but all our power to think, is supposed to be produced by the phenomenal universe as we conceive it. Hence the value of all the experience is made to depend upon an initial knowledge of things, the supposition of which renders the supposition of the subsequent experience superfluous and unnecessary: only that the knowledge of things is made to reappear at the end of the experience as a result of it, which is the *circularity* I complain of. If we know the experience to be an experience *of things*, and build our estimate of its truth and value upon that, then we know previously that there are things, *i.e.* the great groundwork of our thought is independent of our experience. Thus experience is wrongly represented as giving us an account of the genesis of our power to think, or of the great features of our knowledge, though it may rightly give an account of the growth of our particular knowledge. If, however, Mr Spencer's 'experience,' though he may describe it as 'experience of things,' (or rather, in his own language, as cohesion of consciousnesses produced by persistences of coexistence and sequence in what is around us) is still not to be supposed to depend for its truth and value upon the reality of the existence of the things, but is valuable, and resulting in truth, because it is the course which intelligence goes through—in this case experience means simply mental experience, change of thought and view, and we have that positivism or 'historicalism' of which I have before spoken[1]. Our belief in the 'incounterconceivables' (as, suppose, that two straight lines cannot enclose a space) is then *really* based on the authority of all past intelligence. I suppose Mr Spencer would have us believe these, (1) because we cannot help it: (2) if this does not satisfy us, because our not being able to help it is one of the results of the experience (*i.e.* historical change or supposed progress) of all intelligence since intelligence began : and (3) if we are to go further still, because the above *mental* experience, or progress of intelligence, has been an experience *of things* or has been produced by the actual things conforming intelligence gradually and more and more widely to them, or to use his own language, developing 'cohesions of consciousness' corresponding to their persistencies of coexistence and sequence—some such cohesions being abso-lutely indissoluble, and the notions belonging to such cohesions being the 'incounterconceivables.' Now, I think that Mr Spencer *wants* us to believe, say, that two straight lines will not inclose a space, for the first and for the third of these reasons, for the third *most*, the main value of the first being to justify and make possible the third : one of the things which, Mr Spencer thinks, we cannot help believing being the existence of 'things,' or an external world. All that I have lately been saying is to the effect that, as it seems to me, in spite of the singular clearness of view of Mr Spencer, it is impossible

---

[1] *Expl.* p. xviii.

that the *intuitionism* (so to call it) of the first reason and the *experientialism* of the last can go together: and since they each vitiate the other, any who derive from Mr Spencer's book a clear and single view will in effect come to the middle reason— the positivist. In the progress of universal intelligence we have come to think as we have: the habitual thought of the most advanced intelligence is what we call 'truth.' It is no use saying about this that we cannot conceive any one thinking otherwise. Since we have *come historically* to think so, the thinking *not* so must be as a matter of fact *conceivable,* however absurd. Nor is it any use saying on the other hand that our thought or what we call truth is in conformity with things: the fact is, things, so far as we can conceive them, are in conformity with *it,* so that the other statement is merely a truism. We have therefore to rest, as facts, in our 'cohesions of consciousness,' nor, as to the notion of truth, can we get any further than that 'so intelligence now thinks.'

Mr Spencer speaks very quietly about what he calls 'the experience-hypothesis,' as if it were a something well-known to everybody, and as to the meaning of which there could be no possible uncertainty. What I have said as to the ambiguity of the term 'experience' may throw some doubt upon this supposition.

The most general meaning of 'the experience-hypothesis' seems to me to be, the supposition that the earlier, more rudimentary, more fundamental processes of the mind (so to call them just now) are to be explained and described after the analogy of the later and more particular ones, which we can to a certain extent follow and understand. Thus we have found out by experience, we will say, that the earth turns round the sun: we have had experience of the earth and sun, and have found out that this is their mutual relation in respect of movement: we might *a priori* have supposed it would be otherwise, in fact men once did so: this however is what we now find to be the case. Now the *point* of the experience-hypothesis, the sting and value of the phrase, is in the supposition that the fundamental notions, which lie at the root or stand at the beginning of all our knowledge,—as (say), the notion that there are *things* or an external world at all,—are arrived at in a manner which may be considered analogous with the above. But experience of the above-mentioned kind is of necessity the hanging on fresh knowledge to previous: it supposes a course of thought: it will not account for the *starting* of thought. I know by experience that nettles sting: *i.e.* I know by experience that there is a painful sensation possible to me called stinging, and that the things which I call nettles will produce it. The first of these is the mental experience, and derives its truth simply from itself: if I feel it, it is: the second is the experience of fact, and derives its truth (such as it has) from the reality of the fact: I mean by it that I know, from my feeling, *this* as to the nettle, that it has something about it, prickles, poisonous juice, some power or quality, which causes *its* contact, in a manner differing from that of other plants, to be followed by the sensation of stinging. But there would be no meaning in saying, not only I have the experience of feeling stung (the mental experience), but I have the experience of the nettle stinging me (the experience of fact), unless I had some knowledge of the nettle previously to, or otherwise than by, the sensation of being stung, unless I saw it, or handled it, or some way or other knew there was such a thing. When therefore the term 'experience' is applied to the early or first steps of knowledge, it can only mean mental experience—the fact that we feel and think, or change our thought and feeling, so and so. It appears therefore to me that the use of the term experience is faulty, when we are said to know by experience that there are things or an external world, and again, building upon this knowledge, to know by experience that the earth turns round the sun. Does the word mean the same in these two places? If it does, there must be error one way: either we mean by experience experience of fact, and then rudimentary knowledge, such as our knowledge that there are things or an external world, must be supposed to have the same guarantee (against the supposition of its being mere dream or imagination) of actual hanging on to previously known fact, which our particular pieces of physical knowledge have: or else we mean by experience mental experience only, and then we come to the special positivism which I spoke of a short time since; and all we should *then* mean by saying that we know by experience that the earth turns round the sun is what nobody *would* mean, viz. that this, in the advance of human intelligence, is what men *have* come to think, and being the last birth of progressive intelligence, it must be the truest. If however the word does *not* mean the same in the two places, then it seems to me that the ambiguous term 'experience' had better be disused, and the phrase 'experience-hypothesis' is both unmeaning and misleading.

It may make the matter clearer if I put down here very summarily my own view: all our knowledge is founded upon certain great imaginations, (so first to call them) one of which is the conception of our own phenomenal existence in a surrounding phenomenal universe, or, as it is more commonly called, the notion of things and of an external world. Is this, which I have thus called to begin with an imagination, *mere* imagination, or something more than imagination? is it knowledge? Or, on the other side, is it something less than a mere (*i.e. perhaps* unfounded) imagination? is it an imagination which we can know to be unfounded, an illusion? Now *here* it seems to me to be entirely vain to think we are giving any trustworthiness to these early and fundamental imaginations by using in respect of them terms such as 'experience,' 'acquired' &c., which we use in respect of the following on of one portion of our later knowledge to another. To a certain degree, though not I think entirely, the proceeding of those philosophers whom Mr Mill would call intuitionists is the same. The phenomenalists seek to rescue the great imagination above mentioned from being *mere* imagination by calling it 'acquired,' in the same way as we acquire our knowledge that the earth moves round the sun. It is a similar effort which is made on the other side when it is called, *with significance*, an intuition, *i.e.* when the feeling which we have about it is compared with the feeling which we have about our later or particular sensation or perception, the implication being that it is communication with an object independent of us, whose reality is shown to us by this communication. These primary imaginations must, it seems to me, in some manner justify *themselves* from being mere imaginations, for no comparison of them with the particular steps of later knowledge can so justify them.

Mr Herbert Spencer says (*Psychology*, p. 192[1]), 'The multiplied phenomena of heat are resolvable into dynamical ones,...on holding a thermometer near the fire, the same agent which causes in the hand a sensation of warmth causes motion in the mercury.' We are here trying, if I may so express it, to strike the line of knowledge in the middle point between thought and what I call phenomenalism: for such is the finding an agent which will produce, on the one side, a sensation of warmth to consciousness, and on the other side this motion to matter, body, or whatever we call it. My doubt, in all this sort of language, is as to the use of the word 'produce.' The agent, as Mr Spencer calls the heat, is a sort of motion, and that it should produce another sort of motion is well: but its production of consciousness must be a different sort of production. Suppose by production we mean simple antecedence and sequence, as I noticed in regard to Stewart: then we destroy the significance of the other 'production,' of motion by motion. The two productions cannot be similar. It is the same when Mr Spencer says in the next page[2], 'A certain form of activity in the object, is the efficient cause of a sensation of smell in the subject.' All this logical language, 'object,' 'subject,' 'efficient cause,' is what I am jealous of. That is to say, though there is no harm in using it, yet the only way in which I can understand its force is by resolving it into two co-ordinates, what it means in phenomenal fact, and what it means in thought. Activity (*i.e.* I suppose, motion) in the object being the efficient cause of a sensation (*i.e.* consciousness) of smell in the subject, is what requires much consideration. It seems to me that we are not here in what we may call *true* phenomenalism: we have got a cause causing, in a manner quite out of relation with the manner in which we understand causes causing in proper physics or phenomenalism: we are incorporating into physics or pheno-menalism something which has no business in it: by doing so

---

[1] vol. II. p, 138, ed. 2.　　　　　　[2] *ib.* p. 139.

we do but vitiate our phenomenalism, and puzzle our notion of physical causation.

The same is to be said about the following[1]: 'The subject undergoes a change of state, determined in him by some external agency directly or indirectly proceeding from an object.' I am unable to understand what *world*, as I should say, these logical entities belong to. They are sometimes personalized, as 'subject' is here: it is called 'him'; the 'object' here apparently is an actual physical thing: then 'external' to *him*, is that same language I have several times commented on. In my view, *I* think, feel, do, &c.: on the other hand the physical thing acts on me (if we like so to call it) through 'my' corporeal organization, to which it is 'external.'

The same in p. 195[2]: 'Eyes, ears, nose, and the diffused nervous energy through which temperature is appreciated, are inlets to the influences of objects more or less distant; and the ability that distant objects have thus to work changes in us, again exhibits their inherent activity.' *Into* what do these 'inlets' *let* 'the influences of objects'? When the influence has got inside the body as far as it can go, what then? And then again, 'the influence' or 'activity' of the object—how is the activity or influence separated from the object? In seeing, what communicates with our physical eye is light, while the *object* of our sight or thought is the sun, say: what is Mr Spencer's 'object,' with its influence and activity?

I might have proceeded to examine Mr Spencer's definition and account of perception in p. 200[3], and some of the same things would have to be said. It is a complicated state of consciousness made up of many[4]: among them, primarily, 'the co-existence in time of the contemplating subject and the contemplated object.' So far I go, understanding 'object' in my own way. But 'we have further that relative position of the two in space which we call proximity.' Here the position of a contemplating subject in space, as I said on a passage of Stewart, is what I cannot understand, except with the previous conception by ourselves (the contemplating subject) of ourselves,

---

[1] vol. ii. p. 140, ed. 2.   [2] *ib.* p. 141.
[3] *ib.* p. 145 foll.   [4] *ib.* p. 146.

IX.]   MR HERBERT SPENCER.   103

as phenomenal or filling space so as to be capable of such
position. I might go on further and examine all Mr Spencer's
account, much of which I might adopt as mine, and should be
glad to be able to express it so well. I just notice this beginning
of the account, because it shows the difference of view at starting.
With Mr Spencer, 'the contemplating subject' is man in a
spatial universe thinking and feeling: 'the contemplated object'
is a tree, say, in a spatial universe transmitting light in a
particular way due to its chemical constitution and its shape.
To him, as to many others, the associating together, in one
manner of thinking, of the luminiferous æther with thought
or consciousness does not seem more remarkable than the
association of it, for instance, with heat: and thought or
consciousness is a phenomenon in and of the spatial universe
as light and heat are. Consequently, the contemplating
subject, the subject of the attributes thought, feeling, &c.,
and the contemplated object, the object which is variously
luminous, branched, green, &c. (*i.e.* the tree), have relative
position, and there is a relation, as between two phenomena,
between the thought or feeling on the one side, and the light,
carbon, &c. on the other. *Here* we differ.

CHAPTER X.

ALL the various lines of thought, the philosophy of the Human Mind, Real Logic, Real Epistemology, and Psychology[1], are more or less concerned with certain *scales*, or *logical* courses or movements, and certain *progresses*, or courses or movements *in time*, which I will enumerate.

There is the scale which I have called the scale of sensation[2], or the intellectual scale which passes, if we view it subjectively, from feelings to thoughts, and, if we view it objectively, from secondary qualities to what we will call now for convenience 'ideas.' This scale, if we looked not only at the intellect, but at the whole living being, might be prolonged downward into feeling which has nothing of an intellectual character at all, and will die away into vital action, so far as we recognize such, of which consciousness cannot be predicated in any way. The same scale might perhaps be considered, in a possible prolongation upwards, to embrace 'ideas' in a higher view, in which I shall afterwards speak of them.

There is the scale, so far as we may call it such, with which Comparative Psychology is concerned, the long gradation of different forms of life, with increasing and various development of intelligence. Whether the forms, which we compare, are co-existent, or whether we bring them together, so far as we can gain knowledge of them from different ages of the world's history, is of no importance as a mere matter of time : it is

---

[1] See above ch. i.   [2] *Expl.* p. 107.

only of importance so far as, in the secular changes, we can trace law, growth, and development. Or perhaps it would be most correct to say that there is, at this present time, a gradation of co-existent forms of life, forming the present ' zoocosm[1],' so to call it, and that there is another course of a different kind, which *may be* a gradation, viz. the past succession of such zoocosms.

There is the course or growth of knowledge in the individual mind, with which also Comparative Psychology is concerned, for there must be a growth of it, in some respects analogous, in each animal, so far as it is possessed of mind. This is a process to be traced as a matter of conjunct observation of the organization, and experience of the action of it and of the consciousness.

There is the course or growth of knowledge in the race. This, at first sight, we might say belonged to man alone, and was out of the region of Comparative Psychology, but though this may be so, we cannot say at once that it is, and indeed much of psychology denies it.

Now the varieties of psychological thought consist to a great degree in what is thought about one or another of these courses, and specially of their relation to each other.

For instance, the view of many is that the scale of sensation and the scale of life (the two first which I mentioned) are what I may call virtually the same scale, and that each step of it contains (in a concentrated form) all that has gone before it, that man *e.g.* unites in himself different ways of living, feeling, thinking, &c., the scale being cut off, for lower organizations, at lower points of it.

Again, the opinion of many is that the scale of sensation and the progress of individual knowledge are the same, the former being a sort of logical expression of the latter, which is an actual fact in time, or, conversely, the latter being in some way a simple result of the former.

Psychologies which compare together in various manner these different scales and successions, may be in an eminent degree either idealistic, which their authors would perhaps call

---

[1] *Expl.* p. 253.

philosophical, or experiential and observational, which their authors would probably call *inductive*.

Taking Mr Morell's book[1] as a specimen of the former, and Mr Herbert Spencer's[2] of the latter, I will shortly observe upon the method of each.

Mr Morell begins with a view of the zoocosm, and having arrived in this at *man*, then proceeds (in the method of an analysis of consciousness or philosophy of the human mind) to exhibit the scale of sensation, in successive steps of sensation (in the sense in which *he* uses the term), of intuition, representation, &c. He then shows to how great an extent, in his view, this scale corresponds both with that of the zoocosm, and with the two successions of individual and humano-generic growth of knowledge : *i.e.* that the inferior animals live a life of simple sensation (in *his* sense), &c.; again that the *individual* passes through successive states of mind, the first of which is in the main sensation, then intuition, &c.; and finally, that the *race*, in its advance in knowledge, passes also successively through corresponding stages.

Mr Herbert Spencer begins with an analysis of the action of the human mind, from its most complicated processes to its most simple : and having arrived at these latter, he recommences with an exceedingly elaborate and valuable *synthesis*, as he calls it, or examination of the zoocosm from the bottom (*i.e.* from the simplest organizations) in conjunction with the circumstances of the universe belonging to it at each stage, or in other words, an examination of the relations of life, in its successive steps, to its environment, till we come to the relation of human life to *its* environment, a part of which relation is human knowledge.

My business is to examine the points of view thus taken : and I will say, that it does not appear to me that in reality any unconfused point of view can be got except one that is really phenomenalist, or one that is really logical.

In Mr Morell's method there seems to me to be an unauthorized change of point of view, or jump, where he passes

---

[1] *Elements of Psychology*, 1853.
[2] *Principles of Psychology*, ed. 1, 1855, ed. 2, 1870.

X.]

from the view of the zoocosm, which view is simply phenomenalist, to the analysis of the consciousness of man, when he
arrives at him in his place in the zoocosm. We pass all at once
from experiences of one kind (of sight, hearing, &c.), by which
we become aware of the existence of a variety of creatures, to
experiences of a quite different kind, by which we become
aware of pleasures, pains, and our own knowledge.

In Mr Herbert Spencer's method we have, in an elaborate
form, that sort of circularity which I have alluded to in
speaking of Mr Mill's phenomenalism[1], and which it is difficult
to know how to draw conclusions from. In the gradational
comparison between life and its environment we come at last to
human life and *its* environment, one portion of the relation
between which is human knowledge: but I do not see how
any conclusions, as to what human knowledge really is (as, *e.g.*,
that it is *habit*), are to be drawn from what, in this method
of investigation, we find out about it; because just as much
as we have human knowledge here at the *end* of our investigation, we had it at the *beginning* also, and the examination of
the manner in which we come to such knowledge as we have
about the zoocosm, is as important a matter as the examination what light the investigation of this zoocosm, when we
have to come to know it, throws upon the nature of our
knowledge.

The great point as to comparative psychology is, whether
we can really hang on human knowledge, as we appreciate
it by consciousness, to the various, and, we will suppose,
graduated, knowledges of the inferior animals, as we appreciate
them by observation. It seems to me, that a more methodized
observation of the kinds of knowledge of the inferior animals,
than, so far as I know, has ever yet been made, is a thing very
much needed. The word 'instinct' is one of those unfortunate
words which are supposed to be understood by all, words which
are more fatal impediments to the advance of science than
almost anything can be. The *generic* varieties of knowledge
(observation and quasi-reasoning) in different sorts of animals

[1] *Expl.* 162.

are so peculiar, that there seems to me to need a great deal
more study of them, before anything of the nature of a
gradation can be admitted.   The most convenient *present
supposition*, I have always thought, in respect of the relation
between brute intelligences and the human, is the assumption
that the human intelligence is typical and that the generic
animal intelligences are variations from this type, in a manner
answering to what, in organization, is abortion of some portions
with special development of others.   The special distinction
between these intelligences and the human seems to consist
not so much in a relation of inferiority and superiority, as in
a generic determination in particular directions of the brute
intelligence, in contrast with a *free generality* in the human[1].

This difference is sometimes described by saying, that, in
the upward gradation of the zoocosm, self-consciousness appears
first (speaking generally) in man.   Again, in the comparison of
the scale of the zoocosm with the scale of sensation, and in the
successions of individual and generic advance in knowledge or
thought, self-consciousness is put high up or late.   *E.g.* as
animality advances, in the zoocosm, to the self-consciousness
which first shows itself in man; so human thought advances,
in history, to the self-consciousness which belongs to the later
ages of civilization.

In reality, what is the nature of the consciousness of brutes
is a thing, it seems to me, which we do not at all know; and
therefore I question the importance of describing the relation
of our own to it by the distinctive name of self-consciousness.
Self-consciousness may mean various things.   It may mean
consciousness with much attention, and with attention strongly
introverted or reflective, I mean called away from whatever
may present itself as the objective part of the consciousness, to
ourselves the subjective part.   It may mean the perception of
ourselves, so to speak, as a part of the universe, with a degree
of perception of the particular qualities which we suppose in
ourselves, commensurate and corresponding to the view which
we are taking of the universe.   To compare our feeling with

[1] *Expl.* p. 179.

that of the brutes in respect of the former of these is impossible.
Of the degree, or even of the character, of such intensity as
there is in any consciousness besides our own, we cannot form
a notion. It is impossible for us to tell whether even plants
may not have something of consciousness. Descartes maintained
that animals were unconscious machines, and the only way of
refuting him is to say that they act as though they had
consciousness, this being the only proof in fact that we each
have of the consciousness of our fellow-men.

The second kind of self-consciousness is really better
described by the term which I used just now, 'generality.'
The view which man has of himself as a part of the universe
belongs to the *general* manner in which he views everything.
A main point of the difference between the human and the
merely animal intellect is the disengagement of the former
from the immediate present, the view of things in connexion
by means of memory and imagination, and the *interest* in so
viewing them. This disengagement is what I termed above
freedom of the knowledge, a character which it possesses in
addition to that of generality. Man looks, as it were, at the
whole universe as orderly, and arranged into *kinds* of things,
as an individual of one of which kinds he views himself; and
he has a sort of permanent notion or consciousness of this
universe as existing, to which, as to a ground, he refers all
particular fresh observations. So far as we can judge of the
consciousness of the inferior animals, they have but in a very
slight degree indeed this free or general view, as distinct from
the impressions on particular occasions.

The mature individual human intellect, and the advanced
or highly-civilized collective human intellect, are by many
considered, in comparison with the immature and unadvanced,
to present something which bears an analogy to the human
intellect considered in comparison with the inferior animal
intellect. And the mature or advanced state is variously
described as a *positive* state (to use a single word for it) or as
a self-conscious state. These two notions mean to a certain
degree the same thing; but at the same time are so far
indicative of different, and even contradictory things, as to

suggest that these various analogies, between the human intellect as compared with the animal, the mature individual intellect as compared with the immature, and the advanced humano-generic intellect as compared with the unadvanced, are very imperfect.

Positivism represents what the brute intellect *is not*, in so far as it represents a wide and comprehensive view of the phenomenal universe with its laws, of which all individual occurrences are looked upon simply as instances. But it represents what the brute intellect *is*, in so far as it represents the restraint of the intellect in its disposition to generalize and freely to expatiate. And in this point of view, so far as we consider the course of the human intellect, individual and collective, to be *through* such expatiations to a perception of the mistakenness of them, and a consequent return to a confined sphere, in which regard is had only to definite wants and enjoyments, the course is not a genuine progress, but is either a circle or a limited, almost self-stunting, growth. The fact is, as I hope we shall see, that with the more general view of the universe there should go other elements besides, which we may call growth of idealist thought.

If we say that in the advance of human thought, individual or collective, there awakes after a time something which had not been (or had but little been) before; such a change may betoken no advance, but the opposite, unless by self-consciousness be meant a greater intensity of consciousness, as well as a clearer view of our position in the phenomenal universe. There may be self-consciousness which is only a more vivid perception of *our circumstances*, not of ourselves in contradistinction from them; these two being radically different and even antithetic. The one self-consciousness is greater knowledge of the circumstances and occasions of feelings, the other is greater intensity and perhaps number, and perhaps higher character of the feelings themselves. And this, so far as it *does* take place in man, individual or collective, comes not of itself but as the result of effort.

It seems to me that the idea of a gradual or successive awakening from unconsciousness to self-consciousness is what

we cannot conceive—is the putting together two views which
are incongruous, and cannot be taken in conjunction.　I mean
here by unconsciousness simple '*materiality*,' or whatever we
like to call it, of which the supposition is to be made that
it has not even capacity for consciousness, consciousness
δυνάμει, in the Aristotelic phrase.　And this is not merely
otiose scholastic language: for the point of what I am saying is
that if you suppose materiality (as I have called it) *historically*
developing itself into consciousness, you must *logically* suppose
consciousness a possible quality of materiality, by the side of
hardness, smell, &c.　This is really the supposition of a previous
real, though dormant, existence of the consciousness in the
materiality, which indeed the word 'awakening' suggests.
But then this seems to me in effect to be saying, that
there has never been unconsciousness: the consciousness is
then a great eternal and universal fact, as well as the materiality: there are the two things side by side, and what we in
effect say is, that there are two sorts of qualities, which cannot
be brought into relation together: there are the qualities
feeling, thought, &c., of which we suppose the subject *I*, a
person: and there are the qualities hardness, shape, &c., of
which we suppose the subject *a thing, matter*.

In reality, the historical, or quasi-historical supposition of
matter developing into consciousness, consciousness into self-
consciousness, &c. is the putting into language of time, that
which Mr Mill expresses in logical language: it is the phenomenalist view, with an attempt to include in it the facts of
consciousness.　There is no harm in giving such a view: only
that, in respect of the facts of consciousness, it is not fruitful.
In reality, it always leads in the end to what it might more
properly and logically have professed at the beginning, a
negation of what, in the point of view of consciousness, most
fully and thoroughly appear to be facts, but which a logic
founded entirely upon phenomenalist principles, is unable to
take account of.　*E.g.* the freedom of the will, or felt liberty
and activity, is negatived both by Mr Mill and Mr Herbert
Spencer at the end of their books, this being put as a result of
the reasonings which they have gone through.　This seems to

me much the same thing as if one was to give an account of the spatial universe, saying, that variety or change was nothing but the difference between one thing and another, and then to deny the existence of *time*, as being incompatible with this view. If we do not take our liberty or activity as a primary fact, we certainly cannot admit it *afterwards* into an universe conceived in virtue of (or by means of) qualities incongruous with it. If mind is only the subject of changing states, there is no room for activity.

And in the same way, when we form a scheme of the gradual development of life, we take a view of life from which we can never rise to the idea of liberty or activity as a part of it, and are obliged, as Mr Herbert Spencer does, to deny this. We may imagine the phenomenal universe gradually separating into two portions, an organized and an unorganized, each having a relation to the other. The life and its environment, like our senses and the qualities of matter, our eyes and light, &c. are, in a manner, two parts, two opposite sides, of the same thing. In this view, the perceiving mind is, as it were, between the two, looking to the one side and to the other, to a certain depth, but only to a certain depth. From this point of view, *e.g.* to take one side only, the feeling (which, so far as our own consciousness goes, we know accompanies the communication between the organism and its environment) is a dead letter to us. As I have said, what animals feel and even whether they feel or not, we do not *know*: we only *imagine* from the outside actions, which we take as signs of feeling. And if we say that these actions are similar to actions of ours, which are prompted in us by particular feelings which we have, we then bring into evidence something (our feeling or consciousness) which, if appealed to at all, must be produced in court altogether, in all its circumstances and to all its depth, and if we do this, we shall be in danger of finding *this* view swallow up the other.

In speaking formerly of the phenomenalist and logical views[1], one way in which I described their difference was that, in the former, knowledge, in the latter, fact, was of the nature

---

[1] *Expl.* p. 59.

of an accident. The relation of life (or organization) to matter
(or that which is unorganized), in the point of view of accident,
is an interesting matter of psycho-cosmology.

It is interesting to compare the two 'counter-suppositions'[1]
(so for a moment to call them) of thought generating matter,
and matter generating thought. This latter supposition would
be described probably as 'inorganism' developing into organization, and organization into self-consciousness: 'developing
into' here would mean just the same as 'generating,' and they
imply both of them an activity in matter, only not such an
activity as we suppose in thought: but in reality something
of this other activity, some *thought*, must be supposed besides:
the notion of 'laws' of generation or development is really a
reference to such. The other or counter-supposition is of
thought, *i.e.* an original thinking being, first conceiving, and
then creating, matter. This supposition will stand by itself in
a manner in which the other will not, because thought we do
conceive as active, while matter we do not. And it is really
also the more comprehensive of the two. It may be said, that
thought will no more embrace matter in itself, can no more be
conceived as having been capable of generating it, than matter
will embrace thought in itself, or can be conceived capable of
generating *that*: but this I think is not so. I will not however
enter into the reason now.

Leaving out of view for the present the higher philosophy
of which I shall afterwards speak, we are condemned, it seems
to me, to think of things in one of two ways, both of which are
imperfect: the intensive way of consciousness, and the expansive way of observation. We can gauge our thought, or we can
measure the limitation of it: mixing it with other thought is
what we can only do in the last resort, the *highest* thing that
we can do.

[1] *Expl.* 23, 47.

CHAPTER XI.

CONNEXION BETWEEN THE SENSE OF SIGHT AND OUR
CONCEPTION OF THE EXTERNAL UNIVERSE. PRE-
SENTMENT AND DESCRIAL.

IT is upon the sense of sight that depends our imagination, and consequently the mass of our conception.

Sight may in certain particulars be considered a modification, or subtle kind of touch, as in this character specially, that it 'objectifies' ourselves, or reveals to us our own bodies as part of the universe, while at the same time we stand, as sentient of it, in distinction from it. Sight, as a vastly expanded touch, makes us know the universe, with ourselves as part of it, vastly more vividly and widely than touch does.

Sight, however, has certain particulars in which it is distinguished from touch, this especially, that there is in it what we may call a double perception, or a sub-perception joined to a perception—a field of view and a proper object of vision in it—an indistinctly seen mass and a something noticed or distinctly seen—in rather different words, a mass of what is barely seen and a something seen with intelligence—a host of things in view and something among them or about them looked at. In touch and in sight there is equally the exercise of volition for attention and notice, but it acts in different ways. Its action in touch (for intelligence) is mensurative, or, as it may be called in comparison with the other, intensive, while in sight it is distinctive, particularizing, singling out, insulating[1]. In the latter there is a double presence, (1) of a mass of objects to the organ or nerve, and indistinctly to the mind, (2) of a particular object more strongly and specially to the organ, and distinctly to the mind.

---

[1] *Expl.* 40 foll.

I shall call the two parts of the sensation by different names[1]: that which belongs to the sub-perception, 'present-ment': that which belongs to the perception, 'descrial.' The first is what is presented to us : the second is what we descry. I do not mean that the mind is all passive in regard of the first, or all active in regard of the second. One must be very cautious as to speaking about the mind's passivity and activity. We may say with equal correctness such and such a thing in a view is what draws the eye, or such and such a thing is what we remark and notice : we may say, either, we look at such a prospect, and such a thing in it is what strikes us, or, such a prospect is before our eyes, and such a thing in it is what we look at.

By 'presentment' I mean the fact of the view being before our eyes, independent of the thought of one portion of it being noticed by us more than another. This is, in my sense of the word, an abstraction, because, unless we are in a reverie, that is, if we are in a normal condition of sight, there is always special notice of one portion of it, and such sight of the whole as we have, varies according to this. It is visual *presentment* which causes our imagination of the universe, and visual *descrial* which causes us to think particular objects in it.

The two great philosophical controversies as to sight seem to be, which of the two, *presentment* or *descrial*, give us the most of reality and truth, and which of the two is most properly to be called sight.

On the former of these controversies, those in favour of presentment would say that descrial is all imagination : those in favour of descrial would say presentment is all illusion. 'You must interpret presentment,' say the latter, 'before you get any reality': 'If you do begin to do this,' say the others, 'you will lose your hold on reality, and get a world of inventions or creations of your own.' The distinction between presentment and descrial is involved with the deepest philosophical problem which there is.

---

[1] See Crabbe, quoted in *Expl.* 44,
> It is the mind that sees: the outward eyes
> Present the object, but the mind descries.

This problem or question is, whether (taking the suggestion probably from consciousness of what we call our own existence) we believe *à priori* in the existence of something (or, as to the action of our mind, *look for* things): or whether we conceive of existence of things because we find them (what we call) to exist. The question lies at the root of all thought. A great many of the difficulties of logic and grammar turn upon it: and it is perhaps by a mental reference to these subjects that some will best understand the problem.

We speak, *e.g.* of 'the visible world,' 'visible things.' Do we mean (I will put it in various ways) things of which visibility is the essential character, or of which it is one character, possibly along with many others? things *as* visible, or things, more than visible, which we know by means of their being visible? things as they seem to us, or things which seem to us this or that, whatever may be their real nature? Is all that may have to do with sight what constitutes to us the reality of the thing, or is it *our* way to the knowledge of the thing (which is itself something beyond and independent)? Is it the seen, τὸ ὁρώμενον—what we may call the gross visual reality— or is it what we imagine, which constitutes the net and pure reality, when what we think has meaning and the medium is forgotten?

It is not easy to see the question here, but it is most important. It is equally important, more generally, in regard of the term 'object' of knowledge in any application. Do we, as we first think and use the word *know*, mean by it a *transitive* word, certain beforehand that there is something to be known, that there is what I may call an *objiciend*, which may present itself as an actual *object* of knowledge? When it *is* an object, of course its separateness or independence is ended by the particular manner of the knowledge: had it ever, or could it ever have such independence? *Verberat hominem, Servit servitutem:* in the former case, the object is independent of the verb, and need not have been object of it, in the latter case the object has no existence except in dependence on the verb: philosophers are continually using the term 'object' of knowledge without at all explaining in which of these (so different) senses they are using it.

CHAPTER XII.

ON THE THEORY OF VISION.

THE account which I have given[1] of the action of sight as compared with that of other senses, may perhaps make it appear why men have spoken of the *visible* world or universe in a manner different from that, *e.g.*, in which they have spoken of the audible universe, as conceivably possessing a reality which could not be even thought of for the other. Yet the audible universe is the universe of *sound* in a manner quite analogous to that in which the visible universe is the universe of colour: and though there is much difference in degree, yet in substance the ear lends itself to adjustments indicating primary qualities, distance, direction etc., and associating themselves with other corporeal movements more fully indicating such qualities, just as the eye does.

We may say that there are three heads of controversy about the visible world, or visual fact, which however I shall not try to keep too separate: the first is the controversy as to the right application of the word 'see,' which is a verbal controversy, but like most verbal controversies involves something more than words.

The next head of controversy as to visual fact is the nature of the reality which, according as we use the word 'see,' belongs to what we consider the objects of sight.

The third, and most important, is the actual nature of the fact which we may call *in general* 'visual.' I say 'in general,' to keep this part of the subject as clear as possible from any

---

[1] *Expl.* 21, 39.

controversy as to the use of words, or as to their logical meaning,
or as to the ultimate meaning of 'reality.'

I have already indicated to a certain extent my own views
as to this third question[1], and shall now proceed to speak a little
upon the actual controversy which there has been about it,
which is involved to a certain degree with controversy upon
the second head.

The name of Bishop Berkeley is intimately associated with
all this controversy, in a manner, it appears to me, most
mistaken. There are two ruling doctrines, so to call it, in
Berkeley's *Theory of Vision* : the one, which is for the most part
taken for granted, is that we see what I will call ' perspectivally';
that what we see, in one sense at least of the word 'see,' is not
the actual or tangible thing in its proper shape and its true
position, but a representation of it, indicating these; and that
the proper shape and true position are to a considerable extent
matters of judgment.   All this, in the main, Berkeley explains
and illustrates, but takes for granted : while, as his own new
doctrine, he superadds that the suggestiveness, by visual fact, of
tactual or real fact, is not in virtue of any connexion between
the different senses, nor again in virtue of any resemblance
between the so-called distances, magnitudes, shapes, in the one
case and in the other ; but is the result of what he (and others
after him) have sometimes represented as an arbitrary arrangement of the Creator, brought about by means of an *association*
in our minds, similar to that which makes the word ' lion,' when
we see it written, call up to our imagination the actual four-
legged creature.

Berkeley's advocacy of the latter of these doctrines as his
own, naturally leads him to put forward very strongly, and to
illustrate very vividly, the fact (which is far from new or his
own), that it is by judgment, and not by anything which can
be called actual sight as distinguished from judgment, that for
the most part we become aware of distance, magnitude, and
position : and hence his treatise, as an account of vision, has
a permanent value quite independent of his own theory.

[1] *Expl.* 39 foll.

Putting forward, as he does, what would undoubtedly be considered a paradox by people in general, he misconceives the reason why it would be so considered. He thinks people are all but irrecoverably prejudiced to regard the things which they see as the real things. Now in reality, it is not *here* that he would find people differing from him. Of course people in general do not turn their thoughts much to the subject, but so far as they do, they would perfectly agree with what he goes on to say about 'immediate' and 'mediate' vision, and would be quite ready to allow that, while in one sense of the word vision (called, if he will, 'mediate') they see the *things*, in another sense ('immediate') they do not see the things, but *representations* of them, a shaded circle for instance instead of a sphere, an acute angle instead of a right angle made by a receding line with a vertical. They would not differ from him, nor would the paradox begin, till he came to say, These representations which you see are not suggestive by resemblance or for any reason in themselves, but only arbitrarily and by an association, which might as well have made anything else represent the things, if so it had been. And in my judgment *they* are right, not he.

These two doctrines, the doctrine of our *perspectival* sight and of its need of correction or addition from something other than sight, in order to be sight of *the real*, or sight which we can act upon—which doctrine seems to me as old as human thought or human language—and the doctrine that the former, or immediate, sight, stands to the latter, or mediate, in the relation of an arbitrarily significant symbolism, well represented by the words of a language—these two doctrines have been put together by many philosophers into a supposed Berkeleian discovery with singular result. With some, the charm has been in the arbitrary association or experience: and Berkeley, endeared by the degree to which he has insisted on this, has been credited with the entire discovery of our perspectival vision. The view thus set on foot has been acquiesced in by others, to whom association and experience were matters of more indifference, and by others again (it appears to me) who in their dislike to this doctrine of association have been led on to attack things by no means necessarily concerned with it or with Berkeley. Mr Abbott's book[1] seems to me an attempt to prove in fact, that the visible world or visual fact is *more* real, *more* the universe to us, *more* representative of the truth of things, than the tactual or tangible : from which it would seem to follow that in view of action we should correct our touch by our sight.

I do not think the controversy has been carried on in a very philosophical manner. The impugners of the supposed Berkeleian theory are treated with a kind of contempt, somewhat in the same manner in which we might treat an impugner of the Copernican system of the heavens : and they for their part, or at least Mr Abbott, conceive themselves as maintainers of common sense and natural human judgment (called possibly by them 'the evidence of consciousness') against paradox and philosophical refinement. This again their opponents allow in somewhat of a different view, considering that the universal persuasion of ordinary human nature is opposed to the universally received opinion of philosophers, which latter, of course, they hold for truth.

Nothing can be more unlike the real aspect of the question than all this. In a general way, we had better in philosophy say as little as we can either about persuasions of ordinary human nature or generally received opinions of philosophers ; for there has gone more discussion to settle what is the actual persuasion or opinion, than might have been sufficient to settle the point itself independent of these matters, if it had been directed to that end. Or in default of such discussion, there has been what is worse, simple repetition of one philosopher by another, which is the common way in which an opinion gets the character of being generally received.

In this question, however, at any rate, all appeal to quasi-authority either of human nature or of philosophers is alike out of place. Involving, as it does most intimately, the entire question of sensation, it is equally unphilosophical to bar it as settled and done with, or to fix the ground to argue it on by

---

[1] *Sight and Touch*, Longmans, 1864.

reference to a consensus of philosophic authority in favour of a supposed Berkeleian theory.

In examining Berkeley's argument it is important to observe his manner of dealing with *distance* as compared with his dealing with magnitude and situation, on account of the great misapprehensions about it. He is supposed to have *discovered* that we do not *see*, but only *judge* of distance in a right line from the eye[1]. But instead of its being Berkeley's argument *to prove* that we do not see distance perpendicular to the eye, his argument is to prove that we *do* visually apprehend it, in the same way in which we visually apprehend anything real, viz. mediately by signs. The '*perspectival*' fact (so to call it) of foreshortening, which he speaks of as known to all, is opposed to his argument in one respect, while it is helpful to it in another. He makes it helpful in this way : ' You allow,' he says, ' that you know, by exercised sight, the direct distance of things, while yet you have no proper *visual* means of doing so : *i.e.* you know it by signs or mediately : I am going to prove that it is this same way in which, so far as sight goes, you know *any* reality, not only distance, but form, magnitude, situation. You grant the possibility of knowledge of this kind, in the case of distance : I will show you how widely it extends.' In this way Berkeley uses the manner of sight of distance in support of his argument : at the same time his argument in many respects would have been easier if our visual apprehension of distance perpendicular to the eye had been *more* analogous to our visual apprehension of figure or length in front of the eye. He has not been able to prove to people what he wanted to prove (that we do not see real figure in a plane in front of the eye any more than we see real distance perpendicular to the eye), because people have always stuck at the difference between our manner of seeing these, and have said, ' What you say applies in the one case, distance : it does not apply in the other : we will therefore understand your argument of the former only': which is misunderstanding it.

Supposing Berkeley to have made out that seeing is not by

---

[1] *Expl.* 40.

any natural geometry of lines and angles present in some way
or other to our judgment, but consists in sensation or feeling on
our part, feeling of movement of the eyes and feeling of various
distinctnesses or definitenesses of nervous affection, which
varieties of feeling come by experience to represent to us what
we call various distances, forms and magnitudes—we find that
the result of the interpretation which we thus put upon the
visual *feeling*, is to create before us 'the visible world' or a
variously shaped and coloured scene, the particular portions of
which we call visible things, saying of them that they have
form, magnitude, distance.   What relation then, in Berkeley's
view, does this scene, its separate portions, and the ground or
canvass of it, which for the present we will call visible space,
bear to reality ?

The visual scene, says Berkeley, is really at no distance
from us, it is in our eye or, at least, in ourselves: it is only
in consequence of our tactual experience that it and the several
parts of it begin to stand off from us, or that there begins to
arise what has been called '*outness*'[1] : this tactual experience
interprets the movements of the eyes and the variety of distinctnesses of objects into different distances of objects from
us, and this is the first step in the transforming that which
is really at the eye into *the scene before us*.   Hence to one
suddenly recovered from blindness it must appear, says
Berkeley, not the perspectival scene which it appears afterwards, but a confused mass of colour close to us or not
distinct from us.

Berkeley's saying this is remarkable, inasmuch as it is
chiefly since his time that observations have been made on
persons fresh couched, and it has appeared that they do, more
or less, see as he said they must.   But still his way of putting
the matter involves difficulty.   Experiments of the kind just
mentioned are not of *much* value, for this reason.   Of course
the eye, on being first called suddenly into active existence,
cannot *use itself* (if we may employ the expression), or put out
its *own* powers : its condition is for the moment, perhaps for

---

[1] *Expl.* 47; Berkeley *Vision*, § 46.

some time, mazed and abnormal: the man sees things no how
(so to speak), can make nothing of anything, like a man
suddenly cured of complete deafness in the middle of an
instrumental concert. But this is really not the same thing
as the seeing everything, previously to experience, immediately
at the eye, which is what Berkeley says must be. What is
superinduced may be only orderliness of the confused, as the
eye begins properly to perform its functions, not anything new
to the eye, or generically different from the first instant's vision,
like the supposed *outness*. The newly couched man has an
orange set before him, and is told to take it with his hand,
and makes all sorts of bad shots before he succeeds in doing
so, coming to know its distance thus by tactual experience.
What we want to know is, how far, if he had two oranges set
before him, one a little further than the other, whether in a
right line from the eye or not, his hands tied behind him, and
leisure given him to accustom himself to things about him, he
would be able by the use of the eye or eyes alone to form any
opinion as to the distance of the oranges the one from the
other, and correspondingly of their *offness* or distance from
himself. This question is one of 'psychophysiology,' not as
Berkeley puts it, of philosophy. No doubt the perspectival
scene before us is really at no distance, really at the eye, in
this respect, that were our retina suddenly diseased, all else
remaining the same, we might see (in this use of the word), a
scene or supposed prospect entirely different from what we saw
before: and since the eye cannot tell its own disease, we could
form from mere vision no judgment as to the comparative truth
of what we saw. To alter the scene then, we have only to
affect the eye: there might be imagined medicaments for the
optic nerve which might enable us to live in a visible world
of our own, perpetually varying and of whatever beauty we
pleased and could pre-imagine. But all this gives us no reason
to consider that a person beginning to see will see things as at
the eye. What is in the eye is nervous agitation, and corresponding to this in the world of consciousness is true sensation
or thought, and according to the nervous agitation this thought
creates the visual object and projects it into space which it has

created likewise, and this is its locality as a part of the visual
scene. It is at the eye in quite a different sense from the
sense in which it has this locality, and no experience can make
a bridge between one and the other.

The supposition then that the perception of 'outness' is a
putting things off from the eye or ourselves, which at first sight
appear to be at or with us, is an unphilosophical one. But of
course there is no doubt but that the visual scene, as it is
looked on by the mature eye of any one of us, has its history,
having been once merely rudimentary, and that this history is
a succession of what if we like we may call 'experiences,' which
are first of ocular movement associated with our colour-taste[1], so
to call it, and then of general corporeal movement associated
with this. How the visual scene, which we seem to have before
us, is exactly to be conceived in relation to other things in a
manner like it, is hard to say. I mean in this way. Those who
say, like Mr Mill, that it is a vertical plane in front of us, or like
Dr Reid, that it is an equiradial concavity in front of us, seem
to me to be teaching that natural geometry which Berkeley so
much dislikes. It is representable pictorially by means of such
a plane, but it might equally be described as a series of receding
scenic pictures, and in other ways. That which we employ to
suggest to another by likeness what we see or imagine, must of
course be like what we see, but *how* like is hard to say. Again,
how far may we say that the painter's task is to unlearn much
that is added in the visual scene to what is pure matter of
vision, and see things, so to speak, with the eyes alone, without
the intrusive imagination or mind? Does the child really see
that the lines of a house at a distance are in perspective, since
if you tell him to draw them, it is very unlikely that he will
draw them so? Might Berkeley have given as an argument
against 'natural geometry' the fact that perspective lines and
angles have never till this moment, it would appear, impressed
themselves upon the Chinese eye, and that in drawing a thing,
they never imitate it as our eye, at least, would see it, but
some other conception of it?

[1] *Expl.* p. 41.

But to keep at present to Berkeley's view. It seems to me there is want of clearness in his description of the object of what he calls immediate vision. It is 'light and colours': again it is visual extension, form, magnitude, etc. only that these are to be considered specifically distinct from, merely *homonymous* with, the tangible extension, form etc., which bear the same names. I think it will appear, if we watch, that in all this there is a confusion of what I call philosophy on the one side and physics or physiopsychology on the other. Light and colours, *i.e.* light with its own laws, and its relations to our nerves of sensation, is an actual physical existence: there is no other question as to *its* reality than such as belongs to the reality of phenomenalism in general. But the question what sort of reality belongs to the visible scene which we suppose before our eyes, is one of quite a different consideration, and so of course is the question, what relation its reality bears to tactual reality, whether it is the same, or different.

We may be said to see what we ultimately (in Berkeley's phrase 'mediately') see, viz. what Berkeley would call the *real* moon, the *real* tree, the *real* geometrical figure, by all sorts of intermediations, the confusing of which together is fatal to any sort of clearness of conception. We see it by the inter-mediation of our sensation as nervous agitation and ocular volition; by the intermediation of light and its optical laws (the action of which, as sensally known to us, we call colour), and also its geometrical laws (the maintaining that these, if *visually* known to us, must be so by sensation, *i.e.* nervous disturbance, not by reason of their mere existence, is the con-troversy against natural geometry), including under these the image on the retina; by the intermediation of the visual scene, which is a sort of compound of these two last intermediations with experience of touch and movement and more general thought. But these intermediations (and others might be mentioned besides them), are intermediations in different ways. The question may be best understood by considering in illus-tration of it, whether we see form in a plane in front of the eye. What has been said about this shows the odd misapprehensions, as it seems to me, of Berkeley's doctrine. Berkeley says of it, as of everything else, we do not see it, and we do. We see so many *minima visibilia*, or units of visible extension, and we put them together, making up visible magnitude or form : but this is not real or tangible magnitude and form, but something specifically different from it. It may very likely take *time* to put them together, so that we come to see this form by a process : but then this is not wonderful. So, by a process, we come to apprehend visually comparative distance of objects even in a direct line from the eye. There is a face of cliff two miles off, and a large tree one mile off standing in relief against it. We see the cliff with one degree of distinctness, the tree with another, and notice the difference without knowing that it *means* anything. Similarly, in the former case, we put the *minima visibilia* together, and notice them all together thus, without understanding that *this* means anything. Afterwards we walk up to the tree and the cliff, and find they are a mile the one from the other, and we say, Now we know what the difference of distinctness means, and call it visible distance. And then, guided by the collection of *minima visibilia*, we put our hand (say) to a ring on the table or the surface of a round table itself, and finding that our hand travels round it with a certain amount of effort, with no direct resistance, with uniform change of direction, returning to where it started from, we say, Now we know what that which was before our eye means: it means this actual tangible figure which we will call a circle.

Berkeley puts together the heterogeneous intermediation between our visual power and that which we ultimately or mediately see into one notion of symbol or sign, and does not seem to me to deal quite fairly by it. He uses what he considers the entire unlikeness between variety of visual distinctness (the sign) and traversable distance (the thing signified) to establish (so far as it is established) that it is by signs entirely unlike the things signified that we see these latter things: at the same time he acknowledges that there is an aptitude in some signs to represent some things signified[1]. But this notion, if carried to

---

[1] Cf. *Essay*, § 142, "it must be acknowledged the visible square is fitter than the visible circle to represent the tangible square."

any extent, is destructive of the previous argument: for the only reason of the aptitude must be that there is some sort of likeness between the sign and the thing signified, or picturing of the one by the other: whereas his fundamental point is the *specific* unlikeness (so he calls it, I should rather say '*generic*'). He tries to escape this by some very odd reasonings about language, for as I have mentioned, he considers his signs to represent the things signified in the same way as the words of a language represent the things they stand for. Better reasonings would have been of this kind: the visual form of a square in front of the eye has a natural fitness for representing the actual form, more than the visual variety of distinctnesses has to represent actual distance in a line from the eye, in the same way as βομβεῖν, or 'to hum,' has a natural fitness for representing the noise of a bee, more than 'hive,' or 'house,' have for representing the bee's dwelling or ours. But if we make this more than exceptional, there is an end of all notion of specific or generic dissimilarity between the seen and the real, the immediately and mediately seen: and it is clear that the mass of the visual scene will come under the case of aptitude for representation, which is in fact likeness: our seeing direct distance from the eye in the peculiar, *specially* symbolic or merely suggestive way in which according to Berkeley we do see it, without anything corresponding to it upon the retina, has reference at most to only a third of our vision— one dimension.

Berkeley's paradox comes in where he tries to prove that the visual scene before our eyes is nothing more than a vast tablet of symbols, with no more reason (subject to such qualification as we have spoken of) why they should represent the different things which they signify, than there is why the letters l-i-o-n should represent the beast, or an ordinary long-used and well-worn Chinese word-symbol, for 'house' say, represent what we live in. We may feel the most cordial admiration and reverence for the religious application which Berkeley makes of his theory, when he speaks of the visibility of things as a language in which the Creator communicates with us about them: but we are now concerned with the philosophical aspect of his theory: and on this surely there is only to be said that it either means nothing (*i.e.* a very slightly applicable metaphor) or is altogether wrong.

Of course we may say the visible *expresses* to us the actual or tangible, and we may develope the metaphor into a detailed simile, more or less interesting: but this mere use of language has existed from the beginning of the world and needed no Theory of Vision to enforce it. If Berkeley means anything new, he means something wrong—and in fact we have seen how he went wrong: he thought of language as made up of gestures and inarticulate sounds, till the artificial language of arbitrary symbols, *i.e.* sounds and written words, was invented as more convenient: and it is this artificial language to which he compares visible things. When we come at all to consider what language really is, we shall find that the philosophy of vision and reality is in no possible way benefited, but only cumbered and confused by reference to it.

There is one most interesting illustration given by Berkeley, which seems to show us better than anything else what he means by his *dissimilarity*, and which more than anything points the way to our forming a notion of the truth[1].

It is quite possible to conceive that the different parts of our nature might have been ill-fitted to each other. We might conceive this as to the eye on one side, and as to the hand and the other members of the body on the other. There is a world, we might almost say, in every grain of dust and every drop of water: and the visible scene for the optics of the fly or other small insect corresponds to this world. It is quite possible for us to conceive, as to ourselves, that we had eyes adapted to this (imagined) scene and world, while our arms and legs remained as they are, and adapted as they are. What should we judge then about *that* visible scene, which we could not bring into

---

[1] The reference is probably to § 62, 'Our eyes might have been framed in such a manner, as to be able to see nothing but what were less than the *minimum tangibile*. In which case it is not impossible that we might have perceived all the immediate objects of sight the very same that we do now: but unto those visible appearances there would not be connected those different tangible magnitudes that are now.'

relation with our touch and our movements? Should we judge
it to have tangible existence, when no *touch* suggested or could
test its having so? Should we not then be really *blind* as to
the real world of our action and movements, and would not the
eye be to us a sense like the ear, causing in us a sensation of
variety of form and colour, as that of variety of pitch and
quality of sound, but no more suggesting to us any real
universe of which we form a part than the ear does?

In this case we should have before our sight a visible scene,
with microscopic animalcules for cows, sheep and lions, and
with cells and tissues in the place of the forms and shapes
of what we now call things—a scene possibly interesting and
beautiful: but we should be in regard of it (let the reader
remember that in all that I have said I have been speaking
from Berkeley's point of view, not from my own) what we may
call touch-blind or touch-deaf—I mean without the sense of
touch, as the blind is without the sense of sight: our imagination would be visual only, and it would never enter into our
head that the animalcules had any tangible magnitude which
our fingers might to a greater or less degree grasp, or the cells
any actual distance from each other which our hand or our
limbs might traverse. On the other hand, our imagination of
the world, which we moved in and in which things touched us
and we them, would be tactual and motional only: we should
be able to trace a triangle with our hand in the air, and should
conceive or remember the definition of it as thus traced: but
we should have nothing corresponding to it before our sight,
nothing visually suggested by it: our sight would be employed,
as we have just seen, in a different sphere and world.

I think this shows us what Berkeley means by the *unlikeness*
of the visual, and the tactual or real forms. On the above
supposition, we might quite well *see* a triangular cell, or three
long animalcules in such relative positions as to make a triangle,
and notice it for a triangle (or whatever name we gave to it).
The next moment we might be moving our hand first hori-
zontally, then obliquely downwards, then obliquely upwards to
where we started from, or might be passing our hand round a
prism, so as to make or feel a triangle, noticing *it* at the same

time for a triangle, or whatever we called *it*. Berkeley's doctrine
is that these two processes, the first or visual, and the second or
tactual, being, by the hypothesis, not uniteable by experience,
would not be conceived as having anything to do with each
other, and that nothing in or about the one would suggest
anything in or about the other. When, therefore, we find in
our actual life that the triangle of sight always does suggest
the real triangle of touch, this cannot be through any resemblance, for we have just seen that they are of themselves
mutually unsuggestive: it must be by an arbitrary arrangement
of the Creator, who has so appointed it that, where we find the
one by our sight, we find the other by our touch : and since the
latter is what we *want* to find—the real—we may fairly consider
the other a sort of symbol, guide, mark, mere memorandum.

In this way it seems to me that this illustration of
Berkeley's shows very vividly what he means. I will now
explain what I meant in saying that it also seemed to me
preeminently adapted to direct us to the truth.

My own view in this matter is given in the former Part
where, speaking of sensation in general[1], I said that I looked
upon the body as all one sense, and that we became aware,
roughly speaking, of distance, form, magnitude, situation, and
other primary qualities by movement of all or any part of it.
We have special organs of particular sensation besides : which
have each more or less the character of members or limbs of
the body (moveable by us and making us aware of something
by their movement) and also of nervous surfaces, each specially
adapted to be affected (with sensation on our part) by some
particular natural existence or agent—light, odorous particles,
sapid particles. The eye is one such special organ: by its
movements, or more properly by our movements of it, we
become aware, under certain conditions, of distance, form,
magnitude : but its movements take place in association with,
and partly at the instigation of, affection of its special nerves
by the light, the result of which is what we call the perception
of colour. The eye thus, in regard of its movement, is a part of
the whole body in a sense in which it is not so in regard of its

[1] *Expl.* 21.

affection by the light. It has the latter to itself, but its movement is a part of the general movement of the whole body,
which all follows, to whatever extent it does follow, our volition.
It handles, or we handle with it, through the intermediation
of light, whatever the variously exciting light stimulates it
to handle.

Wherever therefore in the preceding I have used the word
touch, following other people's language, what I have meant has
been our knowledge (by means of movement of any part of the
body) of something resisting the movement, *i.e.* of something
being in contact with the body, or of the continued absence of
such resistance where we were prepared to meet it (which is the
traversing of space). I have put this with the other because
it naturally goes with it, though I do not know that I have
ever used the expression 'touch' in application to that.

But it will be seen from this, that touch, as it is commonly
spoken of in reference to this discussion (I am not now speaking
of any titillational sense there may possibly be different from
the feeling of resistance, nor considering *how* delicate this latter
may be), is by no means one special sense to be set by the
side of others, but is the general corporeal sense, the judging
in respect to any supposed thing that it has an existence more
or less like that of our body, because it communicates or comes
into contact with it, and according to the manner in which it
does this. When therefore I said that we might perfectly make
the supposition of our sight and our touch not being properly
matched together, or of our being touch-blind or touch-deaf,
I meant that we might make this supposition on Berkeley's
view, not that I could make it upon my own view. In fact the
great point of my difference from Berkeley and from those
many philosophers who follow and admire him on account of
the pleasure which he takes in arbitrary association and experience, is that I think *things* (our body with its senses and
our faculties of knowledge among them), hold together, with
reason for their so holding, and that we are not on the way
towards truth, but on the way towards error, by making much
of those notions and illustrations which would present them to
us as accidental and unconnected.

We may then individually be imperfect as regards any one
of the special senses (blind, *e.g.*) but we cannot be *touchless*, for
that would be to be incorporeal. Again, imperfection in a sense
like sight is of a double nature : it may either be want of sensibility of the passive or sensor nerve—this is peculiar to it as a
special sense—or it may be malformation of the portions of the
organ connected with movement: this is not peculiar to it as
a special sense, but is analogous to malformation, *e.g.* of the
hand. Now, we are each one of us *one* organization, and the
supposition of Berkeley's which I have been expanding is a
supposition of abnormalism, which might be made with just as
much or just as little reason, in the form of a comparison
between the organs of the (normally) same sense, as in the
form of a comparison between different senses. How should
we manage *e.g.* for visible picture, if our eyes were of quite
different adjustment, and if with the one we saw, and could
not help seeing, objects five miles off or more, and none nearer,
and with the other only objects at a distance measured by
yards ? and what would be our notions of tangible figure if we
were blind (I make this supposition only to keep the touch
purer) and had for our prehensile organs two hands entirely
out of proportion the one to the other, so that we could make
nothing with the one of small things, and nothing with the
other of big ones, so as to establish any relation between
them ?

I make these suppositions, extravagant like Berkeley's, in
order to show that the question about this association and
experience is not limited to the relation between sight and
touch, but is only one portion of the general question of the
association of any one sensation with another. Were our sight
microscopic only, and our touch what it is now, the two sets of
sensations would be unassociable together; but just in the same
way, if we had one hand fit only for microscopic manipulation,
and the other of a kind to grasp houses and church-towers, and
could not help the matter by sight or movement, the different
sensations of touch would be mutually unassociable, we having
no means of comparing large and small things, and the word
unlike would have exactly the same meaning (or no-meaning),

as applied to express the relation between the small cube of one hand and the large one of the other, that it had to express the relation between the square of sight and the square of touch in Berkeley's supposition of the uncomparableness of the two senses.

I hope to speak in a separate chapter[1] about association and experience, about which I will only say now that by 'experience' we mean experience of the universe through our physical organization, and that every use of the word, to have any meaning, takes for granted the general organization which underlies each part, and which must be one and a whole, or it is nothing. All sensations have to be associated together by experience, different sensations of touch one with another, quite as much as sensations of sight with either of them. The newly couched man beginning to move his eyes in judging of the distance of the orange before him, makes exceedingly bad shots at it with his hands in the process of learning to associate sight and touch, but only in the same way as the infant, in trying we will say to take hold of the same orange, will very likely hit it with one hand when he will not with the other, being occupied, for his part, in learning to associate different sensations of *touch*, or volitional movements of his two hands.

The special senses (as I have called them) in so far as they are special, are each isolated from the general corporeal sense, or perception of the relation of the body (as to form, magnitude, position, solidity) to the portions of the universe about it : we cannot help, at least at present, each having for himself his own world of pure colour, taste, smell, and we can bring these very little into relation with each other. But the sense of sight is very much more than a special sense of the kind I have just alluded to. It is composed of a nervous susceptibility mixed with a complicated organization for adjustment, which makes it in fact a hand as well as a palate, and *starts* that knowledge of distance, form, magnitude, position, which *then* refers itself to our general corporeal sensation, or knowledge of the universe, by the association of *its* movements with the more distinctly

---

[1] This does not appear to have been written.

noticeable and mensurational movements of the hand and other
parts of the body.   I will not dwell on this, as I shall have to
speak a little more about it in discussing 'association.'   The
point now is, that it is in consequence of this double character
of the eye that the visual scene is what it is.   We usually, in
describing sight, say that it is the sense for colour, as a secondary
quality, having superadded to it (if we allow this) some arrangements which enable us to perceive with it certain primary
qualities also, *e.g.* form of some kind.   Suppose we alter the
order of the description of it, and say that it is a hand, with a
special nervous susceptibility in the palm of it, which enables
us to know, about what we handle, something more than the
simple handling would inform us of.   We handle, it is true,
mediately, by means of light: but we handle.   And this is a
truer description of sight in relation to touch than the other in
this particular view : in sight we have tactual knowledge of the
universe, with something superadded.   The true imagination or
mental picturing, whether with the object before us so as to be
sight, or without it so as to be what we more generally call
imagination, superadds to the quasi-imagination, or conception
of his own body and of the universe around it, on the part of
a man born blind, who has touched and moved, but never seen—
it superadds, I say, to this not merely the secondary beauties of
colour but a virtual extension of the sense of touch, by means
of light, to incalculable distances from our body, and continuously
over every portion of body and space upon one side of us, leaving
no gap.   It is *this* which makes us talk of *the universe:* whether
the tactual quasi-imagination of the blind above mentioned
would suggest the notion of the universe I cannot tell, I wish
we knew : but as it is, it is the *visible* scene or visible universe
which makes us talk of a universe at all : there is no doubt of
this.

Sight then may fairly put in a claim to *its* share in giving
us our notion of reality, and may with reason put in its protest
against what I must call the monstrous Berkeleian supposition,
that its objects are nothing but a set of symbols, with no other
value, independent of their beauty, than that they suggest to
us objects of touch.   Their reality, as objects of rightly used

sight, is the same as that which attaches to the objects of
rightly used touch. Sight and touch then, or, as I should
describe it, the particular organization of the eye for purposes
of knowledge, its power of movement and its susceptibility
to light on the one side, and on the other side all the rest of
the general organization of the body, so far as it helps us to
knowledge—each of these may be considered to constitute
about half, or to balance each other, in respect of our gaining
knowledge of the universe.

Mr Abbott seems to me to try to make out that there is
more reality in the visible world (or scene) than in the tactual:
that the former tells us more about reality than the other. As
I have said, sight tells us about reality (as we will speak of
reality now) in so far as it is itself a species of touch, complicated indeed and mediate, and in no other manner. The
notion, that in sight we see space by any manner of special
intuition, is rendered chimerical in an instant by the thought
of the physical necessities, or conditions of light and of the
atmosphere, which go to the sense of sight as we have it. Let
us suppose light to be ' offspring of heaven first-born or co-
eternal beam of the Eternal,' something almost like space itself
in its antiquity, its universality, and its fundamentality,—yet,
for sight as the foundation of our imagination and as what
suggests to us the universe around us, there has to exist the
earth's atmosphere, a something which, whatever it may be
in comparison with actual solid objects, yet in comparison with
space must be held to be in itself of a gross, corporeal, accidental character. What we see when light is present, is
illumination or, if we prefer the expression, illuminated objects.
The groundwork of the visible scene is the illuminated atmosphere. Were we reduced to *space* (which is what Mr Abbott
thinks we see), *i.e.* were the atmosphere to vanish, we might see
objects indeed (if it were so) but without any ground or con-
tinuousness, any bridging between them; *i.e.* our universe,
or notion of wholeness and ' *togetherness* ' of things, would
vanish at once. If we see space at all, *that* is space which we
see when we are in total darkness but with our eyes open, and
when we are endeavouring, so to speak, to use them,—a very

unsatisfactory intuition. Suppose, *e.g.* we are looking out of the window into perfect darkness: on a sudden there appear to us two stars, not very far from one another: we are aware of the interval or apparent distance between them, and may be said to see it: on a sudden the stars vanish, our eyes still watching exactly in the same direction: do we now see the interval—no longer properly describable as an interval? If we *did* see it, surely we must see it still: and if we do see it, considering all is darkness, we may in the same manner be said to see the other dark space about it. The fact is, the eye is here reduced to its function as a hand, and if we move the eye before the dark space, we may be said to see the dark space by the process of traversing and measuring in the same way in which we might be said to feel the vacant space if we moved our hand along it: but this *dark* space, whatever we may think about it, is the only *space* we can see, and we see it with the eye not as a special sense, but simply as a moving member of the body.

Space is vacancy, room for things: cognizable by means of any sense or any part of the body only in effort after the apprehension of things, and as a kind of recognition of the temporary abortiveness of the effort. It is understood by us as that in which things might be, but in which, we find, they are not: it is thus, mentally, a kind of expectation of things or mental anticipation of a reality to be known, and in *this* way it may not unfitly be described as the form or outline (coeval with the sense itself, and to be filled up as to particulars by experience) or again as the subjective portion of sensive apprehension. This is what we may be said to see or handle, when we use the sense so far as our effort is concerned, but no object responds. Simple space considered objectively or as a part of the universe, is neither visible nor tangible: it is simply *traversable*, either by the hand or by the moving eye in their way to what they are seeking: the spatial relations are determined by the amount of traverse. If we like to call this seeing space, well and good, only it is a seeing different from that with which we see objects by means of radiation or reflection of the light from them: space neither radiates nor reflects. Any one who says 'we see space' must be prepared also to say 'we handle it': in a manner we do both: we look or grope, and the *something-nothing*, which meets us in the abortive effort to see or find, is *vacancy* or *space*: it is certainly *something*, for we predicate qualities of it, and as we traverse it, we know we are traversing it, in whatever way, it makes itself felt by us: but it is no *thing*, no object: it is only what meets us disappointingly as we seek an object.

Mr Abbott says against Mr Bain, that space is not mere movement, and that our notion of space is something quite different from our consciousness of movement. Apparently Mr Abbott would wish to make us forget that our philosophy must be good for night as well as for day, and would give us for notion of space that sight, with subsequent imagination, of illuminated atmosphere which we have just discussed. Whatever may be right, *this* cannot be. Whereas Mr Bain is certainly right so far as he goes. Traversableness (or moveableness *in*) is one character and predicate of space, whatever others it may have, and may be *the* one character by which it becomes known to us. I will not discuss now what is the proper or full notion of space, but evidently Mr Bain's is *a true* one.

Not that I wish to make reality *in itself* all dark and dismal, and to look upon the illumination of it, by which we see it, as a mere falsification—in other words, to deprive the beautiful scene of its character of being a true version of reality, reality not only of the tangible objects, but of the space containing them. The two things which have to concur as conditions for our sight as it is, light and the atmosphere, are not simply, in our present concern with them, physical existences, but have each their peculiar relation to us *as* thus concurring in our sensation. The atmosphere, *e.g.* though physical and even tangible, is what we may call a likeness or representation of space to us, since we can readily move through it, and grossly tangible objects readily displace it, in such a way that there seems nothing for them to displace: it is space in a way half-filled, filled but not filled, filled as against vacancy, but vacant as against gross things. And since

the atmosphere is illuminable, as we have seen, we have—not
the impossibility, illuminated or properly visible space, but—an
illuminated likeness or representation of it; not a symbol, as
Berkeley would say, but a *resemblance*, the atmosphere really
resembling vacancy in the manner which I have mentioned
above.

It is not, I think, through any particular partiality for
middle courses that I thus take a sort of middle ground
between Mr Abbott and Berkeley, unable to allow to the visible
scene the amount of reality (as compared with touch) which
Mr Abbott claims for it, but claiming for it myself more than
Berkeley would allow. We should have no notion of the wide
prospects of earth or the vast spaces of the heavens without
sight; but there would be no meaning in the notion of them
as wide or vast, without the humble experiences of our own
individual handling and walking. If we *contemplated* simply,
without return upon ourselves as measure, there would be
nothing to contemplate, no large or small, no solid or vacant.
As between Berkeley and his opponents, I think the question
long ago got upon a wrong issue, and that there is no occasion
to displace it from the ground on which men seem from the
first to have placed it and discussed it, only that we must look
at it carefully, not superficially.

Suppose there were no such sense as sight and (if we like it)
no such physical existence as light, but that we had somehow or
other a knowledge of the real universe as extensive as we have
now: how could we conceive ourselves to have this? or of
what nature would it be? We must then, in a manner, have
touched everything that we know of as existing: we must have
a sort of tactual quasi-imagination of the universe, a sort of
mental figuration, without notion of sight or illumination.
I think we can only conceive this at all by the supposition
of a sort of presence of ourselves at will at everything which
we suppose existing. The universe then would not appear to
stand off from us as it does now, and we should be present, in
a way, all over it. The things which we knew as existing we
should know tactually, *i.e.* all over them, and in their solid
shape: there would be no far-off or near, but we should know

distance in one part of the universe in the same way as in another; and the things which we knew would be the same to us at all times; we should never mistake or fail to recognize them.

Let us suppose (if we can) a being with knowledge of the universe like this, and that it is proposed to him to change his way of knowing for ours now, *i.e.* by sight combined with very limited corporeal touch and movement. What will be the advantages and disadvantages of the change? And how will the proposer of it describe or recommend it to him?

'You will be confined,' he will say to him, 'to one very limited portion of space, and always have to be conscious of yourself as *there*: there will be a new existence in creation, *light*, which will radiate from its source, fill the atmosphere and be refracted about in all directions, and broken into various *qualities* or colours; which will strike against objects and be reflected about in all directions again, or perhaps intercepted: you will have given to you an organ with provision for the discrimination of the qualities of the light when it strikes, and also with provision for self-adjustment, or for your own adjustment, according to the directions in which it strikes. Look then at the advantages and disadvantages of the change: on the proposed scheme you will know at one time one side only of things, instead of feeling them all over, *i.e.* you will *look*, in a manner, only at *half* the universe: the light will strike according to its geometrical laws, which will distort the shapes of things, so that you will no longer know them in their real solid shapes, as you did by the mental handling: one thing will hide another, and you will have very imperfect means of knowing distance along the direction away from your eye, nor any perfect means of knowing any distance, distance being, so to call it, distorted, like shapes. Your means of helping yourself will be your corporeal touch and movement, which however of course you will find very limited. On the other hand you will now be able to appreciate the relations of distance, form, magnitude of things, so far as you do appreciate them, all in a moment or, as you will call it, at a glance: the universe will be *one* to you in a way in which nothing else

could present it as such : the light, owing to the manner in
which it will change its quality in striking on objects, or give
them colour, will inform you of something about them which
you could not have known otherwise : and with all this you
will acquire the sense of visual beauty : you will think of the
universe not only as something to be handled and to be acted
in, but as something glorious and interesting to contemplate.'
More might be said on each side : I am inclined to think, were
I the individual, I *would* change my old way of knowledge for
the new.

In what I am now going to say, I shall put the word
imagination to hard, but careful use, but I think that the
free use of it, with attention on the part of the reader, is the
best way not to mislead.

The above imagination then of a sort of tactual (though
possibly only mental) presence with things may seem absurd :
but what is necessary is, that we should somehow set before
our mind a quasi-imagination of the continuous or wide universe,
not visual but some way tactual, and therefore exhibiting to us
actual reality which is in the tangible, if we would at all make
out the relation of the visible scene to the corresponding reality.
We must have something to compare the visible scene with,
and *then* we shall see what relation it bears to this, whether
symbolic or otherwise. It is plain however that Berkeley for
instance does not dream of anything of this kind, or see the
necessity of it. Steeped in what I have called the bad psychology, which supposes things existing and known before us
and then investigates how we come by the ideas of them, he
considers us to be situated in the middle of the wide universe
of things and knowing ourselves to be so, which we only do by
sight, and then says this sight is only symbolic, a chimera if we
think it true, something quite unlike the reality. Why how,
except visually, can you or do you conceive or imagine the
unitary reality, I mean the reality (as individual things and as
parts of the universe) of things, which are beyond your reach
and too large for your grasp and too vast for your exploration ?
If you say the visible scene is not the reality, that the moon of
sight is not the real moon, but a symbol of it, and that the vast

scene apparently before us, of which it forms a part is a collection of similar symbols,—well then conceive me and describe
me the non-visual or real conception or quasi-imagination which
corresponds to this visual scene and of which it is a symbolic
tablet, for I suppose you have such, since you apparently
conceive the real, and are able, by comparison of the visible
scene with it, to say that this latter is only symbolic. You
have not such a thing? but where then is the second member
of your comparison? are you really conceiving and imagining
reality *visually yourself*, beyond the range of your limited touch
and movement, all this time that you are talking of the prejudice and mistake of people in general in thinking *this* reality,
and are you only comparing sight with sight, or else sight with
something (if we may call it so) which is no conception, nothing
appearing to the mind as one, no presentation, but something of
which it is impossible to imagine a symbol, some description,
perhaps, or catalogue of all the properties of the reality
corresponding to the visible moon. But what we want to
have, *somehow*, in our conception or imagination is the reality
itself: otherwise it is nonsense, unless we know the thing by
divination, to pronounce anything a symbol of it.

The sum of all this is, that we cannot understand properly
the relation of the visual scene or imagination to reality, except
so far as we have a conception of reality not only pure and
non-visual, but corresponding to the visual, so that we may
compare the visual with it. Suppose reality to be tangibility,
and say therefore that we have a pure conception of the reality
of the thing which we touch; yet how can this conception be
considered at all correspondent to the vast visual conception
which we have of the continuous universe with the objects of
it, so as to compare with it? Were there no such thing as light
and eyes, what sort of conception should we have of Mont
Blanc as a thing, a mountain, even if we had passed our life
in walking over it? It is our eyes and our hand *together*, not
the one on the behalf of the other: it is our ocular measurement
of the off-standing and remote, in conjunction with our manual
(or generally corporeal) measurement of the contiguous, which
creates to us reality, or makes things *things* to us.

For reasons involved in what has been just said, I have throughout and carefully spoken of the visible *scene*, thinking this the vaguest word, more vague than *prospect*, a word which seemed to involve (what I did not wish to assume) sight, and different from *picture*, which might give what I think a wrong view of the relation to reality. We cannot say that what we see is a picture of reality, because it seems to me that we do not know, except with the concurrence of this as one important means what reality is, and therefore are not in a position to pronounce this, or anything, a likeness of it; and also because all our notions of picture, likeness, etc. are taken from this, and cannot with any meaning be applied back to it. We should define a *picture* as a reproduction or repetition, by whatever means of the visual thing, or thing as we see it: and therefore it is a mockery of definition to *counterdefine* the visual thing as the picture of the thing. For the same reason I think we can attach no important meaning to the notion of *likeness* between visible things and the real ones: the notion may reasonably suggest itself to us when we read Berkeley's extraordinary language about their specific unlikeness, but the fact is, they are not like, because they are the things themselves. That is, they are a phase, view, side, partial and incomplete manifestation of them under special conditions, or what we may describe in many similar manners: the sort of way in which it is so, is plain from what I said a short time since about the advantages and disadvantages of knowing things specially by sight.

In spite of Mr Abbott's singular language about seeing, not touching, being believing—(he apparently forgets S. Thomas, who was said to have believed because he saw, but whose seeing was not considered complete for its purpose without being confirmed or reinforced by touch), there is no doubt but that there is understood truth in touching and handling, more than in seeing. The latter may be illusion, the other not. In fact, seeing is a complicated handling, which gives us reality, unless there are physical reasons for its misleading us, but in regard of which it is more difficult to ascertain whether there may not be such reasons than in the very simple process of handling a thing with our hands.

BOOK II.

IMMEDIATENESS AND REFLECTION.

CHAPTER I.

SELF-SELF AND THOUGHT-SELF. IMMEDIATE, AS DIS-
TINGUISHED FROM REFLECTIONAL, THOUGHT AND
ACTION.

The self-self.

BY the 'self-self' I mean that which cannot really be
thought of, *i.e.* which cannot be made an object of thought,
but which is *with-thought* (mitgedacht), thought along with,
or included in, our *immediate* thought and feeling, or which, in
other words, is one of the essential elements of such thought or
feeling. There is a sort of contradiction here, for by attempting
to make the reader understand what it is, I am making it an
object of thought: it is therefore to be remembered, that when
we talk of it we are making a supposition only, which requires
accompanying correction in our mind, or the accompanying
thought that, for the purpose of talking about it, we are
obliged to make a supposition about it, which is for the
occasion only.

There is the same difficulty in describing immediate thought
or feeling, of which the *self-self* is one element. I mean by it
thought or feeling primary or by itself, as distinguished from
reflective thought or feeling, which I shall explain. If we use
the word consciousness, it is consciousness as distinguished from
self-consciousness and from perception, *i.e.* consciousness distinguishing only between a permanent, pleasure and pain-feeling,
self-self, on the one side, and on the other, a successive variety
of feeling or thought, which is not pleasure or pain, or of the
nature of them; while yet the successive and different portions

M.

are only distinguishable among themselves, without a possibility, previous to reflection, of their being distinctively characterised. The state of immediate thought or feeling is what we, as developed and educated intelligences, can only by imagination approximate to, or in various ways *suppose* for our purpose. It is *thought*, with the object of it as yet in embryo—the object *distinguished* indeed from the subject, as for any thought, or even for feeling, it must be, but not yet *separated* from it, not yet placed out from us or held out before us to be contemplated (in this *outness* I do not imply space, but only something of which space may be taken as a suggestion), the subject and object not yet set in antithesis the one to the other.

I do not mean to say however that in our developed intelligence, immediate thought is superseded and has ceased to exist, though we cannot present it to ourselves: all thought is properly immediate, or has a base of immediateness in it, but the development of thought is the mixture or conjunction of reflection with this in such a manner that we cannot disentangle them.

The thought-self.

The 'thought-self' is that, more or less distinctly conceived, which I have been obliged inevitably to foreshadow and suppose in trying to describe or set in view the 'self-self.' As soon as we in any degree distinctly conceive of ourselves thinking, it is evident that thought is no longer simple or immediate. We are ourselves then *double*. And we are this as soon as ever we set the object of thought out before us as a separate object to contemplate. Concurrently with this, we necessarily separate (bisect or double) ourselves.

It does not matter, it seems to me, whether we say, with Mr Ferrier, that we only distinctly conceive an object by conceiving ourselves as conceiving it, or whether we say, with Mr Herbert Spencer, that we only distinctly conceive ourselves by conceiving ourselves as an object similar (more or less) to other objects which we have previously conceived. The advance of thought, in my view, is the simultaneous development of the distinct conception of ourselves, or our personality, and the distinct conception of objects of thought as independent of us: and each conception brings out the other. By an object of thought, as distinctly conceived, we mean something standing off from, though connected with, our thinking, and we cannot mean this without a *co-conception* of ourselves, from which the other is relieved: nor is there any means of setting ourselves before ourselves, as something to be thought of, without distinguishing ourselves from something else.

The passage onward from immediate thought to the thought of ourselves and of objects of thought in contradistinction, and the advance still onwards in thought, in the *distinctification* and *characterization* of each of these elements of thought and their developments, I shall call, for my own purposes, by the name of *reflection*.

Immediate thought I have, in a portion of what I have written, called by the name of 'impression,' carefully disclaiming, in the use of the word, any reference to its being possibly impressed *ab extra*[1]. It is probable that no word can be used to express it without some provision of this kind against what the word may imply. The word 'intuition,' or its correspondent ' Anschauung,' is a most misleading word: for by its reference to sight it inevitably suggests an object supposed to exist standing off from us and independent of us, than which nothing can be supposed more incongruous with the notion of immediate thought. Intuition therefore, if used to express our immediate intellectual state in reference to what we call the world about us (as distinguished from our relation to it in our developed state of intelligence, when we look around us and see *things*, as we call them, which we know, and recognise, and name), must be carefully guarded against any suggestion of this kind, or it perverts the whole notion of philosophy. It is the same with the term ' experience,' which I will not, however, speak further of now.

What I have called *reflection*, in its character of the joint perception of ourselves and the objects of our thought, is what has been called 'apperception.'

---

[1] See Book I., ch. v. above.

Immediate, as distinguished from reflectional,
thought and action.

When Descartes, in his attempt to reach the bottom of things, says, 'I think, therefore I am,' what 'I think' here represents, is immediate thought. But the state of Descartes's mind when he says this, is not a state of immediate, but of reflectional thought. Though what he says is 'I think,' the state of his mind is 'I am thinking that (or how) I think.' The state therefore is one of self-consciousness, but not of admitted self-consciousness: it is a state of self-consciousness inevitable in the effort to realize or present immediate thought. And though immediate thought, when made an object of thought (as by me a short time since in trying to describe it), is so far vitiated and no longer immediate, still we may to a certain degree keep our eyes away from this vitiation and come to results about it.

Immediate thought itself is inactive and resultless: we can conclude nothing from it till its elements are distinguished and till its object is developed, and then it is no longer immediate. Immediate thought does not *imply* being, but *is* being—*being* bare, uncharacterized, not knowing itself as being: that is, if there is immediate thought, *something* exists, but *what* it is that exists, is what we have no means of knowing. Immediate thought is that impression, or those impressions (in Hume's language), which is all that in his view there is certainty of the existence of: it is mere confusion to say 'we have certainty,' because there is no certain 'we' in reference to such thought, any more than there is a certain object. His error is in looking upon it as a sort of thought without subject and object, instead of with subject and object as yet undistinguished. The best way in which, in our developed intelligence, we can realize to ourselves immediate thought, is by abstracting mentally from our thought, so far as we are able, the attention and notice of which it is full, and which all belongs to reflection.

Immediate thought may be described as the *feeling* of *being*, in contradistinction to the realizing (or presenting to ourselves) ourselves or anything else, as being or existing. In immediate thought we cannot be said to feel *ourselves* as being, any more than we think of anything definite as the object of our thought: either of these would require attention or notice, which belongs to reflection. But the state of immediate thought or feeling (for it matters not which we call it), is a state of being, and it is what, as our thought distinctifies itself into reflection, is the germ of our notion of being, when we come to present being to ourselves as a notion. Thinking, and being the object or possible object of thought, are our two suggestives of *being*, and both grow from this.

I do not think that the Cartesian notion of thought or knowledge proceeding from primary to developed consciousness, in such a way that what we need to do is to pierce back from the developed to the primary, is so good a notion of it as the notion of immediate and reflectional thought and feeling. And, in this latter view, the 'Cogito, ergo sum' is ambiguous, with truth, indeed, in both the views of it; but truth of different degrees of importance. 'Think' may mean 'think as we all do in our developed intelligence, use our minds'—and, whatever may be the exact nature of the implication or inference, it may probably be said with reason that we could not do this without *being*, or having existence. Or 'think' may refer to immediate thought; and if it does, the whole assertion of Descartes is equivalent to the saying, 'To the extent to which I am able to realize to myself immediate thought, I am realizing to myself—coming more and more to understand what I mean when I speak of it,—*being* also, both my own being, and the being of what I think of, though all involved and confused and (the latter especially) entirely indefinite.'

Immediate (or reflex) action as generally understood is a sort of reaction in the way of a supposed natural sequence, but, as I use it here, it will involve something of voluntary action or movement. There is no need for its being thus confined, except to make its meaning a little more definite, the reactions in nature being so infinite.

The wide region of reflectional intelligence is a region intermediate between,—if we can conceive such—an infinite

creature or universe on the one side, conscious, but actionless
and without change or desire for it, and neither self-conscious
nor distinguishingly perceptive, and, on the other side, a
universe full of movement of regular actions, interactions, and
reactions.   In order to present to ourselves the reflectional or
the developed human intelligence, we must begin with immediateness, either of thought or of action.   If of action: let us
imagine the interaction between the light or air and the leaf
of a plant causing the movement of the latter or the opening
of its pores, and let us follow upward interaction of this kind,
if we may still call it so, to the long and complicated process
which takes place when an apple strikes the eye of a man,
leading him to put out his hand and take it and eat it.   We
have no means of knowing *within* the plant, further than we
can trace the movements: perhaps there is nothing but the
movements; and then the action is reflex or immediate.   What
passes within the *man* is the complicated process of reflectional
intelligence: but there is not much more that we can say
about it except so to name it, when we proceed in this way of
investigation from immediate action.

If we begin with immediateness of *thought*, we can only
realize it, as I have said, in a difficult and imperfect manner,
by abstracting attention and notice.   Our process is then pretty
much the ordinary one of psychologists, which they describe as
the gaining of ideas by successive sensation and association.
It is what may better, in fact, be described as the coming more
fully to ourselves in the universe, the becoming wider awake in
it, the distinctifying object after object in it, at the same time
that we more fully feel *ourselves*.   In all this process, thought
is passing from immediateness to reflection, and as it passes,
we lose, as well as gain: belief, conviction, certainty, is the
persistence, to such extent as it does persist, of that indistinction between ourselves and the object of our thought, which
belongs to immediate thought; and our thought, as it becomes
less immediate and more reflectional, loses some of its force of
certainty; we become divided in ourselves and divided from
the universe.   Not but that our gain is far greater than
our loss, thought, as barely immediate, can hardly be called

thought, and we, till more or less self-conscious, are hardly ourselves.

As in this line of reflection we proceed *from* immediateness of *thought*, so we proceed *towards* immediateness of *action*. The reflection which causes delay and hesitancy gives place to trains of thought so rapid as to be imperceptible, and the impulse from without is followed by action from within so surely and immediately, that it is indistinguishable from action simply mechanical or instinctive.

CHAPTER II.

DEVELOPMENT OF KNOWLEDGE FROM IMMEDIATENESS.
INTUITION AND EXPERIENCE.

IT is a little doubtful whether I have spoken correctly in using the word 'thought' of that which is immediate. The more correct phrase is 'immediateness' simply, for even in thought there is implied *distinguishingness* or reflection. However it is convenient to speak of immediate 'thought' always with this qualification.

Immediate *knowledge* is immediate thought with something of the character of reflection attaching to it, but not very much. By knowledge (which is one kind of thought), as distinguished from thought which is not knowledge, I mean thought which has some guarantee or warrant (beyond anything which is contained in the simple thought itself), showing that it is not caprice or chimera. The word knowledge is under any circumstances a bold word to use. It expresses a particular kind of value which we attribute to certain portions of our thought: we require to have reason to go on, in attributing this value to some kinds of thought rather than to others: and we must have the notion of this particular kind of value (independent of the thought to which we attribute it) in order for there to be any meaning in the attribution.

Immediate *knowledge* then, as different from mere undistinguishing 'immediateness,' is thought with a certain amount of *distinguishingness* or particular notice of an object of the thought, but not so much of this as to amount to a distinct judgment about it, which is knowledge of reflection full or developed. Immediate knowledge of this kind is what I have called in another place knowledge of acquaintance[1]: it is called by some presentation: perception is a kind of it. The point of it consists in the want of development or distinctness in the reflection which it involves: but there is such reflection, and only so far as there is such can the thought be knowledge. This may illustrate what I mean by reflection: I mean 'doubleness' of thought, want of simplicity or uniformity of it. In immediate knowledge there must be reason for the distinction and notice of that which is the object of it. This reason is something independent of the direct or simple thought, superadds something and makes it double: and this reason is necessary for the raising of thought into knowledge. The reason may be of various kinds: it may be of remembrance, that the object has been before us previously, and we recognize it: it may again be of feeling, that some pleasure or pain accompanies the thought of the object: the point is, that there must be something superadded to, or aiding, the mere immediateness or presentness.

Perhaps the best way in which we can describe knowledge is that it is an union of *indistinction* and *distinction* of thought, the indistinction giving the reality or trueness of knowledge, the distinction its point or particularity. Knowledge is thought, with a particular kind of value, which we call trueness, understood to attach to the thought. This value, it seems to me, is the carrying on of immediateness into reflection, while reflection on *its* side supplies another kind of value, that namely of distinction among objects, enabling us to know their relations one to another. Let us take the illustration of slowly awaking from sleep. We have here a sort of resemblance of immediate thought. All is *true* in a way, because error or misapprehension is an intrusion of our liberty (though we very likely do not mean it for such) where it has no business to come: *here* there is no place for it: but still, though all is in its way true, we cannot, with meaning, say there is knowledge till there is distinction, and by it an object or objects of thought set before us to be known. And yet it is not the distinction which gives

[1] *Expl.* 60, 121.

the character of *trueness* to the thought, and in *that* way marks it as knowledge, but it is the *pre-distinctional* immediateness which involved the trueness, and on which, for foundation, the trueness rests and must always rest. The oneness of subject and object, thinker and thought, in immediate thought, is the germ of all after knowledge: it is this which constitutes the life, essence, special character of knowledge, *the trueness* in one word, though it cannot be called knowledge till it is developed.

This may be illustrated by reference to the word 'intuition,' which I just now described as very misleading. Intuition is true, or real knowledge, in its character of immediateness, so far as immediateness can give knowledge, but not necessarily true, or real knowledge, in its character of distinction. We have no proper right to say, we know this or that intuitively, because 'this,' and 'that,' imply a distinction of objects which does not belong to intuition as immediate. We have an intuitional knowledge of the external world: but our distinction of objects from ourselves and among themselves, and our consequent view of their relations to us and among each other, which makes up our notion of the external world in its characters and variety—all this is not at all intuition, though it need not be inconsistent with it. Intuitive knowledge, as immediate, is a state of undistinguished and common being uniting us with what we know: as soon as we separate it off from us, intuition passes into reflection: though we have not quitted truth, we have introduced another and a doubtful element, and the particular distinction we make must have its reason, and must have an account given of it. The intuition, or immediate and necessarily true knowledge (of a tree *e.g.*) if we like to use such language, is something which we may psychologically try, in various ways, to analyse, but of which we can give no proper account, because we have no notions or words in which to give account of it. We, and the tree, and the world of which we are both a part, are all undistinguished in the intuition as immediate, and in this indistinction is the fundamental truth of the existence of the tree: but then we add to the immediateness a certain amount of reflection, and arrive at perception or immediate knowledge: which, to be knowledge, must have in it *distinction* (something more than intuition or immediateness), and this distinction is only caprice and folly, except so far as we can give reason, or (which is the same thing) so far as we consider objective reason to exist, for the making it. We say, we perceive what then we call a tree, but we do *not* say, we perceive as *one* object, nameable like the tree—what may be exactly in a similar manner before our eyes—a bit perhaps of the tree and a bit of the sky and a bit of green grass which may be all contiguous. This is because we have a reason, or we consider that there exists a reason in nature, for our distinguishing the tree, which does not exist for our distinguishing and naming the other mass or combination of visualness to which I have referred. The consideration of all the variety of reason of this kind is the work of reflection. Reflection builds itself upon intuition or immediateness, studying it, and bringing to bear, so far as it can, the whole of it. For instance in distinguishing the tree, an object of sense, it has to bring to bear a portion of intuition, different from that of sense, which I shall soon speak of. Still, as human activity and the result of human will, it has in itself liability to error, and not, like intuition, the necessity of truth : hence, no distinct thing or object can be properly said to be known intuitively.

All knowledge, as *true*, has in it the element of immediateness or intuition, and all knowledge, as definite or distinguishing, has in it the element of reflection. Hence there is intuition corresponding to all developed knowledge : our state in reference to the external world, as an object or objects of sense, is one kind of immediateness, but one only : our state in respect to any kind of existence or possible existence, is in the first instance *immediate thought* and *immediate knowledge* (if it comes to be knowledge at all). What reflection does is, as it were, to digest the immediateness, to distinguish different portions of it and bring them into relation with each other. These two processes, the distinction and the mutual reference, are combined and are in fact one, or in other words they mutually suggest each other. We call the intuition of a tree an intuition of sense, or a part of sensation, but it is only *knowledge* (as we have seen) so far as it is made so by reflectional distinction. What this reflection does is to bring to bear on the *sensal* intuition other intuitions which we should describe as of a higher nature, as of unity &c., and only *then* is there intuitive knowledge, or knowledge of any kind.

What I want to make understood is, that the immediateness, which is the basis of all knowledge, has all the elements of truth in it which the most developed knowledge has, whether these elements are intuitions of sense (what we commonly call sensation or experience) or whether, besides these, they are intuitions such as those which I just referred to as being of a higher nature, intuitions of mind, intuitions of reason. Reflection, or the activity of the mind, has to work, not upon a mass of intuition simply sensal, but upon a mass of intuition of every kind and degree, intellectual and rational as well as sensal. If there is not intuition of these latter kinds to begin with, there is no trueness in any after knowledge, which we describe as rational or intellectual, in distinction from sensal. For the activity of our mind, *qua* bare activity, is the source of error: trueness is something *given* to it, and trueness, rightly handled by it, is what we call knowledge. Trueness, of whatever kind, is all given to us in the first instance in immediateness or intuition, and when we stir and quicken this inactive immediateness by reflection, we add, and can add, no fresh trueness, to whatever amount our knowledge grows.

So far then as there are two elements of our knowledge, they are not thought and experience (that is, what is commonly meant by these words), but immediateness and reflection. Only, it is to be observed, these constitute no antithesis—they stand in no contrast the one to the other. They are not, *e.g.* anything that can be called the matter and form of knowledge, for reflection gives no *form*, no new being or reality to immediateness: all the form and reality is already in the immediateness: they are more like the body and soul of knowledge, except that immediateness has all the *life* of knowledge, though as yet but embryotic and undeveloped: all it wants is quickening: till reflection does this, it is knowledge in the germ, but not proper knowledge.

Intuition and Experience.

In English controversy, the antithesis which I have just spoken of between 'thought' and 'experience' is generally described as between 'intuition' and 'experience,' or else between 'ideas' and 'sense,' the word 'intuition' being not commonly used in English philosophy in application to the intuitions of sense, which we more commonly call 'sensation,' and which are here described as 'sense,' or 'experience.' The word 'intuition' in this antithesis, in its English form, is used more or less to express a combination of two things, which are looked upon as one, viz. what I have called the higher intuitions, and the reflectional activity of the mind. It appears to me, that this analysis or antithesis of knowledge is virtually admitted by almost all English philosophers. That is to say, those who most strongly urge that the former element, the English 'intuition,' is not real or important, nevertheless make their supposition of the other element, 'experience' (from which they derive all knowledge) much as their opponents would, leaving in this way, if we may so speak, the place for the former element vacant, though they will not allow it to be occupied. Or, to put the thing in another way, they keep it (I do not mean with any intentional bad faith) as a convenient ground to which their term 'experience' retires now and then, and we never can precisely be sure whether 'experience' means mental experience, succession of states of the mind, or physical experience (so to call it), successive communications, on our part, with physical nature.

Kant's 'experience' is liable to difficulties of a different kind, which I have already touched on in speaking of Dr Whewell[1], who here is at one with him. Kant does not seem to me to give a very clear account of what he means by 'experience.' But on the whole, when he speaks of 'das mannigfältige,' the manifold of experience and intuition, which the conceptive understanding binds up into unity, it appears to me that what he ought to say is 'das verworrene,' 'das unbestimmte' (the confused, the undistinguished) which then is digested, not by a

---

[1] *Expl.* c. XI.

special faculty adding to it ideas or applying to it categories,
but by attention and notice intensifying and bringing out what
is in the immediateness or intuition already. The picture was
not, as Kant's term would seem to imply, a crowd, but a mist.
As we apply our attention to it, the picture and its parts come
out, whether because our eyes are getting clearer, or that a film
is coming off from it, we cannot tell, and need not: for the
picture and our eyes are always opposite the one to the other,
and when we have succeeded in distinguishing them the one
from the other by reflection, we yet cannot present to ourselves
the one without the other, or discover any principle upon which
we can distribute their interaction between them.   The manifold has parts, too many of them for us, whereas parts are just
what immediateness has not.

This is in substance the same criticism which I made on
Dr Whewell, where he seems to speak of sensation as one degree
or kind of knowledge, upon which ideas are superadded, making
a higher kind. He uses the general term 'ideas' for all
the various things which, being superadded to experience,
make it into intuition, understanding, reason, or give to
knowledge these different characters. I mention this to illustrate what I said, that English philosophers commonly put on
the side of the antithesis opposite to experience, both the
reflectional activity of the mind and the higher intuitions.   On
the one side is the imperfect knowledge of sensation, on the
other side is the mind with its activity, furnished with ideas,
modifying the sensation or experience to meet the ideas,
and again the ideas to fit the experience. I do not see why
we should not call the ideas a part of our experience, as
well as (on the other hand) our experience a part of our
thought and knowledge. I see no principle upon which the
separation can be made. Between the activity of our mind,
indeed, on the one side, and the ideas (if we are to call them so)
and the experience on the other side, I see a very great difference
and am most ready to make a separation. So far as the activity
is absent, both ideas and experience are in the state which I
have called 'immediateness.' But then the activity of mind is
wanted as much for the so-called experience as for the so-

called ideas, to make anything of either of them. When I see a tree, I seem to myself to see it as *one* quite as much as to see it as green, and if I did not see it as *one* I probably should not see it as green: the green is called sensation, the *oneness* idea: and of course there is this difference, that we can discover a particular relation between the greenness and particular nerves of our body, to which we find no analogy in the case of the oneness: but this is not sensive knowledge, it is anatomy (not perhaps difficult). Again, the distinctifications of our confused immediateness go in a succession which we call learning: some are speedy, some take long: some have evident, some more complicated, reason for them. The *point* is, that we do not distinguish the greenness of the tree, any more than its oneness, without attention and notice, and that except we do thus distinguish, we have no knowledge of it, even of the meanest kind. There is not even a 'mannigfältige,' a manifoldness of qualities in the tree, scarcely even a chaos. On the other hand, unless the tree, when it first presented itself to my eyes, presented itself obscurely as *one* in the same way as it presented itself obscurely as green, I should have no right, in my after reflection, to call it *one*: the reason for which I come to call it *one* was present in it at the first, just as the greenness was, whether I saw (*i.e.* distinguished) it as green, or as *one*, or however I saw it.

CHAPTER III.

DEVELOPMENT OF SELF-CONSCIOUSNESS FROM IMMEDIATENESS.

THE vague, involved, half-consciousness of immediateness awakes to full consciousness or self-consciousness on the one side, exactly in the same manner as the remaining portion of the immediateness awakes to perception on the other side.

It is possible, that in true or complete immediateness the subjective might not be more prominent or more brought out than the other portion. But in immediateness, so far as we can at all succeed in picturing it, or as it is any use for us to try to do so, the above is not the case: the subjective element is the more prominent, or, if we like to put it so, we are looking at immediateness from the side of *thought*, and it is as immediateness indeed, but still as something which can be called immediate *thought*, that it interests us. The subjective portion of it therefore is not in so embryonic a state as the objective, because I, the thinker, am *in* the subjective portion of it, and know myself to be so, though I do not, as it were, recognize myself, and distinguish myself, more than rudimentarily. There is much to say another time about immediate or non-reflectional consciousness (so far as it is to be called consciousness) which is connected with our *active* nature[1].

However, there is no distinct consciousness on the one side till there is perception on the other, and the same vice versâ. Consciousness is then self-consciousness: we distinguish ourselves markedly from what we know as not ourselves: we know

---

[1] See below ch. v., on *Sensibility and Activity*.

ourselves as knowing, and we know the object of knowledge as known by us.

There is as much reason to speak of this self-consciousness as a separate faculty (if any person likes that language), as there is to speak of perception, and similarly of—what we come to afterwards—memory, imagination &c., as separate faculties: and no more reason. They are all intentions, applications, manners of exertion, of the intelligence: it matters little whether they are called faculties or not.

The controversy between Reid and Hamilton, as to whether consciousness is a faculty, is I suppose in substance this question: whether the term consciousness is most properly applied to consciousness, as I just now spoke of it, in the *pre-reflectional* or immediate stage, or to this later self-consciousness. If we call what I have termed 'immediate thought' by the name of 'consciousness' so as to make consciousness, as Sir William Hamilton does, the germ of all knowledge, all that I would say is, that there is no meaning in trying to analyse it in this state: we are involved in the middle of it, we cannot get away from it or set it out from us so as to be able to look at it. As soon as we *have* succeeded in any way in doing this, we shall find that we have altered its character: it is no longer the original primary consciousness, but is self-consciousness, perception: *these* are what we are analysing, not *it*: and it is a mere logical fallacy to bring notions which we think must have necessary application to *it*, to bear upon *them*, or vice versâ. It is no better than despotic dogmatism under the form of argument to say that the 'deliverances' of consciousness must be obeyed, and then to take to one's self the power of proclaiming them, and to look upon any difference from one's own view as a contradiction of consciousness. Intuition or immediateness, 'consciousness,' if Sir William Hamilton likes to call it so, is the germ or basis of *all truth*, but does not give us knowledge of *particular truths*, or separated units of truth which we can express in propositions, unless it is mixed with reflection, and then there enters in the controvertible element. The fact is, that in separating or formulating to ourselves the notion which we then describe as true, and in expressing it in

M.   11 words, we have been going beyond the intuition, and though we may very possibly be right, we are not immediately and necessarily right: we must give reason for what we say, more than calling it a deliverance of consciousness.

I will refer back for a moment to what I said formerly[1] as to Sir William Hamilton's view of the external world, just to bind together what I said then with what I am saying now. The existence of the external world, he tells us, is shown to us by consciousness, and those whom he calls Cosmothetic Idealists, *e.g.* Berkeley, deny the testimony of consciousness. It appears to me that this kind of language should be banished from philosophy. Consciousness, if by it we mean immediate thought, is a witness, or rather *the* witness, within us, whose testimony it is impossible to deny, but whose testimony, in order to be brought out to the world, has to be brought out through a formula or notion, and this again through words, that is, through other notions: and there is nothing in the world which anybody who wishes to attain to truth ought to be more ready to deny, and ought to be more suspicious of, than what is brought out, in philosophy, *as* such a testimony. Consciousness, like the spirits of our day, has got to speak through a medium, viz. the reflectional or intellectual disposition and character of the speaker, so that the report of what it says, supposing the best faith, is yet very little to be trusted. In the present case, I have no more doubt than Sir William Hamilton that the existence of the external world is a fact or testimony of our consciousness or immediate, necessary, thought; and it is probable that if he (*quod utinam*), could return to earth to philosophize again, and Berkeley too, the view at the bottom of our three minds would be the same: in fact I do not see how it could be otherwise, that is, in such a cardinal point as the present. But *then* we each begin to reflect: and this 'existence of the external world' (what words we use for that which we are talking of in *this* stage of it is of course unimportant, for none can be fit ones) gets put into notions first, and then into words. By what right does any one of us say to the others that the notion into which

---

[1] *Expl.* p. 94 foll.

he puts our original oneness or matter of agreement is a truer representation of it than those into which the others put it? His assertion is worth no more than theirs: and what we want is not assertion, but reason. The fact is, the immediate thought, in which, we may probably suppose, we are all fundamentally at one, cannot be looked at in itself, but must be studied by reflection, whether that reflection be exercised upon the immediate thought itself, which is the proper philosophy, or whether other developments of that thought be followed, or their method studied, which is 'science.' My look around me at this moment involves in itself the notion of the existence of the external world (so far as the notion is true), if I could but get the notion disentangled or make it out in the mist. But if I say, 'The notion is there, you believe it, for it is a matter of my consciousness,' it may with reason be said again, 'I cannot believe it till you describe it, and if you begin to describe it, you will see very soon you are speaking of things very different from consciousness and quite open to controversy: or if you do not, those whom you think your supporters will see it for you.'

So much for consciousness, so far as we use the term to express immediate thought or the state which I have called 'immediateness,' the state *i.e.* of mutual presentation of subject to object and object to subject, which has to be conceived by us (so far as it is conceived) by reflection, and which therefore we cannot *fully* conceive. We *must* station ourselves on the subjective side, which, in the after development, is that which we find to be ours; and *we* being on this side, we may call the state (as bare and pure as we can conceive it) immediate *thought*, without serious error. But in this immediate state, in which there is the fact of knowledge, previous to the disengagement of its factors,—knowingness and knownness, thinkingness and thoughtness, united in one fact,—in this state the thinkingness is not well described as 'consciousness,' both the notion and etymology of which imply a sort of *doubleness* different from the above singleness or simplicity.

Consciousness is a looking back upon, or a looking into, ourselves, and the term inevitably leads to a sort of ambiguity

11—2

of thought. The one self, as it were, is doing whatever it may
be, willing, thinking, imagining, the other looks at it doing
this; and since both selves are of course in reality one, we say,
we think and we know we think, *we* will and we know we will,
and so on. But it is important to draw the distinction between
the simple doing the thing in question, willing, thinking,
imagining, and the doing it with that attention given to it and
that notice taken of it, which makes our state what may be
called with meaning a state of consciousness. The difference
between the two states is not properly that there is in the
second anything of a new kind added to the first: it is the
difference which I have just now noticed between immediateness and reflection. In the second state, what was latent in the
first is brought out and is distinct: consciousness has *meaning*,
for it is self-consciousness, distinction of oneself from something
else: and there is *doubleness*, for besides oneself there is something
else before us, and this latter we say we *perceive*. This is the
state to which belongs that kind of thought of which a portion
is, or may be, proper *knowledge*. Immediateness expresses the
fact of knowledge, but we are now taking our station on the
subjective side to analyse and develope this fact, and our
distinct *thinking*, the right or true portion of which is *knowing*,
begins when *we*, (first) set before *ourselves* (second) an object of
thought to employ our thoughts about.

We must be cautious here against being misled by the word
'object,' and perhaps our best security will be to remember
that reflection is only an outgrowth from immediateness, adding
nothing to it but attention, notice, distinction. Mr Ferrier
says[1], that the essence or proper notion of knowledge is what
he describes as subject + object, the knowing ourselves as
knowing, and the knowing the object as being known by us.
It is to be observed that when this is described as knowledge,
there ought to be meant knowledge beginning to be reflective
and distinct. With reflection begins a reduplication of the ego
or subject, making it a co-object of thought with that which,
in relation to it, may be called the primary or principal or,
perhaps, direct object.

[1] See *Expl.* c. IV.

Mr Ferrier draws many important consequences from his view, and I do not wish to dispute it. But I think that what seems to me the truth is given with sufficient accuracy, if we say that with the commencement of reflection, thought divides itself into two lines, self-consciousness on the one side, and on the other—what might be called perception, or if we like, intuitive knowledge (as I explained this), growing on into other knowledge, or even, if we use the term with care, sensation: it is in a word all our *extro-verted* thought (*extro* implying no relation of space), our thought which is not turned selfwards.

The great difficulty in the study of thought is this importunate self-consciousness, this self-reduplication, and the constant and unavoidable shifting of our mental position, between our observing and observed selves. But it is no discredit to philosophy that it has this difficulty; for in regard of our view of what we call nature it is worse than a difficulty, it is a confusion. In reflection, we try to set before ourselves our immediate thought, which is, as I said, the basis, and contains the reality of all knowledge: but part of it will not leave us but sticks to us, while part we succeed in setting before us or *objectifying*, and hence the difficulty. Language is like the dove from the ark, unable to find rest for the sole of its foot, when it endeavours to plant itself on some firm notion between us, our senses, and the external world. When we talk of 'seeing a thing,' meaning thereby to indicate a process in which *we*, on the one side, with a very vague notion of ourselves, are considered to stand in a certain relation with something of which we have an equally vague notion on the other, while nevertheless we know most perfectly what we mean and mean most sensibly,—all this falls into utter confusion, as soon as we begin to give our attention to the intermediation of our sense. What sees? what do we see? what is seeing? We can understand the term 'intuitions of sense,' 'perception of things,' so long as we continue to express it in the language of the market-place: but as soon as we begin to study the intermediation, where are we to find the intuition or perception? What is 'we'? Is the body with its

senses 'we,' or is it not? Is the intuition 'our' observation of
the state of the brain, or is it the correspondence of the eyes or
brain, in whatever way, with the state of the thing, or what
is it?

I have, however, a little anticipated here in bringing the
difficulty arising from the intermediation of our bodily self, or
sensive organization, between that which on the one side we call
our thought, and that on the other, which we call the external
world, in illustration of the general difficulty arising from our
adding the consideration *how* we know anything, to our actual
knowledge of it, so far as we may call the latter, without the
former, real knowledge. As soon as we begin to reflect, we can
no longer absorb ourselves in nature, or be sure we have hold
of reality, for we only know nature through an intellective
machine or organism, and as soon as we begin to puzzle
ourselves about the working of this, the first simplicity of our
view of nature is lost. And in the same way our simple
thought of ourselves—our self-accompaniment, self-companionship (if we may call it so), as distinguished from our self-
observation and self-study—is lost also. Instead of being
either at home or in the free air, we are in the noisy and
bewildering manufactory of thoughts and notions.

But I will return from this digression to examine so far
as I can, the nature of the reflective consciousness or self-
consciousness.

Reflection is a kind of attempt to translate immediateness,
and as we do so, it may be either our own part or the part
which is not our own (that is, what appears the one or the
other), which may strike us most forcibly and be first attended
to. The former case is that which I will first examine.

Is there anything *but* ourselves? is what is likely in this
case to suggest itself. All is undoubtedly *our* thought: in
calling the immediateness immediate *thought*, as I did, I
implied that it is *we* who are in some way doing something,
or suffering something: the one thing therefore that we are
certain of is *ourselves* and the state in which we are,—are we
certain of anything else?

Here self-consciousness seems to absorb into itself the whole of immediateness: and its disposition to do so is in a manner the beginning of reflective philosophy, *i.e.* reflection turned in the direction of the study of the nature of knowledge, and the fundamental notion of things. If we use the word 'experience,' a term, from the opposite point of view, thoroughly ambiguous and misleading, exactly in the manner in which I have described 'intuition' to be, we had best begin the use of it *here*, and say, that from the first beginning of intelligence to be *itself*, (*i.e.* to be a combination of immediateness or presence, and notice, the two together constituting knowledge,) it goes through a succession of experiences: or, if we prefer the language, its *being* intelligence *consists* in its going through such a succession of experiences: and the first of such experiences is the suggestion to it of the thought that, after all, when we get to the bottom of things, everything is thought on its part, and that there is nothing more than thought. When we talk of 'experience' in any way which can be properly called philosophical, *i.e.* in any way which does not baldly assume, as a matter of common sense or consciousness, the existence of the external world, in the way in which the mass of men are supposed to realize it, as the basis of reality,—when, I say, we talk of 'experience' for any philosophical purpose going below this, all we can mean by it is a succession of mental states, mental experiences, in a sense analogous to the religious application of the word. The word 'experience' here carries with it a notion of value or importance in the mental state, which I have no wish at all that it should lose, if only we remember that in *this* region we have no private revelation of an external world to lean on, when we are charged with meaning no more than mere imagination and illusion.

However, I think there is significance in using the term 'mental or intellectual experiences' for our thoughts, in the way which I will endeavour to explain. The feeling strongly, that the one great fact which we are aware of is that 'we think,' and the subordinating everything else to this, in such a manner as to convert all that seems to be around us, from objects independently existing (as ordinary practical thought is supposed to consider them) into objects simply of thought—this is what is generally called by the name of 'idealism.' It is often charged with reducing thought to mere imagination, any portion of which, for all that we can know, may be illusion; because if there is nothing besides objects of thought, there is nothing independent of thought to test thought by; and to say of thought that it is one thing or another, true or false, when there is nothing else anywhere but itself, is absurd: it is everything, which is as good as being nothing: it has no predicates. And yet there *is* such a thing as thinking incorrectly or falsely. If there is no such thing as illusion, there is no such thing as knowledge. What then do imagination, error, knowledge mean?

I think the best way to have right notions about this will be to rescue the word 'experience' from the application of it which is made by many, and to apply it from the first in the manner in which I have just done. When we say, 'we know things by experience,' what many philosophers mean is, that we know them as a part of the physical order of things in which we live, and that our senses have some way or other, directly or indirectly, made us aware of them. Now when, from this view, we endeavour to pass to the manner of our conception of this whole physical state of things, and to the nature of our sensal perceptiveness, we get into difficulties. Mr Mill speaks of our conception of the external world, or of nature as a whole, being *acquired by experience*, in the same manner as he might speak of any portion of our knowledge of the physical universe, *e.g.* that cows have horns, or that arsenic is poisonous. Now I am at one with him in readiness to use the word 'experience' in both these applications: only I would take, as the type or propriety of its meaning, its meaning in application to the earlier and primary knowledge, which is the more full and general; whereas it appears to me, that the whole point of its significance with him comes from its application to the later or simply sensal knowledge. But in reality, if we take the meaning of such words as 'acquired' and 'experience' from the manner of our gaining our later knowledge, and then, with our minds full of that, apply the words to our earlier or primary knowledge (or thought), all that results is that this earlier thought *does* resolve itself into little other than imagination, and I do not see what principle we have to go on in distinguishing it from that. It is the positivist or experientialist idealists (if I may combine such apparently contradictory terms) who seem to me to be the real visionaries. In our later or physical knowledge, we judge of any particular portion that it *is* knowledge, and we call the mental change 'acquisition of knowledge,' rather than simply 'change of thought' (which in itself might be towards error), in virtue of its coalescing, according to certain principles or laws, with what we already know. When we are speaking therefore of a stage before the chain of this latter experience has begun, and before we have any means of distinguishing an acquisition from an illusion, and when yet we have no other notion of experience to apply than that which we get at this later stage,—then it does seem to me that all at the beginning is imagination, and nothing more. Our so-called knowledge is a vast imagination which we take care to make self-consistent: and fresh imagination which possesses this consistency we call experience. '*Insanimus*' at the beginning, but we take care that all the progress of our dream shall be '*cum ratione*.'

As a matter of fact then, when the mutual presence of subject and object begins to be verified by dawning reflection on the side of self-consciousness, the fundamental experience of the awakening intelligence, which stands nearest to immediateness, is the feeling that all is *our* thought, that whatever, beyond oneself, we may or can ever come to perceive, owes its existence, for us, to our perceiving it; that it is our own creation, which can never stand independently or on equal terms against us.

It seems to me that, whatever may be the extent or importance of our discoveries in the line of physical experience, we can never get away from this initial self-consciousness. I shall endeavour to explain how in the progress of our thought, we come to consider that in reality we depend on the universe rather than on ourselves, and that this is the right way of thinking. But whenever this our dependence is urged upon us as an entire dependence, and the completeness of our view of the physical universe is put in such a way as to include *ourselves*, mind and body, within it,—then, it seems to me, there rises up within us in opposition this first self-consciousness, this first reflectional thought or experience, with such a voice as this: 'After all, that things exist, means, for me, that I think they do: my thought is, for me, prior to their existence: it is now apparently proved, from the manner of their existence, that my thought is only a part of *that*: but how can this be? how can my thought at once embrace their existence and be embraced by it? how can the universe come to generate that out of which it was itself generated? *I think,* is to me the first of realities: that the universe exists is to me a secondary and dependent one: how can we come round to make *this* reality the source of the former, to make the primary depend upon the dependent?'

Supposing it to be the case, as Mr Mill says, that physical research could demonstrate that consciousness or sensation was a function of matter; while at the same time it is the case, as he in another place says, that matter or 'things' is only 'possibilities of sensation' on the part of sensiveness; where are we to find firm ground to stand on? In the circle, which makes sensation a function of matter, and matter a possibility of sensation, where are we to find either premiss or conclusion, principle or result? I cannot think, as I have said formerly, that any possible physical discovery can affect or alter the import of our primary self-consciousness. And though in *language*, one has to use metaphysical and scholastic-looking terms, the *feeling* seems to me to be one of the simplest and most immediate which can be present with us. The sentiment is so close, so intimate, that one can hardly put it into words: it is, that *feeling* (that which we express by self-consciousness, that which suggests to us personality or our own existence) is something, in virtue of the very feeling of it, heterogeneous to anything which we conceive as existing *for* the feeling, meeting it from what we call 'without,' and which we know, and call reality or things, owing to this meeting. However, words are of but little use on this subject, and I will not dwell upon it.

In speaking of the genesis of definite or reflectional knowledge, I use terms whose signification is taken from time, without any, or with but little, reference to time, and it is as well perhaps that I should in passing notice this; I have done the same in reference to space. I hope afterwards to speak of the growth of knowledge in individuals, which is what we call *learning*: at present I have only to do with what might be called *logical* time or space, *logical* priority or order. In philosophical speculation, we must speak of *within* and *without*, of *before* and *after*, in reference not to space and time, but to conceptions which we may consider space and time as suggesting to us, as arithmetical notation suggests the more general algebraical. To space and time themselves I hope to come speedily.

CHAPTER IV.

SELF-CONSCIOUSNESS AND PERCEPTION IN CONJUNCTION.

I HAVE already spoken of these in conjunction, for it is not possible to avoid it, nor do I wish to do so, but I will now speak of them fairly in their companionship, and contrast the one with the other, and of the next step in the experiences of our intelligence.

Self-consciousness is the becoming, more or less distinctly, aware of ourselves. But can we fairly say, that it is the becoming aware of our own existence? How do we know that our supposed self-consciousness is not a dream? that there is anything consistent about it, any ground for it?

The truth of 'cogito, ergo sum,' so far as it has truth, is not, as I have said, argumentative, but consists in its being an expression of the union of thought and being in the primary stage of what I have called 'immediateness.'

Perhaps what I say may be better understood by a reference, for a moment, to Hume. He says that nothing really exists, or can be considered reasonably by a philosopher to exist, except what he calls 'impressions': and in saying this, he perhaps appeared to himself, and in any case has appeared to a great many, to be saying something very sceptical. But observe upon what the notion of this being sceptical rests. Leaving out of account, as in fact we ought, the metaphor in the word, Hume is only liable to the charge of scepticism in the same way as Mr Mill (as I have mentioned) might be liable to a charge of visionariness. To what extent either charge is valid, depends upon the extent to which either philosopher makes his standard of trueness or reality to be what some philosophers, as I have said, mean by experience, viz. the possibility of hanging on and the call to hang on, consistently and satisfactorily, to what we knew before, an alleged fresh fact, in a world of regular co-existences and sequences. No one can doubt but that this, or something like this, is the way in which, in developed intelligence, we do judge as to a great deal of alleged fact. If, then, it is the only way to judge of truth, and if we are to carry it back to our speculations on fundamental truth, then the impressions have no claim to truth, and there is scepticism.

But supposing I say, The impressions have no claim to truth or substance as *you* choose to characterize truth, and therefore you speak depreciatingly of them : but they are anyhow themselves facts, true and valuable so far as that: let us see what they mean. To me, the whole Berkeleian and Humian controversy is a matter of wonder, for, had it not been for the wrong psychology, I cannot imagine what people could have expected to find at the basis of thought, other than what they slightingly called impressions, or perhaps ideas. It is said all that we are ultimately certain of is, not minds on the one side, not things on the other, but only ideas or impressions. Be it so : then those ideas or impressions, and their existence, are one great fact to begin with. *As* ideas or impressions, they are not ideas of minds, *i.e.* conceived by minds, nor ideas of things, *i.e.* expressing or representing something purporting to be beyond themselves. Here then we have a second great fact, after the fact of their existence, viz. that they grow or develope themselves into conceptions *by* what, in virtue of self-consciousness, calls itself *mind, of* what that mind, in virtue of the conceptions, calls *things* : and hence, we have the whole forward road of knowledge open before us. This at least is fact, and I cannot understand what more complete and funda-mental fact we can want or expect. So complete is it, that all after fact seems to me but a portion of it: our mind here makes its first experience, and the point of the significance of the term 'experience' afterwards is that it is the succession of states which the mind goes through, keeping to the course thus begun.

I have taken the above view of Hume's, as to all that in the last resort exists being ideas or impressions, to illustrate what I mean by 'immediateness.' As I view it, it seems to me anything but sceptical, anything but paradoxical. If we at any moment endeavour, in the most distinct manner we can, to set before ourselves what we call our mental state, we get, it seems to me, according to the clearness of our thought at the time, further and further along the way towards a view which is in substance this—not simple self-consciousness, the consciousness of our own existence—but this consciousness in union with the state of things in which we are, the circumstances in which we find ourselves, the objects we are thinking of: we do not exist by ourselves, but in union with all this, as a part of all this: and so it all exists in union with us, as a part of us. In the same manner, if we are trying to form a notion of what we mean by a fundamental conviction of the truth of a thing, it seems to me that we endeavour to pierce back, if it may be called so, to a state in which our separate self-consciousness, as distinguished from the thought of that which we have conviction of, disappears: a state in which we and it are in a kind of (not spatial) presence together, and this mutual presence is the fact which exists. It is impossible to use language about this without its seeming abstruse, and perhaps visionary or mystical, but the thing itself is simple, so far as anything is to be called simple. We may illustrate it by what we sometimes feel in observation of nature, when we have been for a moment lost in our thought: the observation perhaps loses distinguishingness as the mind loses self-consciousness, but all the more there is an intensity and truth in it which, so far as we can carry it out into self-consciousness and distinguishingness, is what constitutes the reality of knowledge.

I have used the word 'phenomenalism,' and hope to use it again, in a particular sense which I have carefully defined. The distinction made by many philosophers between 'phenomenology' and 'ontology' is one which I do not admit. Nor, consequently, do I consider that there is significance in the terms, there being no contrast or distinction. Ontology has now rather a bad name in philosophy, what is called 'phenomenology' a good one : the former, the older term, seems to me to have *a certain* significance and application of its own, independent of the above contrast : in the latter, the newer term, I see no proper significance at all.

To me, and I say it without a thought of paradox—for there only wants a startling manner of statement to make any philosophical truth seem paradoxical to those who are not in the habit of thinking philosophically—what we call 'appearance' seems to involve in it both thought and being, and Hume's 'ideas' or 'impressions,' *my* 'immediateness,' might each be called, if we prefer the term, 'appearance.' The word 'appearance' has a double implication, involving something which appears, and something to which it appears. This implication we may conceive as in either direction abortive : there may be appearance without what we will at present call 'substratum' of it : this is what we term hallucination or dream—appearance *of* nothing : there may be appearance without any intelligence to which the appearance is—appearance *to* nothing. To me the appearance seems in either case like Ely Cathedral without its Northern transept or Achelous without his horn—maimed and but half itself.

Complete appearance is impossible without *ourselves* for the appearance to be to, in the same way as it is impossible without something to appear. There is abundance of *partial* separation between intelligence and object mutually ready and expectant : but can we entertain the notion for a moment of a total separation of this kind ? And if not, then the true and first reality is the conjunction, which I have called appearance.

We may call with equal truth the entire mass of appearance all 'thought,' or all 'being.' And either of these, in its own point of view, may be made the principal.

Being is the first, in regard that the appearance itself, the idea, impression, immediateness, is a fact or reality, in the manner in which I have described, the fundamental or the first fact. And as the appearance resolves itself, in thought, into the intelligence perceiving things, the intelligence itself has *being*

as much as the things, or the appearance would be nothing--
would be the one-sided abortion of which I have spoken.

But thought is the first again in another way, in regard
that, however we try to keep the point of view of a philosophical
speculator or observer *ab extra* of the fact of appearance, we
cannot really *keep* this point of view : we belong ourselves to
the fact of appearance and are a part of it, and when we come
to speak of thought, we have to reinforce the one side of it
by our own speculativeness, and take our place within it.

This last is what I have tried to express, in what I have
said hitherto, by speaking of 'immediate thought' rather than
immediateness : the Humian words 'idea' and 'impression,'
which both have primary references to the intelligence, carry
the same. We cannot of course arrive, in conception, at that
fusion of intelligence and thing, of subject and object, from
which, it seems to me, truth of thought germinates. We are
on the side of thought, and must keep there, and must therefore still describe the utmost that we can arrive at as thought
or idea.

I do not think that the above identification of appearance
with being and truth can be considered as idle, and notional—
what if true, can have no result,—when we think of the
endless philosophical discussion which there has been and is as
to what—say in our sensive intuitions or perceptions—is called
'subjective,' coming from the mind, on the one side, and what
is called 'objective,' coming from things on the other. We
have no notion of things at all, except what the mind gives us.
On the other hand, if we prefer a different mode of expression,
and take this *givenness* for granted, we may say things present
themselves to us as they are. In either case I see no possible
way in which we can make a division between something as
belonging to the mind and something as belonging to the
thing : I do not see what region of thought the principle which
should guide such a division is to come from.

In my view, a thing is what it looks, and looks what it is :
we see it as it is, and it is as we see it. I am here using the
sense of sight as the type not only of all that we commonly
call sense, but of all intuition or what I have described as

immediate *knowledge*. The *looks* of a thing, if we might extend for a moment the use of the word, are the various manners of its presentation to each possible faculty or instrument of knowledge, and these 'looks' (if we use a different language) are simply the qualities of the thing as a substance. The thing is no more than the combination of its looks, the substance no more than the combination of its qualities. In this momentarily extended meaning of the term 'looks,' what I mean is that a thing looks to the sight in this way, smells in that way, tastes in a third, measures so much across or round, stands off so far from the body, constitutes or composes, say, such and such a máchine or system, serving such a purpose—which last is quite as much a 'look' or presentation of it to the higher intuition or perception, as its form or colour is to the lower—and it is the combination of all these 'looks' together which makes up the thing for us: it is the combination of the whole possible amount of such for every possible variety of intelligence, so far as such a conception has meaning, which would constitute the thing in itself, the absolute thing. The thing as it is to us then is not a possibly fallacious representation, not a dress of something underneath, but simply a partial view. Whether a *complete* view exists, or the thing has a proper self or absoluteness, except in face of the Divine Intelligence, is a matter which we may speculate upon, with or without result. *Knowledge* is of the complete view, and is all *absolute*, not relative: we have amount of knowledge according to the amount of completeness of our view; mistake, of which I hope soon to speak, is want of knowledge—but of this presently.

I said that the thing was the combination of its looks, not the sum or aggregate, and in respect of this we have to notice that the looks of a thing are in degrees, and of very different values: and that the difference between a combination and an aggregate is that, as to the former, we understand there is *reason* for it, *meaning* in it, not as to the latter. The looks are of greater or less value according as they tell us more or less of this reason or meaning. In fact, this reason or meaning might be described, if we like to use the language, as the look of the thing itself—it is what I have formerly called[1] its 'thing-hood.' Its character is this, that it is of necessity the same for every possible intelligence, answering the description I gave just now of the thing in itself, so far as this can be supposed to exist.

I have introduced the words 'meaning' and 'reason' here for the purpose of drawing attention to the manner in which they illustrate what I am now endeavouring to show, viz. that the proper reality is the relation of subject and object, or that which I have called 'appearance.' We 'mean' whatever we do mean; a *thing* again or a notion 'means' this or that: we possess 'reason'; there is 'reason' for this or that thing. The usage of language is exceedingly various about all this, but I think it all goes to make us think that the sort of naturally suggested view, which language may be supposed to express, is that things before us in the universe are neither 'phænomena of noumena,' which is pretty much the same as deceptions, nor things which have their being independent of any intelligence conceiving them. Nothing but their 'looking' in the way they do, suggests to us their 'being' at all. The notion of their having a being beyond what they look is purely gratuitous: their looking as they do, is sufficient reality, and in fact all possible reality: the notion of their having possibly another reality seems to me to belong to that false realism, to which the language of Hume which I have quoted is necessarily sceptical.

If we apply what I have just been saying to the Cartesian 'Cogito, ergo sum,' it will appear more strongly than before that such truth as it has must have reference to that primary indistinction of knowing and being which exists in immediateness. If we explain it, *Cogito, ergo sum conscius,* we have not advanced a step: if we interpret it, *Cogito, ergo vivo,* we have advanced too far. And I cannot understand what the absolute notion of being, here apparently involved in 'sum,' is. *Being* is being *something*: being something is looking in some way, or, in grander language, possessing some character presentable to

---

[1] *Expl.* 106, 123 &c.

intelligence. It may be more than this, for it may be intelligence itself as well: but this is what is contained in the 'cogito,' or what the 'cogito' means. In order to get a step beyond the 'cogito,' we want the addition of some property, some character, something for us to be: and it is quite impossible for us to proceed from the bare 'cogito' to this. I do not understand the seeming predication of this absolute 'being' to carry any meaning. Now, as I have mentioned, the primary fact is not 'cogito,' but is what I have called immediateness, of which, so soon as we begin to reflect or wake, we notice 'cogito' first: but we do not 'think' absolutely, we find ourselves thinking *some how*, we have an object, embryotic perhaps, but still enough to make our thought not absolute, but determinate. Hence the first *definite* thought after immediateness, is not 'I am' 'sum,' absolutely, but 'I am some how,' 'I exist, find myself existing, in a state of things': 'I think in a particular way, this or that seems to me or is thought by me.' The immediateness in which we wake to consciousness is a portion, a part, of the state of things. We think in a determinate way of something determinate, and therefore, if we must conclude something, we may say, we are something in a universe. Being is something which we share with the universe in which we find ourselves (or in which we are one with it), and our determinateness is something differencing us from the rest of it. I do not think 'being' would mean anything to us, unless something else 'was' besides *we*, and unless *we* 'were something' differencing us from what that 'something else' was.

This primary imagination, the true 'Cogito, ergo sum' of reflection, which follows on the 'cogito' of immediateness (as near, that is, as we can approach to the expression of immediateness), where we mean by 'sum,' I have a certain being of my own in a certain state of things, I call a primary 'experience' of the mind, on account of the supposition of the existence of this state of things, into which we, by reflection, wake. In developed intelligence, 'true' is equivalent to 'not false': when we assert anything, we are said to mean it more or less forcibly, according as we have more or less in our mind other alternative things which might be and which are not:

we are denying a counter-supposition, and excluding from our notion the *ground*, from which it stands relieved or distinguished. In regard of primary notions, the supposition of truth or non-truth of this kind is impossible. When we first begin to consider ourselves to *be*, and the universe to *be* about us, is this what some people understand by an intuition, *i.e.* a per-suasion carrying necessary conviction, or is it a mere imagination, or is it an experience? It is each or any of these, for here these terms have no distinctive significance. The word 'con-viction' has no meaning when there is no supposition of a possible alternative presenting itself: the word imagination, in the signification of 'illusion' has no meaning, except on the supposition of our knowing reality in some way otherwise than by the way of which we are speaking: the word 'experience' has no meaning except on the supposition of a continuous state of things, and of previous knowledge on which to hang the new. Still, of the three words, the word 'experience' seems to me to approach the nearest to appropriateness. It seems to indicate to us this, which we ought to consider, and which I will express thus, that as *thought* is identified with the subject, so knowledge or truth (*i.e.* true or right thought, as a species of the genus thought) is identified with the object. When we speak of a non-ego, of something besides ourselves, the lowest foundation, the most intimate meaning, of the notion, is not the existence of anything at all like us by the side of us—that may be or not—but is the notion of something controlling or determining our thought. If we were the only existence, there would be no truth or knowledge for us—there could not be even deter-mination or characterization of *ourselves* without an external reference. I call then our feeling ourselves what we are, in an universe in which we are, by the name of a first experience, to express that from the first we feel our thought determined by (that is, to have a particular character in accordance with) something without us and so far independent of us: we wake into a state of things which therefore we understand as anterior, as to some of its characters, to our self-recognition. And yet we ourselves are anterior to it. *Immediateness* is the primal fact to us, which our self-consciousness and perceptiveness have got, in the language which I have used, to digest.

If we use the word 'perceptiveness' loosely to express notice, or apparent notice, of any facts which we may suppose to be in the universe, whether abstruse or simply sensal, it may now be said that self-consciousness and perceptiveness go hand in hand from our first experience, the one setting forth and bringing out the other. We might roughly say that there are two great and separate regions of thought into each of which both enter, or in other words (which I abstained from using before in order to avoid the notion of any reference to time) two stages of our thought in this respect: there is our *full* consciousness of ourselves as thinking, and there is correspondingly with this, perceptiveness of what is frequently called 'the relations in the universe which are the object of thought,' which I hope to speak of more fully soon: and there is what I will for the present call our semi-consciousness of our corporeal and phenomenal selves and our sensive organization, and correspondingly with this there is perceptiveness of those things which are commonly understood as objects of sense.

It will be observed that I called this a rough division, and I am perfectly aware that in making it I am laying myself open to the charge of encouraging the division between ideas and sense, thought and experience, which I have condemned. That division, made so extensively as it has been, would not have been made without much to suggest it. I make myself the above rough, and in fact incorrect, division, to express more shortly and summarily what I have in another place[1] expressed by means of a scale, and because it is convenient to make the distinction, which really represents a *gradation*, between full and semi-consciousness, and correspondingly between thought and sensal perception: but there is no line of demarcation between the two, and every perception, speaking generally, has elements in it from the top to the bottom of the scale.

---

[1] *Expl.* ch. VI.

Our advancing knowledge is a growing and endlessly rami-
fying conception of ourselves in correspondence with the universe,
and of the universe in correspondence with ourselves. This is
knowledge in virtue of its uniting trueness with definiteness : it
is true so far as it is a real development of the original trueness
or fundamental experiences : it has definiteness given to it, and
is thus made into knowledge by reflection, which reflection or
distinctification must not be such as to alter the trueness.

We conceive ourselves on the one side as thinking, and
perceiving through the medium of an intellective and sensive
organization, which we call mind and body in accordance with
the rough division which I made just now, but which is more
fitly represented as I have done in another place by a scale of
mental and corporeal process : I have there called it all sensation. We cannot make a division, *i.e.* *one* division, between
mind and body. Mind and body together form one intellective
organization, of which what we call the lower portion (to what
extent upwards we cannot tell) involves in it an element
heterogeneous from intellection. I call it so, because intellection, being what we conceive a state or action of ours, is
something of which we can be fully conscious, though consciousness is not its being : whereas of our body we have only
what I have called semi-consciousness, by which I mean that
we have the knowledge of it jointly by consciousness and by
perception, and that, while consciousness is our instrument for
knowing ourselves, what we know by perception is, so far, not
ourselves. In respect of our arm, *e.g.* we may be conscious of
it, if we like to use that language, in virtue of a pain in it, at
the same time that we see or perceive it with our eyes.

I do not use the word 'soul,' or any similar, because I am
not analysing what the nature of our existence is objectively,
i.e. what we properly *are* in view of an intelligence which could
thoroughly know us, and what is the fundamental fact of our
life, meaning by *life* the combination in one of all the states or
processes of which we are capable, among which thought is
only one. I hope before leaving off to come a little nearer to
considerations of this kind, but at present *thought*, our manner
of knowing, is all my business. And in view of this I say that

we, whatever *we* may be, think and know through mind and
body, without being able to divide the two. In immediateness
of thought we are conscious of mind and body in a certain
gradation.

Correspondingly with this self-consciousness on the one side,
we conceive the universe (or *a* universe if we like the language
better—if we say *a* universe, we are in danger of the error, that
we are acquainted with the genus of things 'universe,' and are
now coming to the knowledge of a fresh individual of it—if we
say *the* universe, we are in danger of the mis-psychologic error,
that we see the universe plainly before us, while yet we have
got to form the conception of it)—we conceive then the universe as answering to our intellective organization along all the
scale which I have mentioned, as answering to our mind or
thought with order and law, and as answering to our body or
sensiveness with what we call its mechanical and chemical
properties. Where the universe and our intellective organization properly meet, is what we cannot tell: it is the same
question, in another form, as that of the division between mind
and body. That is to say, we know perfectly well how far into
the spatial universe our sensibility extends, and how far in the
same our activity has, what we may call, immediate command,
and the limits of these mark similarly the limits of what I have
called our sensive organization. And also, what is most important, we know that our consciousness and the universe, by
the very notion of them, can never fuse: it is their nature to
stand in antithesis or contrast the one to the other: each gives
to the other its distinct meaning by this contrast: if they did
fuse, we should not know what either meant. But our body is
composed of what we call matter of very various kinds, the
different kinds standing in most peculiar relations to consciousness, which difference is the cause of our various sensiveness.
It is probable that this sensiveness exceeds in subtlety the
utmost conceptions that we can possibly form: that what we
call imagination, *e.g.* is real sensiveness, the sensive nerves being
in action or disturbance correspondingly with it, exactly as they
are in perception. To what extent we may think with what
we call our body or our corporeal organization I am sure

I cannot tell. At this time, when we are perhaps drifting away from the old mispsychologist errors, the error we are possibly most in danger of may be that of supposing, that in finding more and more the importance of matter as an instrument of our thought, we are breaking down the distinction between it and consciousness. I do not see the least how this can be. Ever since men have been, we have talked of 'the eye seeing,' without having been led by our language to doubt but that it was *we* that saw, and that the eye was only our instrument. Even if we should get now to talk of the brain thinking, or perceiving generally, I do not see why anything different should happen. The fact is, that when we think for a moment, we recognize that what we call thinking, seeing, tasting, are what can only be done (or felt) by something which we call 'I,' or 'we,' the expression of consciousness: if there had not been in thought and in language such notions and expressions as 'I,' 'we,' there would not have been such notions and expressions as 'see,' 'feel': but of this no more now.

CHAPTER V.

SENSIBILITY AND ACTIVITY.

BEFORE proceeding further in this direction, it seems necessary to draw attention to certain portions of our nature which
I have not yet distinctly noticed.

The immediateness or immediate thought is what it is in
virtue of our whole nature and that of the universe, and
involves therefore the elements which I am going to speak of
as well as those of which I have spoken. I am going to speak
of the manner in which they come into recognition in reflection.

By sensibility I mean capacity of pleasure and pain, and
I carefully distinguish it throughout from *sensiveness,* by which
latter I mean the general operation or instrumentality of the
nerves of our body in giving us *information* of what we then
call external things. Sensiveness, as I use the term, is a
portion, the nervous or corporeal portion, of the more general
operation or faculty 'perceptiveness.' We are perceptive as
intelligences : we are sensive as corporealized or incorporated
intelligences.

It would be very convenient if we had one word which
would express pleasure and pain together as two species of a
genus 'disturbance' or 'affection' or whatever we might call it,
instead of having to speak of them constantly in conjunction,
as I shall have to do. I think I shall venture to make a term
for the occasion, and as I have called the capacity of pleasure
and pain, sensibility, shall call the fact of pleasure or pain being

present, *sentience*. 'Sentience,' then is the actual feeling of pleasure or pain.

In speaking of the immediateness at first, I used variously the expressions 'immediate thought' and 'immediate feeling,' using more, as I went on, the former, as I have been speaking more of consciousness in its relation to perceptiveness.

As we disengage 'ourselves' however from the immediateness, it is quite as much in the point of view of sentience as in that of thought: some might say more. Some will say that pleasure or pain is all that we are properly conscious of: in fact, that consciousness *is* the feeling of pleasure or pain, and nothing more. I have no wish to dispute about the meaning of the term 'consciousness.' Myself I prefer the term 'self-consciousness,' meaning by it what is sometimes called 'the feeling of personality,' *i.e.* the reflective of thought or notice of ourselves, as existing and as distinguished from something else also existing, which is not ourselves.

But so far as we do use the term 'conscious' as distinct from 'self-conscious' (independent of its later, more or less moral, use, as when we say 'we are conscious of such and such a good and bad feeling, or of having done such and such a thing'), it is perhaps in reference to sentience it might best be used. The application of the notion of 'immediateness' to sentience is not exactly the same as its application to thought. Pleasure and pain only exist as we feel them, *i.e.* in this use of the term, are conscious of them: *here* therefore, till there is consciousness, there is nothing: pleasure and pain are the foundation of the subjective, of ourselves. This is true: but there are two things which we must bear in mind: one is, that there is all the difference in the world whether pleasure and pain are, or are not, *attended to*: and the other (which is what, as well in regard of thought as of sentience, makes it fit to start from 'immediateness') that when we are speaking of any *felt*, *i.e.* of any particular, pleasure or pain, we must make a supposition, or have something in our thoughts, beyond the pleasure or pain itself—the supposition viz. of a reason for it in the existing state of things. One way of realizing what I have called 'immediateness' might be to conceive it as the actual

state of things present on any occasion of our beginning to be
'ourselves,' to reflect, be self-conscious, notice, attend. There
is no pleasure or pain till we are more or less distinctly
conscious, but there is, independently of the consciousness, the
occasion of it: our becoming conscious is not the cause of the
pleasure or pain, but is the waking, if we may speak not quite
accurately, to a state of things in which pleasure or pain are as
it were awaiting us. In a somewhat similar though reverse
way pleasure or pain may be said to vanish, when something
occurs entirely to absorb the attention in a different direction,
though all the occasion or reason of them exists in full vigour.
It is important to consider, about sentience as about thought,
that in mentally isolating it in order to conceive and talk about
it, we must be aware all along that it is not really isolated,
that it is a part of what I have called a 'state of things,' and
that thus it has its reasons *without* our consciousness, though
it exists only as a part of our consciousness. By what I call
immediateness I want to represent the state of things logically
prior to our distinct consciousness, which contains in it the
reason why our consciousness, when it begins, is what it is—
whether of pleasure or of pain.

Under the circumstances in which we suppose reflection,
attention, notice, fairly operative, we may say that self-
consciousness is always accompanied, more or less, by sentience
or the feeling of pleasure or pain: and I do not know that
there would be great harm in saying that this is what we are
really conscious of. But we must mean, then, a very great
deal by 'more or less.' During a large part of our thinking
existence, pleasure or pain, supposing them to exist, are what
we are not in the least attending to, and our attention is given
to all sorts of things different from them: so that if we say
that pleasure or pain is all that we are really conscious of, we
are leaving very little meaning to the word consciousness. It
is more convenient to use the word 'sentience' only when the
pleasure or pain are sufficiently prominent to be real objects of
attention.

Sensibility, the capacity, or, if we prefer to say so, sentience,
the actuality, of pleasure or pain, is the great fact of our nature

in view of action; though I put this, as we shall see, in a more qualified manner than many would. And our *intellectiveness*, as we shall soon also see, is closely wrapt up both with our sensibility and our activity. Of the latter I will speak now.

It may be remembered how some time since I said, that what I called 'reflectiveness' was intermediate between immediate thought and what I called 'immediate' or 'reflex' action. Immediate or reflex action, speaking roughly, is where there is action of one thing upon another, and continuous or spontaneous *re*-action from this other.

I only allude to this for the purpose of pointing out the difference—a difference, however, entirely gradational—between this and an action from without upon what we call an intelligence, with will leading to an action on its or his part, no longer to be called a simple re-action, but a consequence through a complicated intermediation. What I am saying now is from the physical point of view. We are comparing what takes place when an object, for instance, touches the tentacles of a zoophyte and they close upon it, or (what I suppose is similar) when a warm current strikes on the pores of our body and they open or relax to it—we compare this with what takes place, say, when somebody throws a cricket-ball at me striking me with violence and I throw it back at him with the same. Between the first action and the response in the former case there is nothing intermediate, in the latter a great deal: and into this, from our physical point of view, we, as spectators looking on, can pass to a certain limited extent. We are able to know that the impact of the cricket-ball produces strong pressure upon the flesh and nerves, and we know, taking up our thread again, that there is contraction and movement of the muscles of the arm in picking up the cricket-ball and throwing it back. For all that we know from *this* point of view, it might be immediate or reflex action: I might be what is called an automaton in it: the pressure of the flesh by the ball at first might touch a spring and cause all the following motion.

Here we look at action from the point of view of physics or motion: let us change our point of view, and look at it from another side.

Immediateness, or thought in so far as it is immediate, I have described as inactive. We wake, in the language which I have used, into *a state of things*. We are in indistinct presence of what is not *we*, and *it* is in similar presence of us. This indistinct presence cannot become distinct without what I have called 'notice' or 'attention': and this means, that we choose out and direct our thought to a portion of what is present to us and not yet set off from us, and this effort is 'will.' I am not here concerned to consider the nature of this 'will' or what is called the 'freedom' of it. It is certainly not arbitrary, and our attention to one part of what is before us rather than to another is suggested by something independent of us: the nature of the suggestion is not matter for discussion now. All that is of consequence now is that, alongside of our self-consciousness and perceptiveness, and again of our sensibility, there is going on within us a fourth something, which is the determination by us of our attention hither and thither. These four things are not independent of each other: they enter each into each. Though I divide them in this manner, there is no particular principle in their being just so many or just so divided: numbers and sharp divisions have no place in philosophy. There is a sort of contrast or counter-concurrence between self-consciousness and perceptiveness, and there is something of the same between sensibility and activity. The first two go together for our intellective, the second two for our active, nature: but we are each *one*: we should not perceive in the particular manner in which we do, if we were not sentient and active in the particular manner in which we are: so that our general feeling (or, if we prefer the word 'consciousness') is made up of all these things more or less at once and in conjunction.

We pass onward from one experience to another, in respect of our activity, just as we do in respect of our self-consciousness and perceptiveness. As our self-consciousness is extended to that semi-consciousness, as I called it, which we have of our corporeal organization, so the experience of our power in directing our attention is extended to the experience of our power in directing corporeal movement, or (what is the same thing) to the experience of our body not only as a sensive organization, but as an active organization or machine for producing mechanical effects. Our experience of it in this way is exactly analogous to our experience of it in the other: we can move it partly, but it can be moved without our moving it. In moving the portions of it, we move them as partly ourselves and partly not ourselves: that is, the movement of the arm for instance is a contraction of the muscle, resulting from our will and moving the matter which composes the arm, according to the same mechanical laws which regulate the motion of any matter. Our body stands to us, in regard of our motion of its parts and of anything else by means of it, just in an analogous relation with that in which it stands to us in regard of the sensiveness of particular portions of it and our perceptiveness through it.

I have described sensibility and activity as standing in a special relation to each other, but this relation is difficult, and involves another element, upon which I do not want to dwell at length now. I have approached towards the consideration of it in speaking of the relation of sensibility to immediateness.

Activity, like sensibility, has its root in immediateness: that is, in order to understand activity, we must begin with the supposition of *a state of things*, which (though that is not a matter of our knowledge, more than implicitly, or involvedly) contains a reason for the activity (when it comes to be recognized by us) being what it is, and no other. The common parent both of sensibility and of activity may be said to be ' *want* '—' *want* ' as a fact, which we must carefully distinguish from want as a feeling, or the feeling of want[1]. Want, in what I have called immediateness, exists as a fact, and when this immediateness passes into reflection, this *fact* of want passes into *felt* want or uneasiness, and *concurrently* with this (*not* as a result of it) the *fact* of want impels action. What I call ' immediateness ' is the presentment to us of *a state of things*, in which things *are* as they are, but in which, beyond this, things are also *not* as they *ought* to be—by which *ought* I do not mean

---

[1] See this developed in his *Treatise on the Moral Ideals*, esp. p. 26 foll.

any reference to morals (though this principle is very important in its application to them), but I mean simply that the state of things is to be looked at, not merely as it is in itself at the moment, but as it contains or implies what is coming or should come next. This is what 'wants' to be (speaking of *fact*), what there is (the fact of) want of. If we suppose the state of things passing into the next state of things without reflection, this want acts of itself to supply itself, and the *next* state of things is accordingly what *it* is. If the state of things passes into *reflection*, or comes, as some would say, into consciousness, then the want, concurrently with its tendency to supply itself, is also *felt* as want, *i.e.* as uneasiness, passing, with further reflection, into desire. This account of the commencement of our sensibility is in substance, I think, only more fully, the same which I said about it before : except that here we have it in relation with activity.

I have expressed in another place my dissent from the view which makes activity a *result* of *felt* want or uneasiness, as if it were something which we were better without, a necessary evil. It is better, I think, to consider activity and sensibility as equally initial principles in our nature. The importance of the question depends very much on the manner in which it is put. Variety, change, particularity, on the one side, and imperfection on the other, are in a manner synonymous terms : the *change* in a universe thus made up is a continued course of want, (as I have described the fact of want,) and of the supply of it. We may say simply, the same is the case with *us* : but the point I think to be observed is, that even on the supposition of the fullest reflection, we are not entirely put into our own conscious hands, so as for our action to be dependent only on want which we feel. I do not speak here in reference to our corporeal nature (as to which the matter is not of consequence) : I mean that our nature takes pleasure in its active impulses, independent of the conscious pursuit of an end with our activity : these impulses have their reason, and betoken in this way want *as fact*, but they are quite different in their nature from the desire of sensible gratification.

If we now recall to mind what I said a short time since

about action viewed from the side of physics, and compare it
with what I have now said about action viewed from the side
of immediate thought, we seem to see two portions, which put
together, make up intelligent or volitional action as a whole.
But this is not exactly so, and the supposition that it is so
seems to me one of the errors which, in the present state of
philosophy, we are most in danger of. We have to remember
that they are seen from different sides. Looking from the side
of consciousness and from the side of physical fact is like
looking at a carpet, hung up, from the one side and from the
other. What we see is the same, and yet not the same: and
those who add the facts of body and facts of mind together as
two constituents of the universe seem to do very much as if it
should be said there are two carpets, which make up all of
what we see: the one carpet rough and unfinished, the other
smooth and polished: the one with a man in the pattern of it
who has got a sword in his left hand, the other with a man
who has a sword in his right. In a way, it may be said that it
is two carpets that we see: but though we may *combine* them
together if we know how, we must not *add* them or put them
side by side with each other, for they are viewed each in a
different manner, and cannot in *this* way be brought into
relation.

Action upon anything and response to it, so far as we can
see them from the side of physics, are one side of the carpet,
and sensibility and activity, which we may put together as
volition, are the other. Corresponding with pressure upon the
nerves on the one side, there is feeling of pain upon the other:
and, after more or less of mental complication, we come to
what, on the one side, is will to move the arm, and on the
other, is contraction of the muscles, actually moving it.

The side however of consciousness or of thought depends,
no less than the other side, upon immediateness, *i.e.* upon
actuality or state of things. Our initiation of anything on the
side of feeling is not capricious or arbitrary, nor does the
supposition of its being *our own* involve that of its being *this*:
it is determined to be what it is, and not something else, by
something existing: and this concurrence of self-initiation with

existing reason for it is what I have endeavoured to express by waking to something, or by commencing reflection.

By saying, some time since, that reflection was intermediate between immediate thought and immediate action, what I meant was this: that reflection, as we have seen, brings us into a region of what I called 'semi-consciousness,' which is the state of feeling in which we stand in regard of our body. From the other side, if we follow immediate action upwards or inwards, we come to a region of more refined physics, of vital physics, where there are phenomena of a very peculiar nature. This region corresponds, from the other side, with the semi-consciousness. In this region of the study of life we have consciousness and physical fact in very close proximity and entanglement. But for all this, we never can get both into the same view, any more than the two sides of the carpet. We may, and in fact must, deal with self-consciousness as a fact of the universe, because we want some means of expressing, in language of such fact, the *interval* between action upon sentient beings and reaction from them. But when we deal thus with self-consciousness, we simply make an assumption: we do not any more, for our thus dealing with it, know or express what it is. If we say it is physical fact, we seem to me to be simply, from the nature of the case, misusing language, much as if we should say 'space is time.' Because, from another point of view, we do perfectly know what it is, know it better than we can know anything else, for it is of all things most intimate to us. And from the side of *this* knowledge of it, physical fact looks entirely different to us from the way in which it looked from the other, and we at once seem to put out of the question the notion of resolving consciousness into *it*.

However, I will say no more of this, because it is a matter where, from its very ultimateness, there cannot be given much reason, and where this is so, mere reiteration is useless.

CHAPTER VI.

SPACE AND TIME.

In speaking, as I go on, about the *distinctification* of our notions, which is the process of reflection, I shall have to speak about the meaning of a counter-notion or ground[1]—that which a notion is specially distinguished from or relieved against. I think, however, that I shall be understood, if instead of waiting for what I have to say then, I a little anticipate it in speaking of the idea or notion of *space*.

Space is in reality the counter-notion of matter or body, that from which, *as* matter or body, it is distinguished. When we say, 'There is something there,' we mean 'There is *not* empty space,' and when we say, 'There is nothing there,' we mean 'There *is* empty space.' In using this language we are speaking in the manner which I, in another place, have called 'phenomenal,' *i.e.* we have in our reflection come fully into the notion of our being corporeal beings in a physical world. It is with this notion possessing us that we use the language which I mentioned above : phenomenally space is nothing. Our observation, or notice, or recognition of it, or however we describe our coming by the notion (for to me it seems unimportant), is in fact the notice of absence of response to our sensiveness, the effort to handle or see (with therefore the presence of the feeling that there is or ought to be something to feel or see), but the finding nothing : the perception of space is in fact abortive sensiveness.

When we phenomenally perceive, or in other words exercise

---

[1] See *Expl.* pp. 23, 24.

sense, and yet do not perceive anything, what we perceive is space. We are seeing, and yet do not see; we are touching, and yet do not touch; because there is nothing to see or touch: and yet the state of things is different from that which it would be with us at the same moment if there were no such things as eyes or touching power. This seems to me the simplest way of conceiving, as I understand it, pure or bare sensive perception, as I translate the Kantian 'reine Anschauung.' With Kant, 'Empfindung,' that is, taste, smell, the being affected by colour &c. constitute the matter of 'experience,' and give us the notion of reality: we, in virtue of the constitution of our perceptive faculty, *spatialize* these, perceive them as in space, and *hence* proceeds the universe as we are aware of it. So far, then, as we exercise our perceptive faculty without *these* to apply to, we have 'reine Anschauung,' pure or bare perception, the spatializing (or the perception as in space alone) without anything to spatialize or to perceive. This agrees with my own description given above.

All discussions about space are in one point of view unprofitable, namely, because space, so far as it is an idea or notion at all, is preeminently what Locke would call a 'simple' one, and these simple ideas of Locke will not bear much talking about. They cannot be defined, and for their reality in any way Locke has to appeal to the individual consciousness of each one: when we are talking about them, therefore, it is hard to say whether the word 'space' represents the same notion in the mind of each, and hard to know how to come at the knowledge what it ought to represent.

The fact is, we can tell, in many respects, how we ought *not* to apply the term 'space,' and we can find out what we may call various relations of space to other notions: but we cannot at all find out and be sure that when different people use the term 'space,' even thinkingly, they mean the same thing by it; that is, in other words, we cannot tell whether there is any one meaning of 'space' for us to find out. The word is important in philosophical discussion, not for its own meaning, but on account of its being one of the terms which go with others to exhibit various philosophical views of the universe— that is, it is important in its relations.

It is important, however, that we should remember that we can tell in many respects what space is *not*, or, to speak more correctly, when the term is *misapplied*. Thus I believe the greater number of people misconceive the notion of space by identifying it with the illuminated atmosphere which forms the groundwork or canvas of the visual picture before their eyes. I call this a misconception of the notion of space, because it is plainly something different from space, something physical, as I have above described it. And yet, if a large body of people have, as I believe they have, *this* notion of space, to what purpose are we to talk of space as of a simple idea which each has in his mind the same as others, and about which men are sure to understand one another without mutual explanation, and without definition ?.

In Mr Abbott's argument against Mr Bain on the subject of space, where in answer to Mr Bain's saying (as I should also say) that we get the notion of space by movement (of the arms &c.), Mr Abbott says that the notion which we get in this way is not that of space, which we get rather by sight &c., I do not exactly see how the question is to be settled. In order to agree which of these is the true notion of space, we must have agreed first what space is, *i.e.* upon a definition or description of it, but this is the very point in question. Our various muscular movements leave in our mind, we will say, a certain remembrance, experience, or notion : and again our sight of various objects and their apparent intervals in the visual picture leave us another remembrance, experience, or notion : how are we to know which of these is the notion of space unless we have a *third* description of space to compare them with ? And if so, is not *this* the notion of space, rather than either of *them* ?

The notion of space is an important ingredient or part of our notion of the phenomenal universe or external world, and we mean by space a supposed something which (speaking from the subjective point of view) enables us to unite in one conception our heterogeneous experiences, or (speaking from the objective point of view) which gives a basis or bond of connexion to our heterogeneous sensations (or occasions of sentience); which experiences or sensations are what make us aware of the so-called qualities of matter. According as we conceive the phenomenal universe, so we must conceive space. It is *that* in the phenomenal universe, which, existing with whatever sort of existence we attribute to that universe as a fact or whole, nevertheless gives us no sentience and offers to us no resistance, so that it does *not* exist in the manner in which we suppose particular portions of that universe to exist. To unite Kantist language with mine, it is pure or bare phenomenalism, and we must assign to it a *subjective* or *objective* existence according to our general view of the phenomenal universe. We may regard it as that by which we create to ourselves the phenomenal universe: or we may regard it as that which contains, holds, gives a frame or canvas for, the various sensal objects which we come to know—their 'continent' as I have elsewhere called it[1]: were it not for this these objects would not be a universe to us.

In reality then, so far as we have *one* notion of space, what we mean by it, or should mean by it, to think about it to any purpose, is, that which is wanting to our sensiveness, the Kantist 'experience' (or, if we take the other view, to the qualities of bodies which our sensiveness informs us of), in order to make up the phenomenalism of the universe. I say 'the phenomenalism of the universe' rather than 'the phenomenal universe,' because to the making up of the phenomenal universe altogether there go some other notions, higher in the scale of knowledge than that of space, which are not before our consideration now: but, though it is owing to *these* that we conceive the phenomenalist universe in the manner in which we *do* conceive it, yet these are not a part of what makes us call it phenomenal, space and sensiveness being what are essential to this.

The reason why I do not here make use of what might be thought the easier expression, 'external world,' is because the word 'external,' in the proper use of it, *supposes* space, and is therefore better avoided in trying to come at this true notion of space. It is wrong to describe space in any way as 'externality,' because 'external' means 'external *to* something';

---

[1] *Expl.* 10.

but externality to our bodies will not represent space, because
our bodies themselves have magnitude or occupy space : and
externality to our minds can only mean independence of them,
which does not represent anything like what we want to mean
by space. Externality is a derivative notion from that of space.
Still, if we keep this in mind, so as not to be misled, the
expression 'external world' may represent without harm the
system of material objects in which we find or imagine ourselves,
and so is equivalent to what I call the phenomenal universe.
It will be remembered, that *my* use of the term 'phenomenal'
depends upon that of the term 'phenomenon' in science for
an object or fact of nature. I do not admit any meaning in
'phænomena' as distinct from 'noumena,' or in 'phænomenology'
as distinct from 'ontology.'

It will be seen, from the above, that space is a general
expression for the aggregate or summary of those relations in
the phenomenal universe, which are not matters of sentience or
resistance. For these relations we have the various names
position, direction, distance, shape, magnitude; possibly others.
By space we mean a combination of these into one notion, a
combination which they are evidently susceptible of. This
notion we represent to ourselves *imaginatively* (but, if we take
the representation for the notion, *illusively*) by means of what
I have called the groundwork of the visual picture before our
eye, the lighted atmosphere which intervenes between the
various objects which we see; this is simply a material *picture
of space altogether*, just as a piece of white paper is of space
horizontal. Again, the various relations which I have spoken
of above are coordinated by mathematicians, and in virtue of
such coordination we speak of space having three dimensions :
these relations altogether we call relations of space, and unite
them into one science.

We perceive space then in any way in which we become
aware of the magnitude, position, shape, &c., of anything (in
which case the perception of space is combined with sentience),
or when we become aware of interval or distance; in which case
it is unconnected with sentience during a portion of the perception, being so far perception of space pure or bare.

Time and space are constantly put together in philosophical treatment as a sort of pair or couple, and though this is what one should be very jealous of, yet still it is evident from various considerations that they *do* form a pair of this kind. One such consideration is *language* : the when and the where of a fact are what we chiefly want to know about it.

Time and space in a manner meet in a point, the present or immediate, and then, as thought of, diverge. That is, the notions of them are two different directions which our reflection takes. This will appear if we look for a moment at the notions of time and space in this way : they are both of them, as I just pointed out about ' space,' combinations of notions of relations rather than anything else, and this is more apparent in some other languages than our own. In Greek τόπος and χώρα, place or position, and room or extension, are indicated by different words, and in reality are quite distinct notions : and similarly as to time, that which answers to position in space, ' a point of time,' is quite distinct from the notion of interval or duration. This is important in regard of the relation of time and space the one to the other. It is in respect of the *points* that they may be said to *meet*. These, in the ἀπειρόκοσμος[1], or ' great universe ' not of being only, but of being with all its vicissitude and change—the universe of occurrence, of *history* in that objective sense in which we often use the word history, viz. for that which it is the business of history to set before us—are so to speak the latitude and longitude of a fact, the two coordinates which sufficiently fix it. In respect of these *points* then, time and space meet *in a fact*, in an immediateness. But if from this immediateness we begin to *reflect*, and conceive our point of time extended into a duration, and our point of space expanded into an amount or magnitude of it, we get into two different lines of thought, in fact, into two different worlds. Magnitude of space and duration of time are two notions in themselves heterogeneous and disparate, which unite nevertheless in a manner most difficult for us to realize in what we call the sameness or identity of a phenomenal thing, which I hope at a future time to speak of.

---

[1] Formed on the analogy of μικρόκοσμος &c.

The relation together of time and space in our consciousness is no less peculiar and difficult. They come out of immediateness into our reflectional view in a different way, or, we might say, from opposite directions. As they do this, space has the appearance to us of being the more objectively real and necessary, time of being the more intimate to us. If we could conceivably get *out of ourselves* for a moment, and look at immediateness as immediateness, it would involve space, but not necessarily time. If, on the other hand, we abolish altogether the supposition of what I have called immediateness, and consider, as is very constantly done, what we call 'our feeling' only, without any concomitant supposition of there existing a state of things, in which is involved reason for our feeling being what it is, and no other—then the passage of our feeling must necessarily have suggested to us *time,* though our feeling might have been such, that the notion of space or of things in space should never have entered into our heads. Time belongs to us independently of the world of which we are a part: space belongs to us as a part of it. Of course the making for a moment the supposition of time without space, and space without time, is tearing *our* reality asunder into two absurdities: I have done it merely to exhibit the relation between the two.

We begin to have the experience of time (to use the language which I have used before) in virtue of our beginning at all to reflect, or to be sentient of pleasure or pain, or to obey impulse. To say that the experience of time is our earliest experience, is of course little more than uttering a truism. Our experience of space comes later in the way that I have mentioned. Corresponding with this we may say with truth that our feeling is more essential to us than our spatial or phenomenal existence. Spatial or phenomenal is one of the things which, in growing reflexion, we find out we are: we could not have been otherwise than in time, we might have been otherwise than in space: space might not have been at all, and yet *we* might have been. Still when we speak of ourselves as real or existent, a large part of the significance which we give to those terms is due to our notion of space or phenomenalism, so that if space had not been, it is a very slight conception that we can form of what or how *we* could have been. But of this enough.

CHAPTER VII.

KNOWLEDGE OF ACQUAINTANCE AND KNOWLEDGE OF JUDGMENT.

I HAVE spoken on a former occasion[1] on the two different sets of words which there are, in a great many languages, to express what we call knowledge. And a few pages back I very slightly referred to this matter again.

In all philosophy, this division has been more or less recognized, and the two kinds of knowledge have been called, the one intuitive or immediate, the other mediate, conceptual, symbolic, representative, and by various other names. These terms have almost always involved special theories, and different views in regard to the nature, application, and limits, and also as to the mutual relations, of these two kinds of knowledge. I shall not dwell upon these differences here, but shall proceed to speak of the two kinds of knowledge, as they enter into the line of thought which I am now pursuing.

The first I call knowledge of acquaintance, using this expression for my own purposes, instead of the terms 'intuitive' or 'immediate,' for reasons which I have already partly given. This is knowledge which, to use a homely expression, would be immediate if it could, or in other language, is *as* immediate as is consistent with the recollection, that the subject is in a sort of contradictory position, that it is a part of the

---

[1] *Expl.* 60.

entire present fact and yet not a part of it. *Trueness* is the transference of fact into a different world or region, which we call *thought*: and *that* portion of thought is true, which is (or is the result of) such transference: our thought has trueness in it, to the extent to which it can be referred back to such a transference, and no further. Now, as I said before, there is no thoroughly immediate knowledge; because we mean by knowledge a portion of the thought of a special or individual intelligence (or of our consciousness, if we prefer the expression), and there is no *à priori* necessity or guarantee for this being a simple transference of the fact: not to say that it cannot be so, the whole fact comprehending our knowing as a portion of itself. Except so far as we have got this portion of the fact *into* the knowledge, the fact is not complete, and we cannot tell how far this uncomprehended portion may affect the *whole*, which is what we ought to have, to be sure of truth. This is hard to put in words, but not, I think, hard to *see*, and it is variously expressible. It is the principle, as it seems to me, of Mr Ferrier's[1] view of knowledge, that what we know is 'our knowledge of the object of knowledge.' That is to say, that we cannot get into distinct thought the object of knowledge separated from the fact of our knowing it. *Ourself* will get in the way. We *want* to have reality, as it would be if there were no such thing as thought or knowledge in the world, or if, having existed (if we suppose that necessary) for the production of the reality, they had then ceased and vanished. But yet we want the reality to present itself *to us*: *i.e.* we add our being to the reality, and *then* the reality without our being is no longer the complete or simple fact: its imprint is not immediate or trueness.

However, not to dwell upon what language can represent very inadequately, immediate or intuitive knowledge is not properly, and as we should *first* consider it (though we do with reason come *afterwards* so to look at it for convenience) the standing of *us*, the subject, face to face with the object, and a certain relation (that of knowledge) existing or arising between the two. What it expresses properly and first is the nearest

---

[1] See *Expl.* ch. iv.

point to which we can come towards that actual immediateness which is a supposition only, the supposition of fact, so to speak, *passing into* thought, of the same thing being at once fact and thought together. This does not differ from what I said before, viz. that immediate or intuitive knowledge is knowledge, with the smallest amount of reflection possible consistent with its being knowledge.

The word 'intuition' is in many respects about as bad a word as could have been chosen to express immediate knowledge, and in fact, it is almost the most confusing word in all philosophy. The looking *into* a thing implies a very high degree of attention and distinguishing, and is thus the mental process almost at the furthest remove from what 'intuition' is intended to mean. No doubt 'intuition' means also 'looking *on*' a thing, the metaphor simply taken from sight, and hence the Germans use 'anschauung' to correspond with it, but even this metaphor expresses very poorly that which we want to express, viz. that blending, so to speak, of ourselves and our being with the known, that intimate contact of it with us and of us with it, which is the groundwork of our confidence in 'intuition' as necessary trueness. Sight is a good sense to typify immediate knowledge, on account of its apparent freedom from gross or material intermediation (as much in the case of what is distant as of what is near), and also on account of the apparent absence of effort on our part in it. Our eyes are open, and in a moment there is in mental contact with us a vast and glorious infinitude. But we must not speak of sight in this manner except with wilful forgetfulness of the manner in which it is analysable, or else we shall be merely misled. We must not draw conclusions from our metaphor, or 'intuition' will have to be changed to 'betouchment' and even that will mislead us[1].

We have intuitive knowledge all along what I have called the scale of knowledge[2]. First (*i.e.* not in point of time, for all is contemporaneous, but simply first for mention, as most easily conceived) we have the lower or more sentient sensation, taste,

---

[1] *Expl.* 122.   [2] *Expl.* ch. vi.

smell, affectedness by colour, and more generally over the body, feeling of heat, titillation, &c. Second, we have the higher or unsentient sensations, the Kantian pure intuition, Dr Whewell's ideas, the notions of space and time. Last we have the highest or, not only unsentient, but super-corporeal, sensations or intuitions of unity, cause, &c. : but of these I will defer to speak till I have spoken of knowledge not intuitive.

Knowledge not intuitive is that which may most simply be called 'conceptive' or 'conceptual,' knowledge not *of* a thing, but *about* it. I have called it in another place[1] 'bi-objectal' knowledge, because there are two things before the mind in it, not one only : viz. that which the knowledge is about, the logical subject of it, and that which is known *about* it, the logical predicate or *proper* object of the knowledge.

This knowledge is distinguished from intuitive by having for its main element reflection instead of immediateness. Both the elements enter into either kind of knowledge—the distinction is in the respective amounts.

It is an error to suppose that, in point of time, intuition comes first, and then reflection. This is an error akin to that of those who consider the action of the senses an inferior kind of knowledge, and conception, or the superaddition of ideas, a higher kind. Knowledge begins when reflection begins, and no earlier, for in immediateness it is dormant. And reflection and intuition go on together : the latter goes on to the end, as the former had begun from the beginning. We might describe knowledge as an elaboration of immediateness by reflection, keeping in mind that without such elaboration the immediateness is not knowledge. On the other hand, it is not thought in general, but only such thought as *is* thus elaborated from immediateness which has in it trueness or is knowledge.

There is however a difference between the higher and lower intuitions in their relation to reflection : the former, though intuitions, and understood as having acted as intuitions, as soon as we come at all to present them to ourselves or to understand them ; yet, *for* this understanding, absorb, as we may say, more

---

[1] *Expl.* 119.

reflection. I shall have probably a little difficulty in making this clear, but I will just illustrate it preliminarily in the following manner.

There is, as I have already hinted, a good deal of confusion in the manner in which 'sensiveness' (or sensation) is spoken of as intuition or intuitive. This confusion arises from the wrong notion of it as a separate or inferior kind of knowledge. We may begin, if we like it, with supposing the mind a 'tabula rasa,' and describing how one idea after another takes its place upon it. So far as we do this, we are simply exhibiting as a series, for our convenience, what is in fact far otherwise: just as we might give a list, instead of a map, of the places in a country, or as we might exhibit in a linear order a botanical classification, which, if we wanted to exhibit the mutual relations of the orders, &c. in it, would have to be exhibited in quite a different manner. The intellectual order of things is not serial, or linear, or successional. We are plunged into the middle of things, we are in the middle of them to begin with. Advancing knowledge is a pattern coming out[1]: whether we consider this pattern to be in the mind or in objective nature does not in my view matter much, only we must not consider it partly in one and partly in the other.

The history of the human mind divides itself into two conceivable branches: the one the history of its reflection, the other, the history, so far as such is possible, of the state of things which its reflection gradually presents to it—the state of things of which it with its reflection forms a part. The history of the change of our mind from being a 'tabula rasa'

---

[1] The name 'Sedgwick' is added in the margin. The reference no doubt is to the eloquent passage in his *Discourse*, p. 53, 'If the mind be without innate knowledge, is it also to be considered as without innate feelings and capacities—a piece of blank paper, the mere passive recipient of impressions from without? The whole history of man shows this hypothesis to be an outrage on his moral nature. Naked he comes from his mother's womb; endowed with limbs and senses indeed, well fitted to the material world, yet powerless from want of use: and as for knowledge his soul is one unvaried blank; yet has this blank been already touched by a celestial hand, and when plunged in the colours which surround it, it takes not its tinge from accident, but design, and comes forth covered with a glorious pattern.'

to being a picture covered with ideas, is the history of our learning, and in this view there is no harm in thus describing the change. By 'learning' we mean the transition from want of knowledge to possession of it, and we may describe the mind wanting knowledge as the unfigured tablet, the mind possessing it as the figured one. But if we are to describe the process of our learning in a wider view of its relations than the view of its being change from non-possession of ideas to possession, we must view the matter differently. The history of our learning is then the history of our reflection: and the transition in our mind is not from nothing to fulness, but from confusion to distinctness. Immediateness is confusion or chaos, which reflection begins to crystallize or organize. And the intuitive knowledge which the senses present to us, begins not with one sensation, so proceeding to another, and adding on and on, but with a confusion of all sensations or all sensiveness: and in proportion as reflection begins to order this, there is knowledge. This primary confusion does not seem to me to deserve the Kantian name of 'experience,' for by 'experience' I understand something involving attention, order, succession. Still less does it deserve the name of sensible knowledge, knowledge of the sense. Intuitive knowledge is the knowledge *nearest* to this confusion, for be it remembered the confusion has the one great value of trueness or freedom from mistake. But such *unseparated* trueness is of little value; we are *possessed* by it, but cannot possess it or get hold of it to exhibit it even to ourselves, of course still less to others: it is the gradual process of reflection accompanied with continual *fresh* experience or new immediateness, which together constitute 'our learning,' that does this.

It seems to me in reference to the above, that both the Cartesian view of knowledge as distinctification, and the Lockeian view of it as aggregation, have their truth and have their error. Descartes' view, that the clearness and distinctness of ideas to us are an infallible evidence of their trueness, appears to me, so far as it is correct, to be the exhibition of an axiom or postulate more simply expressed thus: 'False ideas cannot present themselves clearly and distinctly'; which in the language which I have used would be, that our reflection, in its natural course, may be taken as a faithful exhibitor or interpreter of immediateness. The possible error arising from Descartes's view is, lest we should think that the clearness of its perception in any way *constitutes* the truth of the idea. Against the danger of this error Locke's view as to the aggregation of our knowledge is of advantage, in so far as it sets plainly before us the dependence of trueness on fact : while on the other hand, as I have just mentioned, it exhibits the historical or actual formation of our knowledge far less truly to the fact than the view of Descartes.

I use the word 'reflection' as the general word for the application of notice or attention to the state of things in which we are or find ourselves : it is not a very appropriate word, but probably no one word could be so. In the lower part of the scale of knowledge attention is *sentient* attention, *i.e.* attention to the feeling of pleasure or pain, as I have spoken of it. At every moment, from the first moment of the infant's consciousness, to the present moment with us, there is an indistinct variety of fact present to body, eyes, ears, nose, and we indistinctly know it to be present. Say that we give our attention to something presenting itself to what when understood we call the sense of smell, then there is sentient attention—the observation of the agreeableness or disagreeableness of an odour. Say we give our attention to its being what we understand or experience to be a *part* of us, our nose, where this odour is present and affects us: and say, that our attention being upon this part, the nose, we in our impulse to movement move our hand to it to touch it: we have then active or volitional sentience, that which, put in connexion with notice of what is before our eyes, is to us the dawning of the notion of space. Say we give more special attention to something before our eyes, a flower it may be, and put out our hand to take it and move it and bring it near to us, thereby markedly separating it from the rest that is before us, as all that is before us is separated from ourselves : then we have the dawning of the higher intuitions, as of unity or reality, to the distinctification of which the name of 'reflection' is more properly to be applied.

But to use one word, I have used the term 'reflection' for the application of attention all along the scale, and I do not think it will cause confusion.

Intuitional knowledge may be called 'presential,' reflectional knowledge 'absential': not but that in the latter the object *may* be present, but it need not be. I proceed to describe the manner of this latter or *absential* knowledge, and then the circumstances in our state of things which render it possible or facilitate it for us, after the analogy of the manner in which the sensive organs of our body render possible or facilitate to us intuition.

CHAPTER VIII.

CONCEPTION.

WE must now, after a fashion not uncommon with Aristotle, take a new point of departure.

Reflection is the application to immediateness of a particular portion of our activity, which we will call thought, the thinking power, cogitativeness. 'Thought' I shall commonly call it. I began previously with immediateness because that is the source of 'trueness.' Thought as such is neither true nor false. It may be either.

Immediateness or intuition is also what is fitly considered first, because it is the source of mental picturing, which is what I shall just now mean when I use the term *imagination*. The words picturing and imagination have both of them reference to the eye, but I mean the *notion* to have reference to the whole of sensiveness, to the mind's ear, the mind's palate, &c., as well as the mind's eye. When we seem to see a beautiful prospect, when we think of a favourite air, or when our palate is affected by the remembrance of the taste of anything we like, I use, now, the term imagination.

This imagination is a quasi-sensation or quasi-intuition. The bodily organization is to some degree at least affected in concurrence with it: so far as this is so, it is, as *we* are concerned with it, as much sensation or intuition as what we ordinarily call so, and we require, to distinguish it from such, the ordinary preservatives against illusion, of which I shall speak another time. Intuition, then, has got this shadow of it, this atmosphere or penumbra about it, which we call 'imagination.'

Intuitions or sensations, dwelling in the mind or recurring, are imaginations.

Now we seem to ourselves to understand what perception (this is perhaps a better term than intuition or sensation—all, in the *present* use, mean the same) and imagination are. That is, when we think of either of the notions, there occurs to us a (probably visual) picture : and if it is the notion of 'perception' we are upon, we think of the objects of this picture as before us ; if it is imagination, we think *still* of the objects of the picture, but of something else as *before us*, not they.

But what is our knowledge *as a whole*? for perception, and imagination (supposing this latter true and justified) constitute but a small part of it. What is that thought which is *not* imagination, and of which *the right* portion constitutes the bulk of knowledge ? What is thinking itself ? What do we do when we think ?

We may try to answer this question either by reference to philosophical literature, or by endeavouring to observe what takes place in our own mind.

It is to be supposed that what we find in the former arises from others before us having tried to do the latter, for it is only on supposition of this being so that it can have value. The different theories of logic, in this point of view, are so many results of people's intellectual self-examination, or examination of the value of self-examination, for they may have considered it to have none. I do not want to dwell long on this, but shall just roughly divide philosophical theories on the subject into (1) theories of thought as 'adstance,' (2) theories of thought as 'talk,' and (3) theories of thought as 'conception,' explaining as I go on what I mean by each.

I have pretty well explained on a former occasion[1] what I mean by 'adstance.' It is not perhaps quite correct language to speak of *thought* as adstance, for a theory of adstance is an effort to consider knowledge, as much as possible, without entering into the questions, so perplexing, of the nature of thought. By a view of knowledge as adstance I mean what

---

[1] *Expl.* 157.

some will best perhaps understand by its being called a straight-forward realization of everything.   Mr Mill's is such a view: I have dwelt upon it previously, and will just describe it summarily thus: Everything we want to know or can know is in nature before us: we are spectators only : thinking is *doing* nothing, but being present at nature, or, if we like better to say it, having nature present to us (I employ in this particular application the coined word 'adstant,' merely on account of the various use, and consequent ambiguity, of the term 'present'), or at best thinking (to purpose) is looking as deep as we can *into* nature and as thoroughly as we can *over* it; only that in saying this we must not mean by *looking* anything hard to be understood or requiring examination.

This is in many respects the same view which I have given, where I have spoken of the dependence of truth on immediateness.   But it is a view which is more summary and simple than mine, and which, on the other hand, gives as the whole problem what is in no respect the whole of it.   It brings immediateness by one summary effort out of its original indistinctness into distinctness : but in so doing it spoils the trueness which it values.   What we want to know is at first *between* us and nature, common ground to both, and we mentally construct what we then call nature by making order out of this indistinction.   When we say that we are present to the universe or it to us, that we ought to be a looking-glass to it, there is very much reason in this, but the immediateness here spoken of is what I have called an abstraction.   'We see things' is an ultimate and primary immediateness for ·the work of life or practice : things, as seen, are then the matter of consequence, and the seeing them is of no further consequence than as the proof that they exist.   But this will not do for speculation.

However I will say no more about 'adstance' just now, and will not speak about thought as *talk* (the philosophic 'nominalism') because I think that anything which I have to say about this will be more intelligible afterwards.

Let us say that thought is conception, and ask ourselves what is conception ?

I will first speak about the meaning of conception, then

about the manner of it, then about the objects of it, then about the progress of it.

To begin with the meaning, which however will more fully appear as we go on : to conceive anything is to begin[1] to have a thought or feeling, for which thought or feeling, (or in connexion with it) we use the name expressing what we are said to conceive. 'To conceive a lion,' is to begin to have the thought in connexion with which we use the name 'lion.' But what sort of thing is this thought?

Here we come to the *manner* of conception. But it is to be observed that we have already begun to speak of one thing which, before proceeding with the manner of conception, I must speak of more fully : this is 'language,' or to go rather deeper than language, society, and what I will call 'co-intelligence.'

The state of things in which we find ourselves has an element in it different from anything that is in the individual immediateness of which I spoke before. This element is 'society,' or our being associated with other beings like ourselves, other intelligences.

There is nothing, in my view, which contributes more to what I should call the unreality and inapplicability of much of the 'Philosophy of the Human Mind,' than its non-attention to the *fundamentalness*, in regard of our intelligence, of society and mutual communication, and the wrong views of language which go with this non-attention.

Were we solitary beings in the universe, *immediateness* would be in its nature the same. We should or we might have our eyes and ears open, and fact and we would meet each other as well in solitude as in company. Nor would there, perhaps, be wanting some impulses to reflection, or to the vivifying, by our intelligence, of this meeting of us and fact. But the *great* impulse to reflection would be wanting, namely the impulse to communication. Intelligence is really *co-intelligence*. I have described reflection, or active and living intelligence, as beginning with the double process of self-consciousness and perception, each setting off the other. As

[1] Cf. above p. 28.

self-consciousness is *self-wards* or concentrated, so perception is *self-from-wards* or expansive, and it is this *doubly*, which is the important point to observe; we generalize in it not only the object of knowledge, but the subject. We come not only to know something widely expanding beyond ourselves, but to know it with a knowledge felt as something more than individual, something not limited to ourselves. In fact we have here *another* of our primary experiences, which places us not only in an universe of things to be known, but in an universe of *fellow-knowers*. The universe of what is to be known surrounds not only *us*, but a number of intelligences like us: and our *knowing* has the second character of being not only a mirroring of the universe or of fact, but of being a sympathy with other intelligences. There is a large portion of our thought, in regard of which its being individual or peculiar to ourselves is its being wrong: and thus we arrive at a second criterion of trueness, besides the derivation from individual immediateness. Thought, if it is to be true, must be not only derived from fact, but must satisfy, or be good thought for, other intelligences as well as our own.

This principle, as we come to understand thought, we consider to be true in the highest generality, when we talk of intelligences in the plural or of particular intelligences: and it is upon *this* principle that those philosophers have gone, who have considered truth to be the coincidence of our thought with the thought of God, or its obedience to it, or in some similar manner. Less generally than this, one manner of our waking to phenomenalism, or to the actual universe in which we live, is our finding ourselves in the society of other intelligences, and impelled to communication with them; so that our thought, which might otherwise have rested in the inertia or inactivity of immediateness, is impelled to shape itself into what we may call a transferable shape, and to take a guise which can meet the thought of others.

Thought and trueness would have been different for us from what they are, in a manner to us inconceivable, if we had been the solitary intelligences in the universe: *our* thought would have been different from what it is, in a manner scarcely more conceivable, if men had been dumb or deaf. As it is, it may be said that the whole mass of human thought and language, which, in regard of the trueness derivable from *individual* immediateness, rests upon sight corrected by touch and movement—I use this as a short expression, having dwelt upon the subject at length in another place[1]—rests, in regard of the trueness derivable from co-intelligence, upon the tongue and ear, *i.e.* upon the double capacity, or two corresponding capacities, of the creation of an universe of sound (corresponding to the universe of perception as this latter is thought) and of the perception of this second or representative universe by the ear. Significant sound of this kind, is, if I may use the expression, a second picturing or representation of fact, *following* (in regard of truth of immediateness) the visual picturing or imagination, and with the vast advantage of being so essentially different from this as not to be possibly confounded with it: but having also the advantage, which the visual imagination has not, of ready transference from mind to mind, of being thus the organ or instrument of co-intelligence, and what makes possible the trueness which depends upon *this*.

In the phenomenalist existence then, in which we find ourselves, and as a fact *of it*, conception is as closely connected with the tongue and ear, or with language, as imagination is with sight. It is a part of our nature, as beings possessed of sight, that we represent the immediateness of fact to us visually so far as we can: it is a part of our nature, as beings having what we now call language, that we represent that portion of fact which is not capable of visual representation, by means of *language*—as I should call it, by *noëm* and *phone*[2]—and that we are able thus to apply to it that notion of trueness which belongs to mutual communication.

This man-made universe, or rather these universes, of significant sound (for every separate language is a separate universe, to the extent which I shall in a moment describe) are

---

[1] *Expl.* 39 foll.

[2] That is, by signification and sound. These terms are explained in the author's Treatise on *Glossology*, of which the earlier chapters are printed in the *Journal of Philology*, nos. 7, 8, 10.

something without which we could not think to any purpose :
and they are something which we should not and could not
construct, unless we were beings of society, *i.e.* both living in
it, and with inward and outward organization *for* living in
it. A language is a picture of the universe which has two
characters, one of which resembles, and the other does not
resemble, the visual picture of the universe which we carry
about each one more or less in our imagination, and which
in fact *is* our universe. A language is composed of sounds, and
these, *as sounds*, are, except a small and particular portion of
them, arbitrary : there is no occasion why they, rather than
other sounds, should represent what they do represent. As
sound therefore, speaking generally, the universe of words is an
entirely arbitrary representation of the universe of fact or
reality. Berkeley considered the universe of sight and visual
imagination to be a similar arbitrary representation : I have
stated above why I dissent from him, and why I consider the
universe of language and the universe of sight to be not
kindred manners of representation. But there is another
character of language in which it is in a certain, though partial,
degree akin to the visual picture, which is the point of
consequence to us now about it. If two people are talking
together, commenting, we will say, on what we call a prospect
before them, we may be certain that there is to *some* extent
co-intelligence : to *what* extent is not of consequence : we are
certain that *upon the whole* the visual picture before the one
is the same as that before the other. Suppose them now
talking without any prospect before them, or any thought of
one, but we will say on some abstract subject : and let us
suppose them talking one in one language and the other in
another. If I, understanding French to the extent to which I
do, were talking with a Frenchman who understood English to
the same extent, it might be the most convenient proceeding
for each to talk his own language, and there might be the most
perfect co-intelligence or mutual understanding. Now what is
the vehicle or instrument of this mutual understanding ? In
what does the co-intelligence consist ? What is it that is in
common to the two minds, that is in one as well as in the

other, for 'mutual' or 'common' understanding (we may call it either or both) to have any significance? In the former case, it was the visual picture: here, if we were talking the same language, it might possibly be the sound, a community of ear-picture like the former community of eye-picture. But in the case supposed there is no such single picture: we have each before our mind, so to speak, a double ear-picture, two corresponding portions of two-sound-universes: and these must correspond, or be *one* piece of thought to us, which they are, in virtue of something beyond the sound: there are two sounds going to *one*—what are we to call it?

It is in fact the 'meaning,' and the second character of words is, I will not say *to have* meanings (unless I am prepared on the other hand to talk of them as having sounds) but *to be* meanings as well as sounds. The word is thought as well as spoken: as thought, it is meaning, just as spoken, it is sound. And words, as meanings, *are* akin to the visual picture, though, as sounds, they are not. That is, their connexion, as meanings, with the reality or fact which corresponds with them, is not arbitrary, in the manner in which their connexion with it, as sounds, is.

It seems to me that all those, from the scholastic Nominalists, and even from Plato in the *Cratylus*, down to Mr Mill, who have discussed words and names and their relation to thought, have not quite sufficiently set before them what they meant by the language they used. For there is still a third character of words, which I may as well at once mention, because, though subsidiary to the other two, which are essential, it is still very important. This is the word as written or printed.

In the greater portion of human language writing is simply a sign, or conventional exhibition to sight, of the word as sounded, or, more correctly, of the several sounds, in combination, which are elements of this. But though thus the written word is, for the largest portion of language, the word only at second-hand, I am inclined to think, from the language of most nominalists and those in general who have treated, in application to philosophy, of names of things, that *this* is what has been uppermost in their thoughts. And there is very considerable reason, in the way which we shall see shortly, why it should be. When words are considered, in regard of our use of them in thought, to have a resemblance to algebraic signs, it seems clear that it is *this*, the written word, which is intended: and in general there is a probability that it is so, when words are spoken of as *signs* of things.

The question before us now is, What is the mental object of that portion of thought which is not imaginational or visually pictorial: what is that we have in our minds when we say we are thinking of something, and yet, from the nature of the thing, it is something which we cannot picture to ourselves? This is the same as the question given before in this form, ' What do we *do* when we think? what goes on in us? what *is* thinking, so far as it is distinct from mind-painting?'

This again is the same as the question, What is a word, as ' meaning'? The word as 'sound' is the result of our will moving the tongue and producing an effect which extends to another's ear: this sound, again, may have reference to certain things which we see, and he sees also, to our common visual picture at the time: but the word, as 'meaning,' is or ought to be something distinct and definite, in regard of which it is not enough to tell us what it is about, or that sound is the means of communicating it: what is the meaning of meaning?

But though I have thus recalled to our remembrance the question before us that we may not forget it, there is still something else to be considered in connexion with it before we can fairly meet *itself*.

It will be remembered that I have from time to time referred to what I have called the 'higher intuitions.' By these I mean simply those which would come in the higher or highest portion of what I have called the scale of sensation or knowledge.

There are two great intuitions in this part of the scale, which, for importance, bear a sort of analogy to time and space below them: these are what I will call 'unity' and 'genericity[1].' By the word 'intuition' I mean here simply the dawn

---

[1] *Expl.* 106.

of immediateness towards reflection and distinctness: unity and
genericity awake in us, as existing portions of fact coming to
our notice, just as smell and colour do, or as time and space.
I do not use the term for the purpose of making any assertion,
which is not to be questioned, about them; for though, or
rather because, I consider intuition *the ground* of all knowledge,
I have disclaimed the language 'intuitive knowledge' as it is
often used; we must plead something *besides* intuition on
behalf of everything that we assert to be knowledge. Intuition
may suggest the line of thought: we may be satisfied from
intuition that there is something there to be known, some
trueness: yet the giving to anything that distinctness and
clearness which is necessary to make it knowledge, the singling
out and particularizing the notions which go to the knowledge
—all this is no part of intuition, but of elaborate reflection
digesting it. And so, in calling 'unity' and 'genericity' intuitions, I do not in the least mean to assert 'These are exactly
the notions which exist, and they certainly do exist, I know it
by intuition.' All that I assert is that we do think of things as
units or individuals, and again as belonging to kinds or species.
This is a fact as undoubted as that we smell or taste them:
and since immediateness or intuition is, in my view, the basis
of all truth or fact, anything which is added afterwards beyond
attention or notice, being *not* true, *not* fact;—it follows that
there must be *something* in immediateness or immediate fact
which answers to this our thinking of things in units and
genera. This something, whatever it is, is what I mean by the
intuitions of unity and genericity.

These higher intuitions are, indeed, as I have noticed,
rather more difficult to deal with than the lower ones, because
reflection plays a more *apparently* important part in regard to
them. We make our philosophical speculation with our
developed intelligence, that is, with our attention giving itself
to our sensive perception of the phenomenal universe so
naturally and habitually, that we are scarcely aware any
attention is given at all, or that, in all this which seems so
concrete and immediate, there is anything abstract and reflectional. The notions of unity and genericity become absorbed,

so to call it, in our sensiveness: and when we say, I smell
a rose, we call it a simple intuition or sensation of smell, without considering that our words have no significance except
so far as, concurrently with our smelling, we isolate a certain
red thing in our thoughts from the rest of the visual picture
before our imagination, and think of this red thing in some way
beyond imagination, the way which we have now got to find
out, which is the meaning of calling it generically a rose. Owing
to this absorption of unity and genericity in sensiveness, we seem
to have to make more use of reflection and attention in regard
of them than we have in regard of those lower intuitions. And
hence it has been thought by many philosophers that we
actually do this, and that unity and genericity, with other
notions of a like kind, are something added by the mind,
expressly and volitionally, to the simple sensiveness,—that they
are thoughts of the understanding applied to experience. This
will be recognized as a portion of that which I throughout
protest against, the division of knowledge between nature and
us. To me, the unity and genericity of a rose are qualities of
itself as much as its smell: or if we use the reverse language,
its smell is as much a feeling or thought of ours about it as its
unity or genericity.

Whatever is true, exists, germinally at least, in immediateness, and is noticed or brought out to be knowledge by volitional
reflection. Owing to what I have just mentioned, the higher
intuitions, as I call them, take more reflection to themselves to
bring them out and distinctify them: but they are intuitions.

The intuition of unity is, I think, associated with our
self-consciousness, and is an application to perception of so
much of that as is capable of such application. It is a projection of ourselves upon portions of the universe in which we
find ourselves[1]. Why do we break up this universe, which, as
a matter simply of sentience and measurement, is one continuous complicated whole before us, into separate, mutually
isolated things? It is *here* that the language of the wrong
psychology, on which I have at various times commented, has

---

[1] *Expl.* 48 foll.

been so fatal to all sound thought. I have described elsewhere what is the real state of *fact* which is described in such misleading language as 'The thing, of course, is clear to everybody—why, the tree makes an impression on our eye—a stone lies before me, of course I see it.' But while blaming the mis-psychological language, I am desirous to admit its truth to *fact* in *one* point of view, *i.e.* as against those who would split up our knowledge, as though it consisted in the addition of something from the mind to something given by the sense. 'The tree makes an impression upon *us*,' if anyone likes to use that language : and the language, 'the tree makes an impression on the eye' is nearer perhaps to this than such language as, 'the eye as sense sees the tree, and the mind tells us what it is.' In the complicated whole at any moment before us, there is reason (whatever that reason at the particular time may be) why a portion should isolate itself from the rest and present itself to us, as, we will say, a *tree*. If it does so, it presents itself to us in all its characters together, as *one*, as of the kind 'tree,' as of such and such a shape and magnitude, as of such and such a colour, in a manner corresponding to the whole scale of our intuitions. It presents itself to the whole of us, to our *intelligence*, of which one character is to be sensive, not *to our eye* with any significance in the expression, since all sorts of things besides the tree are printed on the retina, if *that* is what the eye is to mean here. The *point* here against the mis-psychology is, that the philosophical fact on which all rests—the immediateness, as I call it—is not the existence of the tree (which is what the perception, to suppose any meaning in the expression, must be considered first to suggest to us, and which it is therefore absurd to describe beforehand as the cause of the perception), but what I have vaguely described (for of course it can be described in no other manner) as, there being reason, under the particular circumstances at that moment, why there should be to us this particular presentation, which we describe as the tree making an impression upon us.

That which is thus vaguely described as 'there being reason why the thing should be as it is,' which is what I mean by the immediateness, is described, in the expression above, from the objective side: it might be equally well described from the other: we might say 'I see the tree' just as significantly as 'the tree makes an impression on me.' As to the relation between *ourself* and our sensive organs, we must proceed exactly in the same way from this side as from the other. If we talk of the eye seeing, we must talk, with such significance as we may, of its seeing *light, colours,* &c.: it is *we*, by means of the eye, that see the tree, and see it, just as we did from the opposite side, as *one*, as of a kind, as of such and such a shape, as of such and such a colour. Its unity and genericity are intuitions, just as its shape and colour are.

When I have said, as I have said all along, that it is reflection that distinctifies or, as I might have said, isolates and unifies, it might have been more correct to say that the prime operation and act of attention is to notice—we must not say the distinctions, and unities, which exist in immediateness, for no such do exist, but—the reason which exists for them, the germ of them. Otherwise reflection would be adding something new to immediateness, and if it did, this which is added would be false, not true to fact. We must not consider this thinking by us of things as units and in kinds, a way of thinking of ours about the universe, which in that case must be supposed, as universe, independent of this way of thinking. The reason why we think in this way may be in ourselves, if so we like to express ourselves (for I think that this comes only to a matter of expression); but if so, the reason of *all* our thought and knowledge is in ourselves, for there is no principle upon which we can go in dividing it. Or on the other hand the reason for all our thought (this amongst it) being what it is, may be in the object, if we use such language. I do not judge this matter either way, because I do not think we can go further than what I have called immediateness, viz. the existence of fact, which is the reason for *that* taking place which we find to take place. I do not think there is meaning in discussing whether this fact or reason is in ourselves or out of ourselves: it is previous to the consideration of either. It is this fact or reason which suggests to us the distinction between ourselves and what is not ourselves: ourselves and what is not ourselves, so far as they are to be thought of in connexion with it, are blended together in it.

It does not seem to me that the notion of unity can be described, any more than those of time and space. If we are to try to do so, I should describe it as 'reason for distinction.'

Distinction, as I have said, is what reflection makes: *i.e.* it notices (or we notice in it) the intuition, 'reason for distinction,' and distinguishes accordingly. The first great objective unity is the universe itself, distinguished off from ourselves. Putting it the other way, we might say, 'The first thing which'—how shall we describe it?—'is ready to present itself so far as there is any intelligence for it to present itself to,' as a part of the primary fact or immediateness, is *thought* on our part, with something not ourselves for the object of it. In the course of those our first experiences, the universe, or a part of it, becomes distinctified to us as phenomenal or spatial, and as a unity in *this* respect, that we come to think of it as a vast local and (what we call) corporeal system, of which we are ourselves a portion. It is the supposition of there being reason in fact for our thinking thus, which makes us describe our thinking thus as experience, something we *find*, not imagination, something we *dream*. When we come to philosophize, we may speculate about these our early experiences in various ways: as whether our reflection really interprets rightly the reason for them or basis of them, supposing that there is such. The error of Sir W. Hamilton and the Natural Realists seems to me to be the exhibiting as the fact which gives or has given reason for our thought, that which our developed thought apparently presents to us as the universe: this is in fact part of the general mis-psychological error. I say '*apparently* presents,' because if we are to come to describe in notions and words *how* the universe as a whole presents itself to us,—what we mean, or what men in general mean, by its existence and its reality,— we find that we can no more do so than we can describe the original supposed fact, which gives reason of our thought to the philosopher who is not a Natural Realist. The reason of this however will come more fitly another time.

On the distinctification from ourselves of the spatial universe follows the distinctification of the various things which, like ourselves, are recognized as in it: and it is because they are recognized as being, *as in it*, like ourselves, that the distinctification of them is in various ways connected with self-consciousness. The distinctification of them is the higher portion of perception, as sensiveness is the lower. But this distinctification, as taking place in perception, is connected constantly with another notion, different from what I have as yet called 'unity,' though closely related with it. And I will leave 'unity' now in hope to return to it in detail.

'Genericity,' or the existence of things in kinds, is the companion notion to 'unity,' much after the analogy of time and space.

Unless there were *particular*, or as, in reference to kinds, it is to be called, *individual* unity, there would be no meaning in speaking of kinds of things: unless there were generic unity, there would be no meaning in speaking of *things*: for by things we mean things according to kinds.

As we start from immediateness and apply to it reflection, we have first particular or individual unity and then generic unity or genericity. But as we start from reflection or notice and apply it to immediateness or fact, we have first generic unity, or *a thing*, next particular unity, or *this particular thing*.

Putting for a moment, and for the better understanding, a sort of exaggerated or caricatured significance into the notions 'pure or bare perception or understanding,' 'the part of the mind in thought,' 'ideas as distinguished from sense,' we may call it or them the anticipations by the mind of its after knowledge, of that knowledge which it has when it comes to experience. What I have said as to reflection may be similarly distorted or exaggerated for a temporary purpose. Generic unity, I said, if we start from the point of view of reflection, is anterior to particular. Experience is by the nature of it particular: the generality of our ideas, which corresponds to the genericity of things, comes with reflection. How is this?

Speaking roughly, we think of portions of the universe in a *general* manner, which is the same thing as viewing them as generic or as things, on account of the impulse to communicate with other minds about them—in fact to talk of them.

This is the first suggestion of genericity in things, which prepares the way for other more definite suggestions afterwards. It is also consistent with a process of learning the distinction between genericity and individuality, which I shall shortly speak of. All I mean here is, that there is a rapid impulse to associate with sound any object of perception, for the purpose of having a mutual or common intelligence, a communication, on the occasion of it, with any other intelligence locally present: this is surely the way in which the mind of infants begins to work. The perceived object therefore at once acquires a second existence before the mind in the sound: and this doubleness of its existence renders much possible in the mind about it which would not be so otherwise.

The *first* existence however of the object before the mind, is neither generic nor individual, but 'singular' or 'proper' in so far as we do not mean by 'proper' something distinguished from general. Soon this 'singularness' is divided into genericity and individuality, and the point of importance is, that it is the existence of the object of thought as something mentally graspable by means of the sound, which renders this division possible.

The sound then comes to represent the object as generic, and is, in fact, the fixed standing ground, the firm holding point, which the mind has in reference to the object in this view.

But then, in the same way as under the unity of the universe comes the distinguishment of things altogether, so under the generic unity of things comes the distinguishment of individuals. And as, sensively, everything is particular, so, reflectionally, everything is generic. Designating the kind, or generic unity, by the sound, we have to add something to this, some other sound, for individual distinguishment. The generic unity, however, is still what makes the thing: this, with the distinguishment, is the thing as it can be perceived: the particular. This is merely 'substantive and adjective': logically, 'substance and attribute.'

To sum up *for the present* what this is all coming to : the question is, ' How, in what manner, do we think ? ' 'think' referring here to that part of our thought which is not pictorial imagination.

The answer is, by three processes united : and I believe it to be an accident of individual minds whether one of the three is more operative than the others : nor would I say but that there might be other processes subsidiary, for I have no faith in numbers in philosophy. The processes are, (1) Imagination of sounds, *i.e.* of the sounded word, which in people who read and think much is probably a good deal superseded by quasi-visual imagination of the word as printed : (2) Pictorial imagination subsidiary, or as it were circumvolitant, presenting to the mind types, examples, or illustrations, and very frequently one special, almost permanent type : (3) Thought, again (like the thought of the whole as I am describing it, but somewhat irregular, like the last-mentioned operation of imagination), of the attributes that distinguish the generic unity (which is the object of thought) from other generic unities, or which constitute its qualities and make up what is called its definition. Every generic unity has the character of being a quasi-individual, or what logicians call a species, relative to other generic unities more wide than itself : and has its own distinguishments therefore or qualities, as the individuals under it have theirs.

The last of the three processes which I have described is the most important, and may be said to constitute the essence or reality of thought, the other two being only subsidiary. But it will be observed, that in speaking of it, in an attempt to *describe* thought, I could call this by no other name than thought, and *it* would have to be described again by means of imagination verbal and visual, like the whole. So that it comes to this, that if we are asking what is in the mind, we seem not able to get beyond its being this imagination, the *thought* being, in a manner, a sort of *using* it.

Roughly, this third process may be said to express the object of the thought-word : the two former, the manner of the thinking it.

The thought-word, or meaning of the word, is that to which most correctly belongs the expression 'concept,' 'notion,' 'idea,' as Locke uses this latter.   In speaking of *words* here of course I am speaking of what we should call *general* words as distinguished from proper names.

There is the word as imagined and thought, and also the 'thing' as imagined and thought.   The word is imagined or mind-painted variously, the thing more variously still.   The *thought-word* and the *thought-thing* are the same, and are what is called the 'concept.'   The thing in question is thought, by regulated imagination of what I have described as its attributes or qualities: and the thing is *subjected to thought* (so to speak) by means of a supposition of it as independent of its attributes, that is, not as without them, nor yet as with them, but as, for a moment, without consideration of them—this supposition is the substantial thing, or thing as substance.   Corresponding with the substance and attribute of thought is the subject and predicate of word: and after the analogy of language which I have just used, 'substance' is the thought-subject of our thought, 'attribute' a thought-predicate of this subject.   These attributes or predicates stand in various relations to the substance or subject, and I do not think that philosophical language has ever been very strict in its manner of speaking of them.   The important distinction of them is into those which are necessary to, or always present with, the substance or subject, and those which are contingent or only possibly present: the former make up the 'definition.'

I hope another time . to speak at more length about 'substance' and 'attribute,' and will now leave this subject with the following summary.

Knowledge is the application of reflection to immediateness, or, in rougher and simpler language, of notice to fact. Knowledge may be called generally notice of fact, or fact presenting itself to our notice, but it must not be divided, and called *at once* both, fact presenting itself to our notice, *and* notice on our part of it, because these things are the same in different words: the division of the whole into *experience* or felt fact as an inferior knowledge, on the one side, and on the other side, pure or bare notice with certain objects of knowledge peculiar to it, which it applies to the above experience, is fallacious.

Still, as I have said, and as I hope to illustrate more at length, knowledge is the application of notice to fact, and we may speak of notice and fact separately, though we must not, as above, divide knowledge between them, nor, according to what I have called the wrong psychology, in investigating the process of notice, assume *beforehand* fact, as it is to us *after* our notice of it is complete.

One way therefore in which we notice the universe in which we find ourselves, as we do, is in virtue of our impulse to communication, which is the mental source of the formation of concepts, and this formation of concepts is in fact a viewing of reality as composed of substances with their attributes, a way of viewing it corresponding to, and yet differing from, the viewing it as composed of particular things in their kinds.

In saying that we notice what we find ourselves in, as we do, I do not intend these for two independent things, which would be the error that I protest against. It is the noticing *as we do* what we find ourselves in, which makes us consider that this *is* what we find ourselves in. And the *finding ourselves in* whatever it is, is in fact the noticing it. Only, as we look at knowledge from the one side or the other, it presents itself differently to us, and to understand it, we must look at it from both. Thus, by substance and attribute is specially the way in which we *conceive* things, and by subject and predicate the way in which we *speak* of them. This way of conceiving is neither discordant from the fact, nor is it to be considered in such a way giving us the fact, that we are bound, so to speak, to find a separate reality for 'substance' and for 'attribute.' It is the doing of *this* which produces the notion of 'things in themselves,' things, by their very nature as things, beyond our knowledge.

Both our noticing things as we do and things being what they are for us to notice are parts or outgrowths of the *one* immediateness or general fact, out of which we and the universe awake to understand and be understood.

The way in which we think about things and the way in which things present themselves to us are two *views* of knowledge : and they (1) must not be considered as two things, nor (2) be confused together when we speak of knowledge, or be applied the one to correct the other.

The former is the proceeding (erroneous as I think) of Kant and Dr Whewell and other distinguished philosophers. The latter is that of Mr Mill, where he describes the universe as made up of substances and their attributes.

BOOK III.

WHAT IS MATERIALISM?

CHAPTER I.

LIMITATIONS OF MATERIALISM. PSYCHICAL ANATOMY CANNOT EXPLAIN OUR MENTAL EXPERIENCE.

THE word 'progress' may be said to have a triple meaning. It is progress as 'course,' or progress as 'improvement,' or progress as 'advance.'

The 'course' of philosophy, as the history of man goes on, is 'improvement,' but is not necessarily 'advance.' By which I mean, that, while the course of physical science is improvement and this improvement is advance (*i.e.* our cyclopædia of actual knowledge in it increases every day in bulk, and we can distinctly mark each step), it is not so in philosophy : we may understand philosophy better than the ancients did without knowing *more* about it : perhaps even seeming to know less.

There exists in modern times one great branch of physical science which scarcely existed at all among the ancients, but which now enlarges its dimensions, and increases its discoveries, every day. This is the application of anatomy to psychology, psychical or psychologic anatomy, physiopsychology or psychophysiology, if we take care of the meaning which we give to this latter expression. This claims to take the place of philosophy as hitherto treated, on the double ground of this latter having been non-advancing, which, according to a manner of thought usual with us now, is taken for the same as wrong or false, and also (a view considered in close connexion with the other) of its dealing with notions and unrealities, whereas the psychical anatomy deals with facts.

In order for philosophy to hold its ground it is necessary, in regard of the former of these views, that it should either show itself advancing, or else show that *its* improvement does not necessarily involve advance: and in regard of the latter of the views, it should be prepared to question the claim of the psychical anatomy to be the sole domain of *fact* in regard to thought and knowledge, it should be able to make good a *higher* notion of *fact*.

It is one of the principles upon which I have wished to go from the first that, whatever the psychical anatomy can make out upon its own proper scientific method, is to be, not grudgingly admitted, but cordially welcomed, as what must really help philosophy, so far as philosophy is the pursuit of truth. I regard the jealousy felt of researches in this direction on the ground of their supposed leading to what is called 'materialism,' as a very great misfortune. Such a feeling justifies the counter-feeling on the part of those who make the researches, that the road they *are* pursuing leads to something which, as a matter of course, must be looked upon by a large number of people as something to be accepted indeed—for we can do no better—but a something disheartening, cutting off hope, inconsistent with ideals and aspiration, browbeating our self-complacency, and reducing us to our true place in existence from a vague imagination of a higher. All this, on one side and the other, seems to me something quite beside science and philosophy. Vain dread on the one side and vain pretension on the other here aggravate each other.

I may as well preface what I am upon now by saying in general, that wherever, whether on the side of religion, or on a side more or less opposed to it, I meet with a doctrine, one of whose principles is the browbeating and humiliation of any part of our intelligence, I look upon it as being so far wrong. I look upon both religion and truth (to speak of them for the moment as different) as elevators of our thought: and when I am told in respect of anything professing to be the one or the other, 'It is hard, but this is something to which you must bow and subject your intelligence,' 'It is hard, but this is something to which you must depress your imaginations and limit your hopes,'—I feel, if I do not say, that I *believe* in my intelligence, my imaginations, and my hopes, and require whoever claims thus to invalidate them to show a very definite warrant for it. When I am bid to accept, as I am most ready to do, the information which an apparently well-grounded revelation gives me, I say, ' I can only accept this in the same way in which I would accept *any* information or testimony about anything, viz., on the basis of my having an intelligence prepared for it, of my having certain ideas and notions already upon that which the information concerns, or else I can make nothing of it: the information may perhaps put an end to some speculations which, after it, I find to be vain, but its character as a whole must be an enlarging and supplement of my knowledge, not an overthrowing it, and though I *partially* submit my intelligence, I in a much greater degree find it expanded and elevated.'

My feeling seems to me to be the same, with a different application, when I read what is said by many professing materialists. It is all very well, they will tell us, to imagine or to hope : but truth exists not for *us:* that we should like a thing to be so and so, is no reason for supposing that it *is* so : there may be human, generic imaginations, about a spiritual world, about a future life, and much besides, and yet all this may be illusion only, and if we find out the truth to be otherwise, we must confess it *is* only illusion, and must acquiesce in our lot.

Supposing this professing materialist to have followed, as he very likely will have done, what I have called above the proper scientific method of psychical anatomy, I allow fully that, in that to which he calls upon me to submit my imaginations and hopes, there is much of truth. But what I want to be certain of is, how far the truth which he brings me is *all* the truth which there is about the matter. It is very likely that to *him* it will appear so : it is what he has most likely spent his life in investigating, and the study of which has formed his mind : so much the more is what he brings likely to be truth within its range. But I am not so ready, as he would have me, to allow that my imaginations and hopes have nothing to do with truth.

They are facts : they seem to me to mean something, to betoken something : it may be hard to tell what : but then I ask myself, whether the line of thought of this physiologist has been such as to make him a good judge about them, and to warrant him thus summarily to tell me that they mean nothing, and are worth nothing.   To know the mutual inconsistency or contradictoriness of two kinds of truth, we must have a knowledge not only from the one side, but from the other.   And I have a belief (of course such a matter can be *belief* only) that truth is a mistress who reigns by the affection of her subjects, our thoughts, not by arbitrary calls for their submission.   Whenever I hear these latter, I feel a disposition to think that it is not *truth* that is calling, but either something else in her name, or else servants of hers who do not quite know the proper language of her servants.

There is indeed one thing most important to bear in mind about anything in regard of which we have imaginations, or hopes, or fears, that is, that our thoughts do not make fact, and that the truth, whatever it is, *is* what it is, whatever we think about it.   I mention this, because in matters as to which our thought is really so important as, we will say, a future life, we are apt to make it even of *more* importance to us than it really is, by a sort of feeling as if the fact depended upon it, as if the professing materialist not only took away from us whatever comfort (of course also whatever dread) the thought *here* of a future life might cause, but the future life itself.   The future life will be, if it is to be, quite independent of what the materialist, or we, may think about it : and so far as our lot in it is to depend on what we do or believe here, *that* also will be as it is to be, independent of philosophical speculation, only that *then* the possible destruction of our belief by this may be a matter of important consideration.   But, besides the religious belief which we may have, and in a region of thought wider and more elementary than this, it seems to me that the ultimate feeling of our nature (or our reason, for here all such words mean the same thing) is, that so far as we have given to us faculties to imagine and hope whatever it may be, we have, in a manner, given us the thing itself; that in nature there is nothing self-stultifying, self-neutralizing; that it is not science or philosophy which calls for the submission of our intelligence in such a manner as to do violence to it; but that its submission must be to reason, and, so to speak, to reason in the same kind of thought.   However, I am not unlikely to have to speak of this again, and will not dwell longer on it now.

I have used the expression 'professed materialists' here to signify those who, from the point of view of psychical anatomy, consider themselves able to make out that the notions which men have at various times maintained as to another world and a future life cannot possibly have any foundation.   We will now see how far, in the way of this method of psychical anatomy, we do seem to arrive in this direction.

Supposing for a time we abstract and put aside all notion of personality or consciousness, and consider that, on the method of psychical anatomy, all thought, even the most complicated, is explained, that is to say, explained with such explanation as the principles of psychical anatomy allow of.   Let us see what this amounts to.

We will then say nothing about 'I' or 'we,' but simply 'there is thought,' 'there is action,' and so on, in the various degrees of complication and abstractness.   And we will suppose that we are able to dissect or analyse our corporeal organization to the extremest point of subtlety: not only to dissect its composition, but to follow, in their actual occurrence, the most delicate movements of the most refined portions of it.

Were this so, we might conceive ourselves arriving at such a point of knowledge as to have a corporeal movement, or change of state (including in 'corporeal' everything, even the most refined, dissectable, observable, or analysable) for every mental change of state or thought, as we should express ourselves in the now usual language.   As we know at present that there is an affection of the optic nerve corresponding to sight, so we might know that, corresponding to the most abstract or complicated thought (as that two straight lines cannot inclose a space, that Socrates was poisoned, or that there is such a thing as virtue), there was some affection of some nerve, or of some portion, large or small, of the nerve and brain system; particular

according to the particularity of the thought; so that with any
variation of the thought there would be variation of the bodily
state. We might continue the supposition to the passage from
thought to what we call 'action.' Corresponding to what in
language we call the determining to do a thing and the doing
it, we might suppose the minute internal movement, only
appreciable by the psychical anatomist, followed by movements
of hand and arm, &c. visible to all.

If we conceive a theory of this kind perfect, the psychical
anatomist will be able to describe thought perfectly from *his*
point of view. We will suppose for greater definiteness that the
theory is something like Hartley's, of vibrations in delicate
nervous strings all over the body, brain and all: then the idea
of space, as we call it, would be a particular vibration of such
and such portions of the nervous system. It would be just the
same if we took any other theory of what I may call the
corporeal character of thought. We may suppose imagination,
memory, &c. to be, as Hobbes calls it, decaying sense, or sense
persistent in any way, or semi-persistent, or latently persistent
with a tendency to recur should particular associations bring it
back. As there is affection of the nerves in sense, so there
would be similarly in imagination and memory. Again, supposing that abstract thought arises from the various confluence
of imaginations, and the nerves being affected in the imaginations, there would in this case be a similar nervous affection, but
in a more complicated and refined manner. Abstract thought,
to describe it from this point of view, *is* this affection of the
nerves or nervous state. The brain and body altogether is
a delicate organization and system, which, correspondingly
with the existence of thought, is in one state or another, and
its being in this or that state we may say constitutes the
thought.

The point is, how much do we *explain* by all this ? In
saying that the refined bodily state constitutes the thought, are
we doing any more than shutting our eyes to one portion of the
entire fact ? In the view above, there take place in the organization, according to the laws of nature, certain changes, according
to higher laws indeed, but still in the same sort of way, in which

chemical changes take place in some chemical substance; in
fact, in the same sort of way in which physical change of any
kind takes place. Our view is enlarged, and our physical knowledge increased, by the observation of the laws of these changes.
But I do not see how, by observing them, we have got at
all further towards the understanding of *thought* in that meaning
of thought which leads us to say—still not to come to personality and consciousness till we are fairly forced to do it—there
is sight or thought of things, and this sight or thought of things
is something different from anything that is in things, or from
any action or affection of them. Things in reference to it
appear in a different light from that in which they appear in
relation to each other: the expression 'sight' from the first
means something different from the relation of an external
object to a nerve; and all this apparent corporeal explanation
is really nothing more than a circuitous way of altering the
meaning of the word, or, as I have said, shutting our eyes to a
part of the fact which it expresses.

All the corporeal explanation is really only a discussion of
a portion of the fact: what I have called above ' professed
materialism' is a taking of this portion of the fact for the whole.
And the notion of the professed materialists, that they are right
in doing this, seems to me a good deal confirmed by the dealing
of their adversaries towards them. That we see with the eyes
everybody allows: but that we think with the brain is called
materialism. (It may now be seen why I have used the
expression 'professed materialism' with the design of distinguishing an avowed philosophical creed from vague charges of
holding this or that doctrine.) But I do not see why it is more
materialistic, in any important meaning of that term, to call the
brain (or nervous system including the brain) the instrument or
organ of thought in general, than to call the eye the instrument
or organ of vision. The mistake arises, in the main, from that
mistake about the nature of sense or sensation upon which I am
continually animadverting. The eye sees, we say: or, more
generally, the sense gives us experience or inferior knowledge.
Now if, as it is the eye that sees, so it is the brain that thinks,
then where are *we*? Then materialism *does* absorb all. But in

reality sight is thought, and a large part of what we call thought is inward sight, and the so-called materialist is probably right in saying that a large part of it at least (may be all) *is* accompanied with nervous affection, as sight is : only that it is *we* that do it all, sight as well as abstract thought, and unless there was the ' we ' doing it, sight would be no more sight than thought in general would be thought.

The anti-materialists seem to me to strengthen and encourage their adversaries by such arguments as this : 'But then you leave the soul nothing to do—you make it a sort of idle presence by which everything is said to be done, a sort of royal personage in whose name all is done, whilst the brain and body are really what *do* all, and the supposition of the present *soul* is merely otiose.' All this seems to me to be just the kind of mistake which gives possibility of reason to the materialist supposition. The body does not do one sort of work and the soul another, so that if we find the body doing all that we previously supposed the soul did, we have lost all reason for supposing the soul to exist. If ' soul ' and 'body' are the terms we like to use, then the body is the instrument of the soul, and it certainly to a *great* extent is an instrument in all that we call thought and knowledge. The finding it *more* an instrument of thought than we had previously considered, makes no philosophical alteration in the supposition : there is nothing in the new finding to give it less the character of an *instrument* than formerly. The absence of a part of the brain may be accompanied with incapacity for one sort of thought ; this is like blindness as to the eye. Even if we suppose the soul to have nothing to do but to manage the body as its instrument, that very management seems to me to be enough, and to imply what makes the supposition of it not otiose.

I have only however for a moment used this language of 'soul' and 'body,' which belongs to an order of considerations to which I do not wish to advert now, viz. considerations as to the possible existence of the soul independently of the body. I am now speaking of thought *only* : and all thought, as we know anything about it, is at least *connected with* the body and sense. The supposition of the professed materialist is, that it is sufficiently described, as thought, by being called a modification of the more refined portions of the body.

All that can be discovered really by the psychical anatomist is, that there takes place this modification. The modification, or corporeal change, bears, as I have said, an analogy to a chemical change in any substance. On the other hand it is in a way which is not only not physical, but which cannot be brought into relation with physical laws, that we know this modification to be accompanied by what we call *consciousness*. And the important thing is, that this consciousness is not consciousness of the modification (the use—even momentary— of this expression is distasteful to me—*consciousness of* something material): that is, it is not knowledge of the occurrence of the modification, such a knowledge as the anatomist after- wards gets; but it is a thought, knowledge, or whatever we may call it, of something apparently quite different. A modification takes place in my eye and optic nerve, and a part (or the whole) of my brain. I have a consciousness corre- sponding or contemporaneous with it, but my consciousness is not of the modification, or anything like it : my consciousness is something which I describe perhaps as the perception of a beautiful prospect with mountains and trees and houses and sky. *This* then is at least *one* side of the thought, which the psychical anatomist describes as such and such a modification of nerve and brain : and when he tells me again that the thought *is* this modification, and that is the last word of science about it, he does not seem to me to face or to look at the thing which I want explained, which is, how a thing which is on the one side this modification of nerve and brain should on the other side be something so different. He will say perhaps 'This is a mystery: no physical science can tell us this.' That is exactly what I think : but that being so, I do not see what is the use of saying that physical science exhausts, or tends to exhaust, the problem, or that we can have a physical science in any way occupying the ground of the old philosophy.

Let it be observed, that the consciousness is not, as I have said, of what can, by anatomy, be made out to take place, but, apparently, of something different from it. For it is *thus* that

we have the two worlds, of thought and of fact, which, however
they may be coincident, yet are, as thought and fact, mutually
independent, and the relation of which together is, as we shall
see in a moment, most complicated. We might suppose a
chemical substance conscious of what takes place in it, in
consequence of another particular substance being applied to it.
For all that we know, there *may be* consciousness in the universe of this kind: we could form no notion of it if there was,
and therefore it is not with a great amount of significance that
we can say there is not. But our consciousness is not of this
kind. Thought is not present at the nerves or brain and their
modifications: or if it is, it is not as thought of *them*, but
of something which has nothing to do with them; it is present,
as *thought*, at the sun and stars in sight, at Mont Blanc and
Chimborazo out of sight, at griffins and chimeras which could
never possibly be in sight: or rather (and it is *here* that comes
in the difficulty and the complication) it is present, as thought,
at what, in consequence of the thought, we call by these names,
but which, if it were not for the thought, would never be
suggested to us, and which are thus in a manner, creations of
the thought. So that we get into the entanglement, that while,
on the one side, the psychical anatomist says that the thought
cannot exist without the corresponding modification of nerve
and brain, or even perhaps, unphilosophically says, that this
nerve and brain secrete or produce it; the philosopher on
the other side may say, with equal reason, that the thought
creates the universe as we know it, and as a part of it, the very
nerves and brain which are said to produce or be the cause
of itself.

CHAPTER II.

INTELLECTUAL AND MORAL DIFFICULTIES
OF MATERIALISM.

It is possible that the problem which we have been considering may not be soluble for us in its entirety : all I say is, let us not take half the problem for the whole, and give a partial investigation as a solution of the whole, for that is sure to be wrong, and that is what it seems to me the professed materialist does. I think that the view which I have previously commented on, which puts matter (or body) and mind by the side of each other in the universe, or divides the universe into mind on the one side, as a substance with *its* attributes, and body or matter on the other, as a substance (or substances) with *its* attributes, gives us a misleading view of the problem. The universe is more complicated than this. What we have as the two things or elements in the universe—if we can in any way conceive them as two things, and get them into view side by side, which is the real problem— are not matter and mind, but what I will call 'fact' and 'seeming,' and by 'seeming' I do not mean anything standing in contrast to *truth*—that may be or may not be—but I mean what I have described above as the one side of thought: the presentation—to *something* I suppose, whoever and whatever it may be—of things as being, of fact as fact. The difficulty about the universe is, that things not only *are*—we will consent to go with the physical philosopher so far—but *seem*, and that, when we come to examine what we mean by 'they are,' we find that it resolves itself into this 'they seem,' or at least *depends* upon it: and yet, if we start with the supposition that the things *are*, their 'seeming' then is only in virtue of the existence among them of these particular things, with the qualities they have, which we call our nerves, brain, &c. If we consider our nerves and brain, the *seeming* is an accident of that which is: the universe is a great miscellaneous aggregate of things, among which happen to be certain nerves and brains, or intellective organisations; and so the universe not only is, but seems or is thought of: this, its seeming or being thought of, is to the materialist a subject of interest only as a matter of nerves and brain, and when these are anatomized, this accident of the universe is dismissed. But if we come at all to reflect on the 'seeming' or the 'thoughtness,' it is this (it appears to me) which presents itself to us as the main fact, and though I will not say that 'being' is an accident of it, yet still we have to define to ourselves 'that which is' in some such way as this, 'that which seems to us to be, and *rightly* seems': the seeming is the more general, and when we have excluded from it that which wrongly seems, there remains that which is. And, on *this* side, seeming or thought, so far from being an accident of the universe, is the all-important thing about it.

The taking an *abstraction*, in the sense in which I have used the word, for the whole of the view which we should take, which is done, more or less, by many beside professed materialists, is a wider form of the mistake which I have noticed.

But this 'seeming' of things of course implies something more than the existence of things: it implies something—mind or intelligence we call it—to which they do seem as they do. I said just now that the universe was more complicated than that we could conceive it simply to exist, made up of mind and matter, and their respective attributes. This is because, when we introduce mind, matter has a double character, that of being and seeming. This puzzles us. For discussions about the phenomenal world *itself*, and the mutual relations of the various parts of it, there is no difficulty. We consider 'phenomenon' as identical in signification with fact, that is, we think of the universe only with reference to its supposed being, without any reference to its *seeming*, or being perceived. In fact we take our idea of 'being' from it: when we say 'a thing *is*' we mean that it is a part of this universe, with the same manner of being which we suppose as belonging to that. We then have what I have before called the ordinary 'phenomenalist' or physical view of things. But all this is only valid for the phenomenal world itself, and the relations of its parts: and this is what I have meant by previously calling this view 'an abstraction.' That is, we must neither pronounce that there is no other reality besides this, nor must we apply to such other reality, supposing that there is such, the logic or manner of thought belonging to this. However it may be a fact that the phenomenal world *is*, it is at least as much a fact that it *seems*, *i.e.* presents itself as object of thought to something which, in virtue of this very fact, we must consider as different from itself. What is this something? and what sort of existence has *it*? When we come to find that this something is *we*, and that it is only in virtue of this *seeming* of the universe to *us*, parts apparently of itself, that we have been all along talking of its *being*, we get into the puzzle which I have spoken of.

The studying ourselves and our sensations as far as we can on the former or phenomenalist supposition, and the pronouncing, along with this study, that all truth, or all thought of value for us, is to be deduced from this supposition alone, and then the making assertions on this supposition about things which we may soon see cannot be judged of from *this*—this is what I have called professed materialism.

Those valuers of phenomenalist study who are really philosophers meet the difficulty as they can. Mr Mill gives us what I have called a thoroughly phenomenalist logic or method, *i.e.* treats of things in the first instance, for science and life,—with careful putting aside all mention of our conceptions of them,—as if they were reality to us. The consideration of their 'seeming' or being conceived by us he will not allow to disturb the science of them: at the beginning he mentions that it *is* an important consideration, and in fact that it gives a secondary or dependent character to all that notion of their *being* which is assumed for physical science: this is the same thing which

I have meant in calling this an abstraction. In his further development of this consideration, it seems to me that at first he leans to a Kantian or Hamiltonian kind of thought, which may be described thus: we use the expression 'phenomenal' world, for the universe of things which we perceive by means of our senses. So far as the *application* is concerned, there is no doubt about that, and we mean the same thing by the word in *this* respect, which is the important matter. But in regard of the *signification* of the term, or the reason *why* we call the universe before our senses 'phenomenal,' there is a difference. With me the use of the term 'phenomenal' may be taken to imply that I consider that the universe, which we assume *to be, seems* as well; but not at all to imply that it seems other than it *is,* in any possible respect or in any meaning of the term 'being.' In what I have called the Kantian or Hamiltonian manner of thought, I understand the word 'phenomenal' to have more or less, besides its application, the signification of relative as opposed to absolute, of accidental as opposed to essential or necessary, and of attributal, belonging to attributes, as opposed to substantial, belonging to substance. This is the manner of thought to which, I think, *at first* Mr Mill seems to lean.

Afterwards his language at the least is different: and he describes the things of the universe as being really (or to the philosopher) what he calls 'possibilities of sensation.' Here he appears to recognize what I have expressed by saying, that when we come to take into account the 'seeming,' *i.e.* the 'thoughtness,' conceivedness, perceivedness, of things, it is *this* which presents itself as the true, comprehensive, or ultimate fact, upon which what we call their *being* is dependent. But I do not like the expression 'possibilities of sensation,' because it seems to me an attempt to put together notionalism and bare physicalism—I use these rough expressions for the better understanding—making a union which cannot but be incongruous, and which does not seem to me to be suggestive or lead us onward. 'A *possibility* of sensation,' like the old δυνάμεις or other Aristotelian abstractions, is an abstraction which we can make nothing of: on the other hand, the word *sensation*, as

Mr Mill uses it here, seems to me, though I may mistake him, to have an undue concreteness, and to mean something implying the actual physical existence of nerve, brain, &c. If so, considering that these nerves, brain, &c. are *things* belonging to the physical universe, which the phrase 'possibilities of sensation' is to give us a sort of account of, the account returns upon itself or we make no step, and are still in that same bewilderment which 'being' and 'seeming' together, as I have said, must cause to us.

If 'sensation' here means simply a kind of consciousness or feeling, without any reference to physical accompaniments of it, then, though there is no harm in calling the phenomenal or external world an aggregate of possibilities of such sensation, I can hardly see that there is much good in it. At least to make the phrase mean much for me, I must try to translate it a little from its abstractness. I must mean by 'possibility of sensation' a fact, *the* one great fact it would be of reality. There is no doubt but that the varieties of our (I do not mean here any stress on *our*) consciousness are facts, and our consciousness altogether, comprehending these varieties, may be considered a greater fact: and our consciousness is what it *is* (one of its phases being what we call perception of an external world) in virtue, we may presume, of some further fact, probably double: *i.e.* partly fact as to what we are, partly fact as to what something else is. We are the subject of the seeming, that to which the something else seems: at any rate, in our consciousness, something else *seems* to seem to us. This seeming of something to us is equally well described as sensation of something by us (in the *last* meaning which I assigned to Mr Mill's 'sensation'). If then we are to speak of possibility of sensation (which is really, if we are to come to these Aristotelian abstractions, the *fact* of general or potential sensation implying the *possibility* of particular or actual sensation), I should describe it as a fact, implying doubleness, a something seeming (or felt) and a something to which it seems (or which feels), and also implying characteredness or qualitiedness in each member of the doubleness. It is owing to these characters that that which seems or is felt seems or is felt as it does seem or is felt. But this is a rudimentary or embryonic description of reality in general, and possibility of sensation, to mean anything *as a fact*, must mean that. Mr Mill's using the term 'possibility of sensation' as a description of the external world seems to imply that after all he must mean by sensation what I will venture to call 'eye-work,' 'ear-work,' &c. as distinct from the feeling of perception: and if so, we have the old difficulty about the eye and ear themselves (or nerves and brain if we prefer the language), which are at once things which we must have in order to have sensation, and yet things which we cannot have till we have got sensation.

Mr Mill is perhaps led to the describing the external world thus from the previous Kantoidic notion of the thing in itself, unknown substance, or *noumenon*: it is an abstractification of that. As we are looking out from ourselves, we are to understand that beyond the sensations, sensible attributes, or phenomena, there is, not indeed a something unknown of which these are the dress, but a possibility of the occurrence of these, which possibility is the reality. My criticism just now is to the effect that the possibility of this occurrence involves something on *our* side as well as on the other, and therefore cannot serve to describe *that* in distinction from us. As I began with saying, *this* description of a something (to call it a something) behind the phenomena, does no harm (as the notion of a thing in itself does) and it may possibly do some good. The 'possibility' of things seeming to us as they do, I should be more inclined myself to describe, in language which I have frequently used, as *the reason* for it: by this 'reason' I mean some fact, whatever it is, which perhaps may not be known to us, but is not to be supposed (why should it be?) unknowable; nay, which, in part at any rate, is already undoubtedly known to us.

The fact of things 'seeming' or being thought and known in addition to their 'being' (if indeed their being is anything more than a portion of their seeming) is looked upon in one of two different lights by those philosophers who value physical science as the line of thought in which most of advance and fresh knowledge is to be expected.

One of these lights is that of which Mr Mill's view may be taken as an instance. It is a view in which, however I have

criticized it, I to a certain extent concur. Mr Mill has banished
most carefully from his logic of science every supposition of our
being concerned with mere conceptions or notions of our own :
for the purpose of logic we are concerned, he says, with *things*.
But afterwards we come to philosophy, and then it appears that
the *things* are only what I will call unknown occasions (I use
this expression for 'possibilities,' as a little less abstract) of sensation, and all the variety of them is variety of sensation : and
since eye, ear, nose, are among these things or occasions, we
must not mean by 'sensations,' sensations as affections of *these*,
but sensations as *feelings* which we feel, that is, thoughts,
conceptions, notions (for these are only different names of
intellectual feelings) : things at last *are* conceptions or creations
of the mind, and anything they may be besides, so far as we
can make anything of them, they are *through* being this.

I have said that with this view, I to a considerable extent
concur : things are supposed to *be* in the first instance, this,
their phenomenal *being*, being a supposition or abstraction, for
the making of which we forget, for the time, all about their
seeming : and we being thus simply *adstant*, what we know, when
we know anything, is simply the fact which is going on in the
universe. With this fact is all our business.

But then, if we are philosophers, we cannot help considering
besides, that all this, which we call *being*, we can only call so as
seeming to us to be, as being thought by us *as* being : and all
physical or phenomenalist being, all our *realization* or realism,
is wrapt up of necessity in a vast surrounding idealism, as some
would call it : an idealist philosophy surrounds a phenomenalist
science.

I will not criticize this at length now *on the whole*, because
the consideration of it will at various times recur. It seems to
me to be right or wrong, as it is taken. The way of taking it
rightly seems to me to be the consideration of our thought
itself as a great fact : we think as we do (by which thinking
the universe is suggested as given to us) in virtue of fact going
beyond ourselves, or if we like to call it so, antecedent to
ourselves—fact of which all our knowledge is an imperfect and
gradual revelation to us. I think that in this way we may

consider the universe as true and real as well as we : and this is what I call *rightly* taking the view mentioned above: I hope to explain it more fully. *Wrongly* taking the view consists, as I think, in making so much in the first instance of the *being* of the phenomenal universe, that when the independence of this notion is undermined by the superinduced and enwrapping idealism (or notion of *seeming* and *thoughtness*), we lose all notion of *being* or fact altogether, and seem to be in a world of chimera and illusion, or at least in a world where there is no possible way to distinguish between what is illusion and what is not. I think a wrongly taken idealism of this kind does sometimes go with a very pronounced phenomenalism : but of this another time.

By the second light in which the ' seeming ' of things may be viewed in relation to their being, I meant this. Suppose a physical investigator assuming the being of the external or phenomenal world not only as a fact for science and action—a fact, the existence of which, as a fact, is capable of being afterwards philosophized upon, interpreted, qualified—but as the one and only fact which he means to recognize, and all philosophizing about which he sets down beforehand as nugatory : supposing him to say, ' From this my point of view I mean to discuss knowledge and thought, or the *seeming* of the universe and things in it to certain particular things in it : this is a fact or phenomenon of this my universe, and you will see that I can treat it as such.'

In this case, what he does is to treat the phenomenon of thought or knowledge as a portion of the wider phenomenon of ' life.' The support of life, speaking roughly, is by means of action either spontaneous or volitional, and to volitional action there goes, as an ingredient or preliminary, thought or knowledge of some kind. Knowledge is in this view a part of action for a purpose : the beginning and foundation of it.

This line of thought is as important in its way as the other, and though I have, with a view to bring it more into relief, represented it above as taken (what I should call) wrongly, it need not necessarily be so. I will not dwell upon it, for I have only alluded to these two lights in which the relation of

thought to being may appear (in the one of which *being* is more
or less dependent on thought, in the other *thought* is an accident
or particular of being) to compare them together. But I will
say one word on the difficulties of it.

The great intellectual difficulty I have spoken about, and
shall not dwell on more, but it is accompanied by an equal
moral difficulty.

We do not know much about the intelligence of the inferior
animals, but in any case, their intelligence seems all absorbed
in their action, and to go to the support of their life.

But with us, *men*, this is not so : we think about the
universe in general, and about things altogether in a far wider
way and view than we can at all apply to practice, or than we
can at all consider (taking our analogy from other facts of the
universe) to be simply a natural fact of our phenomenal life,
serving us to guide our actions, as the animal's intelligence
serves him, and as our stomach serves us to digest, or our eye
to see.

This *generalness* of our intelligence brings strongly before
us the intellectual difficulty of which I have abundantly spoken.
When we *think* of our thinking, not only do we find it going
beyond all reasonable relation to the support of our physical
being, but we find that, as *thinking*, it alters the whole universe
to us : we should not talk of anything being, were it not for our
thinking.

The *moral* difficulty is this. The physical philosopher who
treats thought or knowledge as a part of *life*, cannot I think
but look upon developed human thought as something abnormal,
something out of relation with that physical universe, of which
he is determined to make it a part, something, in a manner,
unmeaning. Whether for *happiness*, we should be better without it, he might find it difficult to say : it gives us many
pleasures, and gives us many pains : but, strange as it may
seem, I think he would have to say that as reasonable creatures
we should be better without it : we stretch our *thoughts* into
infinite space and infinite time, while our *life* is all limited and
confined, and from *his* point of view, surely all this must be a
sort of superfluous (περιττός), idle, imagination or illusion.

And so he will very likely do that which I have spoken of before (which some, it seems to me wrongly, do in the name of religion, and some, equally wrongly, in the name of materialism), browbeat our thought and intelligence; say it is all that 'forward and intrusive faculty, imagination[1]'; that we must keep at home and on the ground, and cease generalizing and expatiating. Now it is not at all from the point of view of sentiment as occasion of declamation that I think all this is wrong but from the point of view of fact.   Knowledge is a mode of thought and is formed from imagination, and in this thought and imagination I see, perhaps not knowledge itself, but its germ and material: that we do think in these various ways, seems to me a fact at least as important as the existence of the phenomenal world: to say that all our thinking so is folly, seems to me simply what I have called a shutting our eyes to so much important fact.

If then we start with the phenomenal universe, we find thought or knowledge by far the most important fact in it, a fact taking such dimensions, as to force us to do one of two things: either (so to speak) to let it out of the phenomenal universe, in which case we must say, 'The phenomenal universe then is not all, there is something besides it': or else to expand the dimensions of the phenomenal universe till it becomes no longer phenomenal, *i.e.* simply what is in communication with our corporeal organization: or, which is the same thing, to expand our notion of our 'life,' till we mean by it something no longer answering to the analogy of life as lived by plants and animals, but including this, and going far beyond it.   If we expand in *this* way our notion of our life, then we *may* consider all our possible thought and knowledge subordinate to it.

It is *thus* that I mean that we may think wrongly, or think rightly, of knowledge or thought as a part of the universe.

----

[1] Butler, *Analogy*, ch. i.

CHAPTER III.

THE PROVERSE AND RETROVERSE OF SENSATION.

It seems to me that some of the difficulties as to the relation of thought and matter may be looked at more clearly by the following use of the terms 'retroverse' and 'proverse.'

In the sense of sight, which I will take as an instance, there is an affection of the nerves and brain, the nature of which we understand, so far as we do understand it, by anatomy. Correspondingly, or at least contemporaneously, with this, there is a feeling, or as some would say, a consciousness, which we should describe in words as the perception of something, a prospect or a picture. These are two contemporaneous facts, entirely, as facts, dissimilar, or if we prefer so to speak, one fact composed of two entirely dissimilar portions. I shall call the one of them the *proverse*, the other the *retroverse*, of the fact: and the latter of these terms is that which will come into use the most frequently, because by the 'proverse' I shall mean in general the fact, whatever it is, which is being spoken about, and by the retroverse the corresponding fact on the side of mind, or feeling, or consciousness, or whatever we may call it.

Of the fact then which is commonly, but often very loosely and ambiguously, called sensation, the proverse is the physiological or anatomical portion—what I have in another place called, the communication[1] between the nerves of our body and the natural agents of the phenomenal universe. The retroverse of this is our particular feeling, whatever it is, which goes with the particular communication. The retroverse of the communication between the moving substance (or undulating ether) light and the nerves connected with the eye, is the imagination of a

[1] *Expl.* pp. 7, 19, &c.

coloured picture : and so for the other senses. The complete
retroverse of the whole communication between our corporeal
organization and the phenomenal universe, is the conception
which we have of that universe as *one*, we forming a part of it.

I have already spoken of the complication which there is, of
necessity, in this. In what is said above, there is a sort of
fundamental fallacy, or logical circle, which we cannot avoid.
The facts which constitute the proverse are only facts to us, as
a portion of what, again, is only fact to us in virtue of the
retroverse. This retroverse, which is a thought, conception, or
imagination, has an object which is the phenomenal universe or
something belonging to it, and has also a proverse, or accompanying fact *in* this phenomenal universe. But this proverse
is no further fact than as the entire object of the retroverse is
fact : so that we have, in the manner which I have spoken of
already, a return of our view of the matter into itself. We can
only avoid this by assuming the only *certain* fact to be the
conception or conceiving : the nature of this is to suggest its
object as fact also, and *in* this object we find a certain particular
portion of fact, which is connected with the conceiving in a
particular manner, viz. as what I have called proverse to *it*, as
retroverse. Whether this is the proper way of avoiding the
complication is what I am not discussing now.

The *proverse* fact of sensation consists of various phenomena
of the nerves and brain as they are objects subjected to our
physical observation. The *retroverse* fact of it is of a double
nature, in a way which I have already described : that is, it
consists of sentience and perception. By sentience I mean the
feeling of pleasure or pain, the feeling of something as liking it
or disliking it. By perception (which I should prefer to call
circumperception, because, in contrast to sentience, it carries
our thoughts out and away from ourselves) I mean conception
and imagination with the added assumption (and it is to be
supposed, fact) of reality, correspondingly (or contemporaneously)
with the various particulars of the *proverse* fact.

The retroverse of *some* communications of our nerves with
matter beyond them, as of a prick with a pin, is sentience
almost without perception : of some, as of the application of a
sweet-smelling flower to the nose, sentience and perception

mixed: of some, as of movements of our arms and objects by them, little other than perception.

Before speaking of the application of the terms in *this* use of them to the relation between the physical universe and thought, I will speak of another use of the terms, analogous to the above, which I hope will not cause confusion.

Say the fact which we are considering is the physical state of our nerves in communication with matter without; then the retroverse of *this* is what I have described. But say the fact which we are considering is the phenomenal universe itself, and that we begin with simply saying, 'The phenomenal universe exists,' 'exists,' that is, in the manner in which the things and facts of the phenomenal universe exist, is what they are, does what they do. Let us suppose that we begin with the phenomenal universe, because we consider existence and it as co-extensive terms. Now, a portion of the universe, as thus conceived, is all that nervous modification which has itself a retroverse in the manner I described: but just as this has thus a retroverse to itself, so it may itself be considered a retroverse to the universe conceived as above. Our sight of the universe is what it is correspondingly to the optic nerve being what it is: but just in the same way the optic nerve is what it is, correspondingly to light being what it is. Light, vibration of air, exhalations which, communicating with our nose, make smell—these are facts, like any other of the million facts of the universe—facts of the first order, if we like to call them so, in our present view of the universe: there might have been no life or thought anywhere in the universe, and they would have been facts still. Then we find, in the life or organized portion of the universe, these facts of the first order reflected or answered to, if we may so speak, in facts of the second order: light is answered to by an optic nerve, vibration of the air by an auditory nerve: there is a universe of nervous modification corresponding to the universe of fact of the first order, a retroverse of it, after a manner analogous to that manner in which conception and perception are the retroverse of this modification.

I will return now to speak of the terms 'proverse' and 'retroverse' in the first of the uses mentioned.

It seems to me quite possible that physiological research might make out our nervous organization to be of the following nature; brain, with the two sets of nerves, viz., of sensation and of voluntary motion starting from it: the brain a source of force, but of force communicable with, and therefore to a certain extent of the same nature as, the existing physical forces of the universe: this force supported by corporeal nutrition: and again a special adaptation of the nerves of sensation to particular physical agents. We should then have the brain with the two sets of nerves starting from it, both sets in a manner alive and in action: we might call for the moment the sensor nerves 'receptive,' the motor 'editive.' Both sets of nerves are then at work in their way: the *editive* transmitting the force from the brain, and with it contracting the muscles, which is our immediate or proper *motion*: the *receptive* seeking out, as it were, for something to receive. When the proper natural agents present themselves and communicate, the receptive nerves receive and transmit the modifications produced in them by this to the brain and all over the nerves: their receptive modifications or movements may be supposed to associate themselves with the editive modifications of the other nerves, and so a regular or systematic or 'occasioned' contraction of the muscles or movement of the limbs be produced. And all this may be conceived to be *one* force in the nerves analogous in some measure to electricity, galvanism, &c., but still peculiar: I will call it 'nervicity': it is generated by the brain, supported by corporeal nutrition, has the occasions of its energizing supplied to it by the receptive nerves, and passes out through the editive nerves into contraction of the muscles, where it becomes (or produces) mechanical movement.

I have not cared to be very particular in this description, which I intend to represent in a general way the opinions which I conceive to be those of Mr Bain on the subject, and perhaps, in a less degree, of some others. The purpose for which I make the description is the following:

All the above (supposing it physiologically made out, which I can quite suppose it might be) would be to me what I have called the 'proverse' of a double or conjoint fact, to which there was a 'retroverse' of equal importance. It is this retroverse

which all the various terms belonging to what we call 'mind'
express. The retroverse of the more simple action of the receptive nerves is that which we call 'perception'; the retroverse of
this, persisting after the communication with the natural agents
is past, is what we call 'imagination'; the retroverse of the more
complicated and internal action (so we may suppose) of the
same nerves is what we may call 'conception.' Again, in the
manner which I have mentioned, there is another kind of
retroverse of disturbance of nerves, which I have called 'sentience,' feeling of pleasure or pain, liking or disliking: and again
still, the retroverse of the regular, occasioned, systematic action
of the editive nerves in contracting the muscles, &c., is what we
call *Will* or volition.

The use of this manner of speaking is not at all to give an
apparent account of what is not really accounted for, but the
opposite, viz. to obviate the doing of this in a wrong way.
When it is said, *e.g.*, that impression of light on the eye and
optic nerve *produces* sight or perception, I am always rather at
a loss what is meant. Supposing by 'produces' we mean
'generates' in any way after the analogy of generation of
organised beings, a motion or new combination of elements,
after the analogy of chemistry, or anything of that sort: or
supposing we simply mean, 'is followed by,' after the regular
laws and course of nature—what *are* the laws and course of
nature applicable to this? We are making nature for the
occasion: we have no analogy in nature for any supposed
'production' of this kind. Between physical modifications of a
nerve (say 'vibrations') and what we call 'conception' there is
an absolute heterogeneity, or in fact a want of relation going
on beyond heterogeneity. And yet there is a correspondence,
in time if in nothing else: but it is more than this, because,
according to what the one is, so is the other: this is what
I have endeavoured to express by the term 'retroverse.' The
two things belong to different worlds or regions, and yet bear
a relation the one to the other corresponding to the relation
between the different worlds or regions.

Of course if we say, on the one side, that it is wrong to
describe material impression as 'producing' conception, so we
must say on the other, that it is wrong to describe conception

or thought as 'producing' mechanical motion. Upon the whole, I think the *spirit* of professing materialism consists, more than in anything else, in the being broadly awake to this latter truth, while the former, which corresponds with it, is looked on as of trifling importance. 'Volition' is looked upon as the result of physical, nervous modification, because it is said, with truth so far as it goes, Nothing but force can produce force or movement. But in the meantime no notice of the same kind is given to the consideration, that the appulse of light to the eye is followed by that ultra-physical fact which we call sight or perception : or rather, this latter fact is considered to be physical, a part of the phenomenal universe, because it is supposed to be produced by the appulse of the light, while any process in the reverse direction, of production of mechanical effort by anything not mechanical, is considered absurd.

The reason why the treatment of the matter, in some way such as that in which I have here treated it, seems to me of importance, is this : that that part of the entire fact which I have called the 'retroverse' is of more importance than we should judge from considering the nature of the proverse, and is not to be considered a simple accompaniment of this latter, of such a nature as to be thought perhaps even of *less* importance than it.

If one could for a moment imagine oneself, the subject or thinker, placed exactly in the middle of this fact of sensation, between the proverse and the retroverse of it, and looking alternately through the one and the other to see what we see : it is through the retroverse we should see the universe as we do see it, not through the proverse. Of course this rather bold imagination must be dealt with carefully, lest it should mislead us : I am obliged to talk of *seeing*, but that, it must be borne in mind, is metaphor.

I avoid in general the word 'conscious,' just because of the ambiguity attaching to it on account of the fact now before us. In what I am saying now, however, I will use it.

Suppose that there exists, correspondingly with sensation and volition, a current (or it may be vibrations), or something similar, through the nerves and brain in the manner which above, following chiefly Mr Bain, I have supposed. This we know physiologically. It is the proverse of the fact of sensation, the actual physical portion of it. But if our thought were directed *here*, if *this* were what our consciousness was directed to, we should not know the universe as we do know it, or anything like it. Immediate knowledge on our part of a tingling or thrilling in an optic nerve and of a corresponding set of contractions in the muscles of the eye would not be *sight*: so far from it, if we had such an immediate knowledge or consciousness and our attention was directed to it, it would effectually *prevent* sight. What there is immediate knowledge or consciousness of, is the double retroverse, as I have described it, of the fact of sensation—it is merely a question of the use of the word 'consciousness' whether we say there is consciousness of this, or this is the consciousness—viz. of sentience (or feeling of pleasure or pain), and of the exertion of volition, which develops itself into the notions of space and solidity. In the case of the eye there is (speaking shortly) pleasure felt in the colour, and there is felt volitional movement of the eye to follow it. And here what I want observed is, that our consciousness of the retroverse is a fact out of all proportion important in comparison with what our consciousness of the proverse would be: and I think it is the not bearing this in mind which makes another particular of what I have called the spirit of materialism. The phenomenal universe is something very vast: even the whole life in it constitutes but a small portion of it, and human life only a portion of this, and these modifications of the human nerves are therefore only one incidental fact of it, and if *this* were what we were conscious of, it would not be anything we might say very important. But what we are conscious of, in being as above conscious of the retroverse, is not of an incidental fact in the universe, but of something which affects the being of the universe itself. In being conscious of our volition, and aware that it is only the existence of this which makes us speak of there being such a thing as the phenomenal universe, we ask ourselves, are we right in thinking thus? Our thought takes a position of superiority to phenomenal being: and in reference to sentience, it takes a position of more important superiority still. Liking and disliking begins to open the door to *criticism*, to the question, not as above, what is true or fact, but what is good or desirable, and thus to ends and rules of action.

I have always objected to the saying, that the universe is made up of facts of mind and facts of matter, because when this is said, it is scarcely possible but that what is meant is the phenomenal universe, *i.e.* the universe as it presents itself to our perception, but supposed to be more or less independent of it : and if this is so, by counting facts of mind constituents of a universe like this, we are just giving to them that character of minor importance, of quasi-accidentalness, which I have been deprecating. It may indeed be said *after* this that the universe itself is one great fact of mind or sensation. If this is said, the matter is set right, on one condition : that by facts of mind in the first case, when they are spoken of as joint constituents, with facts of matter, of the universe, we mean facts of mind looked at without full attention to the import of the expression 'mind,' thought as one constituent of life, as life is on our globe. Then, if we give full attention to what we mean by the term 'mind' (or we might say 'thought' or 'sensation'), we must alter our language, and say the universe is a fact of mind, the saying which would have no significance unless we consider 'mind' to be more extensive in meaning than, and prior in meaning to, the universe. When Mr Mill describes 'things' as 'possibilities of sensation' he must consider 'sensation' a more primary fact than 'things': and since organs of sensation, or the proverse of the fact of sensation, are themselves.but things, it must be the retroverse of the fact, or the thought, which is thus more primary.

The philosophy, which there is more or less in the thought of all who think even in the least degree, appears to me fairly shared, as it exists now and has existed, between what I have called the spirit of materialism and the counter-spirit. All sensation, perception, conception, consciousness, has got, it would appear probable to me, its retroverse and proverse, its soul and body, its portion in the phenomenal universe and its portion in that region of thought in which the existence of the phenomenal universe is but one phenomenon.

BOOK IV.

Πάντων μέτρον ἄνθρωπος.

CHAPTER I.

IN the controversy between Mr Cope and Mr Grote[1] as to the meaning of the maxim πάντων μέτρον ἄνθρωπος, the former endeavours to prove that the latter is unjust towards Plato in charging him with misrepresenting Protagoras, maintaining on the contrary that Plato's argument in the *Theaetetus* is based upon a right understanding of what Protagoras *did* mean, and that Protagoras is justly condemned.

Doubtless there is force in what Mr Cope urges[2], 'Was not Plato more likely to understand what Protagoras meant than Mr Grote—Plato with the book before him; Mr Grote somewhere about 2265 years afterwards with no other authority than what he finds in Plato, asserting that what he does find there must be incorrect'? We cannot deny that the fact that Plato had the book before him and was himself engaged in the actual controversies of times following close on Protagoras, combined with his extraordinary philosophical powers, makes the probability very great that he *would* have understood Protagoras. At the same time a glance at the controversies going on at this present moment as to the meaning of late and living philosophers, is enough to show that the inference is far from certain: and the idea, that it is absurd for Mr Grote now, with little to go on but Plato's own arguments about Protagoras, to correct Plato's view of Protagoras, is a condemnation of criticism altogether. Mr Grote does in regard of Plato's

---

[1] See Cope's *Theaetetus and Mr Grote's Criticisms*, 1866.
[2] p. 15.

philosophy what he did in regard of the history of the Grecian historians. Criticism of ancient writings, so far as it goes beyond words to meaning and subject, takes as its basis the supposition that many things in the ancient world have been misunderstood by former generations, the true intelligence of them having been reserved for our time : and it is the same in the case of philosophy.

The probability then, which is certainly great, that Plato will have rightly interpreted Protagoras may be rebutted by showing reason on the other side ; and Mr Grote conceives that he has succeeded in producing such reason.

In the dialogue Socrates asks Theaetetus what knowledge is, and receives for answer that it is αἴσθησις, which we will call for the present 'sensation.' Socrates replies in effect, 'This is the same doctrine as that of Protagoras, that man is the measure of all things, and the same doctrine also as that of certain Ionic philosophers, that all things are in a perpetual flux and flow. He then proceeds to treat the three doctrines as substantially the same, and argues against all in conjunction.

Mr Grote's case is that each of the three doctrines is in itself independent of the others, though they may be tenable in conjunction; that there is no reason to suppose that Protagoras joined either of the other doctrines with his own doctrine of *Homo Mensura*; that this latter doctrine has a most important meaning, and is in a high degree true, in a sense quite different from that attributed to it by Plato, when he combines it with the other doctrines.

Mr Grote supports his case by giving what, in his view, is the simple and natural meaning of the words of Protagoras : this meaning, he says, has no reference to sensation or to flux and flow : what it expresses is *generally* the relativeness of knowledge, or *more particularly*, what comes to the same thing, ' the autonomy of each individual mind,' ' equal right of private judgment to each man for himself[1].' The Protagorean 'measured by' is explained by Mr Grote as equivalent to ' relative to,' and the relativeness he explains as above.

---

[1] Grote's *Plato*, Vol. II., pp. 362, 388.

There is indeed, it is to be observed, a very long interval between the general doctrine of relativity (which Mr Grote begins with understanding Protagoras to express) and the more particular doctrine which he proceeds to connect with it. There are many steps necessary between the very abstract philosophical notion that a perceiving subject is necessarily conceived when we conceive an object, and the doctrine of individual judgment, or every one being his own measure of truth and error. To tell what a philosopher meant from a single sentence, however pointed and deliberate, which is all we have to go upon in the case of Protagoras, seems to me an insoluble problem. Very often, the more pointedly a thing is asserted quasi-paradoxically, the more the context involves explanations, which from the dictum itself we might never have dreamt of. Protagoras himself is to us a name, and little more—a man of one saying: what we have in the *Theaetetus* is a Platonic Protagoras, a dramatic creation of Plato. It is a perfectly legitimate supposition for criticism, that Protagoras, like many others, was a philosopher misunderstood from very early times. For that philosophers understand each other in the most various manners, and therefore to a great extent misunderstand each other, can surprise no one who reads the history of philosophy. We know nothing about Plato from which to judge how far he was likely to do, what philosophers do not often do now, *i.e.* use pains and effort to master an opposite view to his own, and see things from his opponent's point of view. Hence it is quite possible that Mr Grote's Protagoras now may be a better likeness than Plato's; and may give us more the actual philosopher, than Plato's. I am not myself disposed to think it is so, because there does not seem to me evidence to rebut the before mentioned probability, that Plato and those for whom his dialogue was written, having Protagoras' context before them, will have understood him better than we, who have only the solitary sentence.

It is on this probability that Mr Cope rests *his* case, and he supports it by endeavouring to show that others in old times, as Aristotle, Diogenes Laertius, Sextus Empiricus, and Simplicius understood Protagoras in the same manner.

In qualification of this line of argument, it ought to be kept in mind that Plato's manner of understanding Protagoras was very likely to govern, in some degree, the manner of understanding him afterwards, even possibly in the case of Aristotle: not that Aristotle disliked differing from Plato, but that we cannot tell how much attention he may have given to Protagoras.

Mr Cope quotes Mr Grote as saying, that the *Theaetetus* is the first attempt of any importance to analyze and classify psychological phenomena, and fortifies this view of Mr Grote's by some very interesting historical remarks of his own. In the view of both it would appear that, at the time when Protagoras wrote, αἴσθησις was undistinguished, scientifically, from other mental operations, supposing such to exist. But to the extent to which we consider this to have been the case, Plato's saying that Protagoras' *Homo Mensura* was equivalent to the maintaining knowledge to be sensation, will have had no great significance. For the term sensation only has force in distinction from other possible mental processes: and if Protagoras had no notion of such distinction, then, upon the whole, he held what Mr Grote considers he did, though Plato may not have been wrong in saying that he held ἐπιστήμη αἴσθησις. We shall have in this case to modify or somewhat generalize our notion of αἴσθησις, and to call it 'feeling' rather than 'sensation' or 'sensitive perception,' and this indeed suits better with the constant references to general corporeal experiences, as of heat and cold, quite as much as to the experiences of what we call the five senses. The point *then* of the difference of view taken of Protagoras by Plato and by Mr Grote will be, that, supposing Protagoras to have said, Knowledge is *individual feeling*, Mr Grote considers the importance of this to reside in the word *individual* ('feeling' being taken vaguely), while Plato considers 'feeling' to mean corporeal feeling (which, he would say, *is* necessarily individual and independent in each man); and holds besides that there are mental processes to be brought out, in psychological analysis, from the vague notion of 'feeling,' which are *not* thus individual and merely subjective; and that knowledge really resides in these latter.

I cannot therefore follow Mr Cope's reasoning from the ignorance of Protagoras in the first paragraph of page 22, where he says, 'Therefore we have the less need to feel surprise at his confining his theory of the subjective standard of truth to the apprehension of objects by sensation, and shall have the less disinclination to believe Plato upon his word when he tells us that he did so.' If Protagoras was 'ignorant of any distinction between sensation and thought or knowledge,' then whatever word he used to express the intellectual process will, I conclude, have represented a confusion of the two, whether it were a word corresponding to our 'sensation,' or to our 'thought.' If he meant by αἴσθησις, a confused mixture of what we should call sensation, thought, and knowledge (which in fact is implied in his ignorance of any distinction), then Mr Grote's view is the correct one, and there is little significance in Plato's criticism.

In short this argument of Mr Cope shows, if it shows anything, that there must have been much scope in the writings of Protagoras for variety of view about his exact meaning. Plato interprets them in *his* way, and controverts them as thus understood. As I have said, his interpretation is probably in the main the correct one. But under the circumstances shown above, it is highly probable that other views of him were taken also, with more or less reason. The position of Plato is therefore that of an interpreter, in conjunction or rivalry with others, who had his books before them as well as Plato, or who could at least readily ascertain their contents: it is not the position of an exhibitor or representer of his view to those who, like us, have little or no other means of knowing about it. If Plato had to *teach* men in this dialogue what αἴσθησις, as a distinct mental process, *was*, he must have been prepared to find some of those who had read anything which Protagoras had said about αἴσθησις *without* this knowledge, (a knowledge which Protagoras himself did not possess) taking a *different* view of what Protagoras meant from that which *he* took. Mr Grote may be supposed in this day one of that possible old minority of Protagorean interpreters revived: and the discussion now, as then, involves both the points, not only what is the meaning of πάντων μέτρον ἄνθρωπος but what is the meaning of ἐπιστήμη αἴσθησις, with a view of ascertaining how far the one involves, or is equivalent to the other.

When Mr Grote and Mr Cope tell us that the *Theaetetus* was the beginning of psychological analysis, they do not, I hope, mean us to consider that it was the beginning of a course, by which all the confusion and difference of view on the subject of the variety of mental processes were got rid of, so that though people before the *Theaetetus* may have doubted what ἐπιστήμη αἴσθησις meant, they could not so doubt now. Mr Grote's commendation of the doctrine of knowledge being sensation, as he holds it, is curiously in point. Mr Grote is maintaining that 'all knowledge and conception of truth is ultimately derivable from the objects of sense' (in Mr Cope's words): and in doing so, of course gives to a certain extent, *his* view of ἐπιστήμη αἴσθησις. 'Counting, measuring, weighing, are facts of sense simple and fundamental, and comparisons of these facts, capable of being so exhibited that no two persons shall either see them differently or misunderstand them.... It is therefore among select facts of sense, care-fully observed and properly compared, that the groundwork of unanimity is to be sought.' Mr Cope, in commenting on these words, concludes that, for this unanimity, we must suppose an objective, or in a sense external, standard: I take his view: and *I* comment on the words with a view of ascertaining what Mr Grote's view of ἐπιστήμη αἴσθησις is. Will *everybody now* agree with Mr Grote that 'counting, measuring, etc. are facts of sense or explicable by sensation?' Will all understand alike this process of *comparison* of sensations, and agree as to the amount of simply *mental* activity which the word is to be taken as implying? Will they agree whether the sensations compare themselves, or whether we, still sensationalists, can allow of a superior faculty comparing them? Will Mr Grote tell us how counting and measuring will give us a basis of knowledge as to *colour*, we will say? And might not some philosophers say what Mr Grote says here, only varying the language, and describing as facts of distinctive sense phenomena of the last kind (colour, etc.), the other alleged facts being styled *judgments* or *forms* of sensation, or whatever it might be?

I call attention to this not the least with the intention of discussing what ἐπιστήμη αἴσθησις does mean, but to suggest as worthy of our thought the question how far, at this moment, if we asked a succession of philosophers, What is the meaning of knowledge being sensation? we should get similar answers. And yet of course, till they were agreed upon their answer, it would be useless for them to discuss whether such and such a person held that knowledge was sensation. Mr Grote to a certain extent, and Mr Cope still more, speak as if, though the meaning of πάντων μέτρον ἄνθρωπος might be matter of discussion, the meaning of ἐπιστήμη αἴσθησις must be *evident*. But if this is not clear *now*, it is hardly likely to have been so in those times of non-analysis.

Apparently it is granted on both sides, that whatever *Homo Mensura* may mean, and whatever 'the Relativity of Knowledge' may mean, they both represent, to some extent, the same notion. Now Mr Mill, in his book on Sir William Hamilton[1], without any thought apparently of Plato or Protagoras, explaining 'the Relativity of Knowledge' in what he considers 'the simplest, purest and most proper acceptation of the words' explains it thus; 'that all the attributes which we ascribe to objects consist in their having the power of exciting one or another variety of sensation in our minds; that to us the properties of an object have this and no other meaning; that an object is to us nothing else than that which affects our senses in a certain manner; that we are incapable of attaching to the word 'object' any other meaning...so that our knowledge of objects and even our fancies about objects consist of nothing but the sensations which they excite, or which we imagine them exciting in ourselves.'

Here we have the doctrine of the relativity of knowledge put forward as naturally associating itself with a theory of 'knowledge' being 'sensation,' and Plato's proceeding in the *Theaetetus* seems to me precisely similar. All that Plato does in reality is to quote from Protagoras the saying which is equivalent to 'knowledge is relative,' and, in view of discussing

---

[1] Pp. 7, 8.

it, to suppose it to imply a theory that knowledge is sensation
—Plato's *exact* proceeding being in the reverse *order*. Now
we need not agree with either Mr Mill or with Plato. When
Plato abruptly, as he does, says that the theory of knowledge
being sensation is equivalent to the Protagorean relativity and
the Ionic flux and flow, I think we are a little startled, and are
disposed to consider that things are brought together at least
rather too summarily and rapidly. And similarly in reference to
Mr Mill's explanation given above of the doctrine of Relativity
(the application of which makes out Sir W. Hamilton in spite
of his own belief, not really to have held the doctrine), we may
be a little doubtful about that also. It is curious to compare
the proceedings of Plato as to Protagoras in old time, and of
Mr Mill as to Sir W. Hamilton now. Plato makes Protagoras
hold the theory of knowledge being sensation, because he held
Relativity : Mr Mill *will not let* Sir W. Hamilton hold Relativity,
because he holds, or is supposed to hold, that we know something of things in themselves, and that there is *some* knowledge
not from sensation.

Evidently therefore there is a great tendency to join the
two doctrines together, not only among the contemporaries and
successors of Plato, but among philosophers still. And the
probability is very strong, not only that Plato understood
Protagoras in the main, but that Protagoras, in enouncing his
Relativity, was thinking rather of its philosophical bearing, if
we may so call it, that is, of its connexion with the manner of
our gaining our knowledge, than of what is rather its *moral*
bearing, that is, its connexion with our taking our beliefs from
authority, instead of thinking for ourselves, and keeping fast
hold of our *own* truth, so to call it, against others. Mr Grote's
commendation of the Protagorean view, as he understands it,
seems to me made from a point of view so very unlike what
the philosophy of Protagoras was likely to have concerned
itself with, that it rather weighs *against* his supposition of
Protagoras' meaning being the correct one.

The relativity spoken of by Mr Mill may be called *generic*
relativity, in contrast to Protagorean or *individual* relativity.
The principle of the former and of the theory of sensation

accompanying it may be described as being, that the senses
give substantially to each man the same information under the
same outward circumstances: but if we suppose another race
of intelligent beings with different senses, they would have
different information given them, and therefore different knowledge: hence knowledge is generically relative, depending upon
the faculties by which it is apprehended. The supposed
Protagorean relativity says, Each individual is, for knowledge,
himself, autonomous, independent.

The *individual* character of the ancient relativity is what
Mr Grote tries to bring out in the strongest manner, and it is
apparently from the wish to make it the single, undivided
point of the Protagorean doctrine that he takes so much pains
to separate off the sensationalism. This latter, as we have
seen, he does not disapprove: only he does not wish Prota-
goreanism, if we may so speak, expanded in *this* direction. For
then we could not fail to come to the observation, which is the
basis, as I have just said, of modern sensationalism, viz. that
the senses, in the main, tell us all (*i.e.* each man) alike: that
the mass of the knowledge which they give us is intercom-
municable and is common property, however it may involve
beneath it much that is not so. The charm of sensationalism,
in the eyes of Locke and most modern sensationalists (curiously
enough, considering how the old *individual* sensationalism was
attacked on just the opposite lines) is the degree to which it
secures us against individual arbitrary judgments. If we
follow out sensation we get away, on the whole, from individual independence. Mr Grote, considering the point of
Protagoras' dictum to be the *individualness* of the relativity,
would rather follow this out in the direction of the entire
process of knowledge, including thought and judgment. Supposing Plato to understand Protagoras thus, πάντων μέτρον
ἄνθρωπος αἰσθανόμενος, we may suppose Mr Grote to understand
him thus, π. μ. α. αἰσθανόμενος ἢ δοξάζων. On the other hand
we may suppose Plato to have understood Protagoras, π. μ.
ἑαυτῷ ἄνθρωπος αἰσθανόμενος, which is true or false according
as it is understood: this is the view expressed in other words
by οἷα μὲν ἕκαστα ἐμοὶ φαίνεται, τοιαῦτα μὲν ἔστιν ἐμοί, οἷα

δὲ σοὶ, τοιαῦτα δὲ αὖ σοί[1]: 'the senses always tell us true,' *or* 'much that they tell us is illusion,' according to the language we use. But, whatever be the real truth or want of truth in this, there is a more important truth in such a phrase as π. μ. (not ἑαυτῷ only, but) πᾶσιν ἄνθρωπος αἰσθανόμενος ἀνόσως. Sensation, under its normal conditions, gives knowledge which is, and is understood by the individual as good, not for the individual himself only, but for all: it is part of his idea of it as knowledge *that it is for all.* To the extent to which there is any notion in his mind that it is not so, but is knowledge to *himself* alone; that something *e.g.* which he supposes himself to see would not be seen by another in his place,—to that extent he doubts of its being knowledge : the notion of its being ἑαυτῷ, to himself as against others, spoils it as knowledge, though it may endear it as imagination.

---

[1] *Theaet.* 151 E., quoted in Grote's *Plato,* II. 323.

CHAPTER II.

MR GROTE, interpreting Protagoras to have meant by his dictum, that every thing which a man deliberately thinks, judges, believes, is true to him individually, and that this is all the notion which we can have of truth, makes many most valuable remarks on the importance of this intellectual individuality. But, as a matter of philosophy, it seems to me that what he does is only to take away all particular meaning from the words truth and knowledge, so that we should have to use our language differently. He speaks himself of one person being *wiser* than another: well then, supposing everybody is in possession of truth, each of his own, we must leave the notion of truth in philosophy, as useless to examine, and must do what will come to the same thing, examine what is the meaning of one person being *wiser* than another. We may call each man's belief *his truth* if we like it: I see nothing in this more than altering the meaning of words. In that case, instead of speaking of a more or less *true belief*, we must speak of a superior and inferior, a more or less *correct, truth*. Horror of authority seems to be rather an *idée fixe* of Mr Grote: but he does not seem sufficiently to consider, that what needs setting against this belief on authority, is, from the philosophical point of view, not hugging our own opinion as *our* particular truth, but belief upon *evidence*, and refusal to yield to anything but that. Whether our belief is on authority or evidence, we must equally go out of ourselves for the materials of our judgment. Our judgment on evidence may even be called *less* individual

than if we believed on authority: we choose our authority
perhaps arbitrarily, but a belief upon evidence implies a supposition on our part that the grounds of our belief are what will,
or ought to, satisfy *another*, and reasonable persons in general.
We express this by saying, ' We judge for ourselves': but this
does not mean, ' We make our truth for ourselves.'   We should
so be led to the worst form of belief on authority, of which
there are some hints in Mr Grote,—following the mass or
majority.   If truth only means, 'that which is believed,' there
is some danger lest we should conclude, Then the best truth,
the truth which we had better adopt amongst the infinity of
individual truths, is that which is most and most widely
believed—the voice of the multitude.

In the Introduction to the First Part of the *Exploratio
Philosophica*[1] I have expressed myself on the subject of the
importance of individual judgment very strongly, and in a
manner which might appear to some at first sight to imply a
view similar to Mr Grote's.   In reality, however, my view of
the importance of individual judgment is very nearly the
reverse of his.

The question may present itself, more intelligibly to some,
if by way of introduction to it I use terms which Mr Grote
just introduces, but which have been more commonly used in
reference to religious controversy.   The difference between him
and me is simply this, that while what is important in *his*
eyes is the *right* of private judgment, what is important in
mine is the *duty* of it.

Mr Grote's view is that, in a manner, a man's thinking for
himself gives him truth, *his* truth ; and since the possession of
this truth is an important and valuable thing to him, his right
of thinking for himself is so also.   My view, while I do not
deny this, passes on beyond it.   A man's thinking for himself
gives him truth of a certain kind, *his* truth, if we so like to call
it.   But he is not to rest here.   His thinking for himself is
important, not only to himself, but to others and to intellectual
society, because all thought and learning is really social in a

---

[1] Pp. xxii., xxxii.—xlvii.

manner which I have at various times explained. To use
Platonic language, it advances in the way of dialectic, by the
comparison of the thought of one man with that of another:
and the thought of any individual man is worthless for this
comparison, unless the thought is true to that man's self, *i.e.*
unless he has been at pains and has been conscientious about
it, and unless his account of it represents something which he
has really inwardly or outwardly *seen*. What is important for
a man is, to get at what he really *does* think and see, a matter
which few people are interested about, and which is the sign of
what I should consider the real philosopher. Knowledge, so
far as it is knowledge, is only accidentally the property of one
man rather than of another; it equally fits all; it is the same
in whatever mind it is; it is communicable and transferable by
language. But all knowledge rests, in the *first instance*, upon
a truth or trueness of *observation* and *thought*, which *is* individual.
As in the case of disentangling evidence we want to find out
what this and that person really were witnesses of, so here
we want to find out, for *sense*, what is the thing which
we really see, and for *thought*, what is the thing which we
really inwardly see or are conscious of. When we do this,
we being all of us *men*, with substantially similar faculties
of intelligence, the individual *is* a measure of truth, in one
way to himself, in another *generally* and for all. He is
a measure to himself, in so far as his actually *seeing* the
thing (I will use the word *seeing* as the typical word) *is* truth
to him: he cannot get rid of it, he cannot substitute anything
as truth for it, it stands *intimate* to him, uncorrectable. But
while he has on the one side the firm persuasion, that nothing
can commend itself as true to him, which is in opposition to his
own *seeing* as above, supposing it careful and conscientious, he
has on the other side equally strongly the notion of knowledge
as something which is only accidentally individual, something
which is no more *his* property than that of others: so that any
conception on his part of what he sees being true to *him*, while
possibly not true to *others*, would be in fact a doubt whether it
was true, or knowledge, at all: his mind would be in an
inextricable perplexity: the notions of truth and knowledge

M. 18

would be destroyed or cease to exist. His feeling therefore as
to his own thought—and not only his feeling, but *the fact*—is
that, as in one view he thinks and sees for himself, so in
another view he thinks and sees for every one. In one view he
thinks and sees as Thomas or Charles, in another as a human
creature or an intelligent being in general: and full truth or
knowledge is the super-induction of the latter of these notions
upon the former. Neither of them will give it separately.
His seeing or thinking as Thomas or Charles, if he does so
conscientiously, will give *a* truth, but it is not till he adds the
notion of his thus thinking or seeing being typical of what
others will think or see, that it is what I have just called *full*
truth, or what he would count as *knowledge*. On the other
hand, his simply following the example and authority of other
intelligent beings, and thinking or seeing (if we may call it so)
as they do, will give him it may be truth, *another* truth or a
different portion of it, to the extent to which the example is
followable: but though he may *adopt* the thoughts of others,
he cannot *think* them except for himself, and knowing, or
thinking *truly*, is a case of *thinking*.

Human experience is all anticipated, if we may so speak, in
the frame of the human mind, which is a part of the general
manner in which things exist for each other, or fit together.
Seeing is knowing that we see, and knowing that we see is
knowing that what we see is as we see it. Whatever therefore
we can say to ourselves that we see,—supposing the care and
conscientiousness which I have spoken of above,—is certain to
us, and derives no additional certainty from the fact that any
number of people see the thing the same as we do. Knowing
that another person sees the thing is the same as taking a second
look ourselves, to be sure what it is that we see, and it is no
more. In regard then of our sensation and thought, from the
first, we perceive and think not for ourselves only, but for all
and any, with the same persuasion of the certainty of what we
see and think as certain, as if we knew for a fact that everybody else saw and thought the same. The fact thus anticipated
in the manner of our sight and thought, viz. that others see
and think the same as we, we find justified by our actual

experience. We may find, indeed, in this experience, that the commencing assumption was *in a manner* too general, that is, that, in our sight and thought, there is something belonging to ourselves exclusively, so that the *first* or individual truth of our sight and thought (as to the reality of which each is μέτρον ἑαυτῷ, a measure to himself) has to be pruned, in order to our arriving at the second or full truth, that namely, of which each is μέτρον πᾶσιν, a measure good for all alike. This is merely a further extension of what I alluded to when, in speaking of sensation, I said that παντὸς μέτρον πᾶσιν ἄνθρωπος αἰσθάν-όμενος ἀνόσως: any special *individuality* of sensation in the body is of the nature of disease : and in one way, individuality of thought may be looked on, in comparison with the knowledge or true thought which is alike for all, as disease likewise. But in *this* respect it is *not* like disease, viz. that, for knowledge, what is needed in regard of it is not to get rid of it, but to allow and understand it, and then to make the proper correction.

This is what is done in the intercourse of life and in that special intellectual intercourse which Plato, I suppose, meant by Dialectic. It is curious to observe how, in Mr Grote's argument with Plato about this, the two sides of truth, its generality and its individuality, are brought out. No step is made, says Mr Grote[1], in the Socratic Dialectic or Elenchus, unless you alter the view of the individual: truth is therefore individual. On the other hand, were truth individual only, why should you *try* to alter the view of the individual? Why should you not keep your own truth, and leave him his? In this dialectic, just as, on the one hand, the requiring of the assent of the answerer at each step, shows that truth must be individual, or that you have gained nothing unless you have made it truth *for him*: so the fact of your discussing and comparing and testing opinions shows that you do not consider this individual opinion or truth for a man's self, as what is to be rested in, but as the *road* towards a *not-individual* opinion, or truth for all. It is most important, in the way to this, that you should have the individual opinion well brought out, and

[1] *l.c.* p. 356.

herein lies the value of the Socratic cross-examination: the individual opinion, if it be a real and conscientious sight or thought on the part of the individual, has of necessity *a* truth, which when brought into contact with *other* individual opinion (either counter-asserting and comparing, or, as in dialectic, suggesting doubts, and leading to distrust, examination, and further thought) will more or less lead on, by the connexion which all truth has together, to truth of more fullness and importance.

The individual view is thus the witness which we have of objective fact or truth, and it is because it is this witness that to me it is of value. Our own individual view is the first thing to us, because it is intimate to us in a manner quite different from anything which the thought of others is; and what we mean by 'objective fact or truth' is a something which we believe *this* to bear witness of to us. But along with our own view we have, as I have said,—and if we did not have it we should not have the notions of truth and knowledge at all, nor, I think, would the words have existed—the thought that it is, in substance, *not* individually or exclusively *ours*, but that it is the view of *intelligence*, of which intelligence we, each of us, are an instance or specimen. It is in virtue of this latter thought that we consider our view to be truth or knowledge, and call that which we believe it to bear witness to, *fact*, this term having its significance to us by contrast with a 'counter-notion,' which we call *illusion*. Experience, as we go on, both confirms and corrects our individual view with its accompanying thought; not indeed by confirmation adding more certainty to it, nor yet by correction altering its substance: but there comes to be formed in us a mass of opinion of every variety of certainty, and with various degrees of insight and belief, which opinion is continually modifying itself according to our intercourse with others, and the comparison of *their* individual views with our own. We make use as it were of their eyes to help our own to see the objective fact: and beyond sight or immediate certainty, the mass of opinion or belief, which furnishes our mind, is of value if it rests on evidence, this evidence being, like the original sight, good for all, if good for one.

It is because individuality of view with me thus stands subordinate to an objective truth which we believe in, that it is able (as I look at things) to maintain itself against any possible view of any number of others. If what I feel is, I *suppose* this or that, I should consider it presumption to put *my* supposing against that of men in general: but if what I feel is, I *see* this or that, then I *could* not, if I would, yield in this matter to others. If I am sure that I see the thing, I cannot get rid of the feeling. It is in the *dependence* of our thought upon a believed object of it, that resides its *independence* of the opinion of others, or its true individuality.

Mr Grote, looking upon individual view as valuable in itself, not as I have done, in its character of witness, has at last, it appears to me, to leave hold of his own view where it is most needed. Taking his view, we seem to have no ground upon which we can maintain our opinion against that of others, or have anything further to say about it, except that it is *ours*. And this being so, unless we suppose no intellectual intercourse and no comparison of opinions, all *support* of individuality of opinion seems to vanish, and such intercourse and comparison is likely only to result in an acquiescence, on the part of individuals in what is most generally believed. The individuality which was at first so strongly asserted thus ends in destroying itself.

To illustrate the relation of *individual* truth of view to *full* truth or knowledge, we might take an instance from sense. I think I see a mountain out of my window. This fact, so far, is full of individuality or *accidentalness*, and in order to be a fact contributory, for me or for any, to full or proper knowledge, has got, in this first state, to be carefully tested. Is it a window that is before me, and not a picture in which a mountain is painted, or a mirror reflecting a mountain behind me? Am I certain, as I look and look again, that the object before me retains the same figure, so that I can be certain that it is a mountain, not a cloud? Is my eyesight healthy, (the ἀνόσως which I mentioned), not liable to films obscuring it or to any other defect? Supposing a man comes out and tells us, I saw there a mountain from the window in such a direction,

there is all the difference in the world whether we can trust
him for having really *looked*, in somewhat of the way I have
described, or whether we have only reason to think that
something has passed before his eyes, which, in his carelessness,
he describes as he does.   In the former case *we* are as certain,
speaking generally, that the mountain is there as *he is*, and our
knowledge through *his* eyes is as trustworthy to us as if it
were through *our own*, and he on his part most likely tells us,
not the *individual* fact, *I saw* a mountain there, but the
general fact, *There is* a mountain there, he meaning by this
not, I *think* there is, or to my view and for individual *me* there
is, but I *know* there is, and in knowing it I know it for *you* as
well as for myself, I know that whichever of us goes to the
window will equally see it: I tried every means of testing my
seeing, and until I had tested it, if you had passed, I should
have said, I *think* there is a mountain there, *to me* there is:
but then I should not yet have said for *myself*, I know there
is.   It may not be possible to make the testing complete,
and of course I may be deceived: it may after all be a
cloud, not a mountain: the point is, that I am no more
certain of anything for myself than I am for you, that I have
no *individual* certainty or knowledge except such as is accidental to the matter in which we are both interested, which is
the existence of the mountain, such *e.g.* as the size of the
supposed window, the shape of the room, &c., which are all
parts of the first fact or the sensation, but are only mediately
important to the full or desired truth.   When I say *mediately*
important, what I mean is this: you might want to know
whether you could trust me for having really *looked* with care
and attention: your way of doing this would be by examining
how distinct the first fact, upon which all rests, was with me.
If you asked whether the window was large or small, and I said
I did not know; whether the room was square or round, and I
said it was square when you knew it was round,—you would
say then my observation was worth nothing, and you would
not trouble yourself about it.

     Perhaps this illustration may help to make it understood
how the furthest point towards knowledge to which we are

able to get for ourselves is the most real knowledge, or the thought nearest to knowledge, to which we can arrive for others, or as general fact. What is individual belongs to a middle region, having a value which I would exalt as much as Mr Grote does, but a value which I have just now called *mediate*, something not to be rested in for itself. We must be true to ourselves in what we see and think : otherwise we shall not be able to add to the stock of general truth, of truth which is good alike for ourselves and for others. We must be each one to ourselves a faithful $\mu\acute{\epsilon}\tau\rho o\nu$ $\pi\acute{a}\nu\tau\omega\nu$, a rule of brass or good hard wood and not of flexible lead or wax, because we each, individually, are the measure of a portion of reality which, when combined with other portions of knowledge, of which others, in *their* life and history, are measures, (the individuality or 'accidentalness' which I described just now being disengaged) results in man being generically a $\mu\acute{\epsilon}\tau\rho o\nu$ $\pi\acute{a}\nu\tau\omega\nu$. The things which *we* see for *others*, as well as for ourselves, are put along with the things which *others* see for *us* as well as for themselves, and thus has been accumulated what we call the stock of existing knowledge.

I do not at all mean to say that it is easy for us to reconcile the certainty of individual sensations and insight with the feeling which we have that what is true for one is true for all ; so that, if we find others differing from us, we can only hold our own opinion with something of an effort and possibly with mistrust. I have before said that, with regard to sensation and individual conviction, we do not wait for others in order to be certain, in the manner which I have described, alike for ourselves and for them. Truth is not deference to numbers, not the generally believed, in which the individual must acquiesce. If we saw the thermometer was at 50, and knew we had looked carefully, we should not be the least more certain because half-a-dozen persons, looking successively and immediately after us, said the same. But, inasmuch as the feeling that we saw it, was at the same time a feeling that others would see it similarly, we should be in very great perplexity of mind if the half-dozen persons, we having reason to trust them, should agree in saying that it was 60. The individuality of observation and the felt generality of knowledge, or the result of observation, would be in conflict. *We* should look again, *they* would look again, we should clear our eyes, do anything we could to test the observation, be sure we all looked from the same point, I know not what,—we might have at last to rest in our perplexity. But it would not at all satisfy the perplexity, with me, for us to sit down and for me to say ' Well, each is a measure for himself : it is 60 for you and 50 for me, both are true, one your truth, the other mine.' Both *are* true, as facts of observation : it is a fact that you see the thermometer 60, I 50 : it is a fact moreover which like all fact, has its meaning and its reason, if we could but get at this, and *points* therefore or is in the way towards knowledge, only that we cannot get further *along* the way: there must be something wrong in you or in me or in the thermometer, though as yet we have not found out what. But if we can go no further, the two true facts of observation only make knowledge about what is accidental and unimportant : they make no knowledge about the thing which we want to know, viz. what the thermometer stands at.

There is a thing which in this perplexity, some might say was the thing to be done, and that is for me to say, ' It is six to one against me : I must give in.' I do not think I should do so. Till I saw reason to mistrust my careful view, I do not see that I could help holding it. If it was said, ' Truth is the generally believed, and the generally believed here is that 60 is the number'; I should say, If I could call it to myself belief or supposition, I would defer : I do not want to set up my judgment : but it is *sight*. The turning my eyes that way and the persuasion that there is before my eyes the fact, which we call the quicksilver at 50, are two things equally unescapable by me : you bear witness with me to the truth of the former, and since the second presents itself to me with equal evidence, I must accept it, though you cannot bear witness to that.

The state of things which I have here described cannot in reality, unless exceptionally, take place in a sensation such as sight, but it serves as a good illustration of what is the normal or ordinary state of things in regard of opinion. We have the constant conflict going on between our own opinion or belief and that of others, and while we try conscientiously to test the former and see if we can justify it to ourselves, we find perhaps on the other hand, as we look, more and more of opinion against us. As to this we may very likely have to come in practice to a view somewhat similar to that of Mr Grote, where he in effect says—I will keep my opinion as truth for me, you keep yours as truth for you. This does not mean that we have arrived, both of us or either of us, at truth, but simply that it is no use saying any more about the matter; that we see no reason to doubt our own opinion, but have no means by which we can persuade the other party of it. But before we arrive at this stage of indolent despair—for such it is, not of philosophical reasonableness—we ought to make sure of our own opinion to the utmost extent to which we can, and (in this view) to have it with its reasons, clear before ourselves, in the first instance, and then, in whatever way, to compare it with that of others. We may be said, each one of us, to hold our individual opinion not for ourselves alone, but for general intelligence. To state the matter strongly, unless we consider that every one ought to think as we do, we do not believe in our own truth : we do not consider what we think, to be real truth and knowledge. The isolation of our thought, and the holding it simply as *our* best way of thinking, and not, so far as it commends itself to us, *the* best way for everybody, is a denying to ourselves the notion of truth altogether. Unfortunately as a matter of fact it is most usually the case that those who least care to justify their opinion to themselves are the most ready to enforce it on others : very constantly even making the latter a sort of substitute for the former. But though, in conscientious thought, we are thinking for others as well as for ourselves, and ought to be aware we are doing so; we have also to remember that they think as well as we do ; and the more value we set upon our own thought the more shall we also, in reason, set upon *theirs*, if only we have reason to believe they *do* think. We here come upon the same difficulty as in the case of the thermometer: men as we all are, with the same fact before us, the supposition involved in the notion 'knowledge' is, that the fact shall represent itself to all in substance the same: yet we are in the unhappy position, that, whereas there are two characters of knowledge which constitute its definition, the one, that it is (say) a faithful representation of fact to the individual, the other, that it is a sympathy or region of communication between intelligent beings,—we cannot make these two characters go together, and therefore are in continual perplexity.

As the discrepancy of opinion is infinite, whereas that of sensation is only occasional and exceptional, so the former has powerful agencies to remedy it, while in the latter we are nearly helpless. Opinion or judgment is formed, speaking roughly, from the putting together sensations or original experiences, which process we will, still roughly, call reasoning. In reasoning, as in seeing, we are (so far as we feel we are doing it truly) doing it for others as well as for ourselves. Reasoning may be described as a mental view on our part of a connexion of facts which commends itself to us as true or as a more general fact, a part of our notion of its truth being that, when put into language and communicated to others, it will commend itself to them as it commends itself to us. We may find that the view we take of the cogency of a piece of reasoning may be different from the view which others take: but this discrepancy of view, while it is more likely to occur than in a case of sensation, has at the same time more remedies against it, because the principles upon which the reasoning should go may be agreed on beforehand, and because the reasoning may be exhibited in various forms so as to be well tested and thoroughly understood. The doing all this is *discussion*, which stops, as soon as we come to the original experiences upon which all rests. And hence it is that discussion is of no value unless there is beneath it a good basis of conscientious and careful individual feeling. It is this individual feeling about which we are autonomous, this which is our 'private judgment.' The question between it and conclusions arrived at from it by reasoning and discussion, on the one side, and belief upon authority on the other, presents itself to Mr Grote and to me (to come round to the point from which we began) in rather a different manner. Where *he* sees a tyranny of authority, I am more disposed to see a want of truth of individuals to themselves. We had better have a belief upon authority, (for the chances are that the authority will be in *some* degree at least worthy of regard) than an individual view, or what we think such, formed carelessly and unconscientiously and only half realized, valued rather because it is *ours* than because it is true, and which, therefore, we do not choose to bring into fair contact with other opinions, fearing that it would not stand the shock of the Socratic elenchus.

CHAPTER III.

RELATIVITY OF KNOWLEDGE, GENERAL
AND PARTICULAR.

WITH Mr Grote the character of knowledge as 'relative' does not at all destroy its character of being real knowledge, it being the fact, not only that *we* cannot conceive knowledge other than relative, but that relativity attaches to the very notion of knowledge—that knowledge is inconceivable otherwise.

The most general relativity of knowledge is described by Mr Grote as the necessary relation of an object to a subject—in other words, the necessity, if we want to conceive a thing or fact, of conceiving a thinking subject with it—in other words again, the necessary involvement, in the notion of an object of thought, of a subject thinking it; the fact involved in knowledge, as it is put by Mr Ferrier, being not simply an object, but a subject knowing an object.

This view of relativity raises the question, Is existence nothing without intelligence perceiving it? Is there no such thing as 'knowableness' distinct from 'knownness'? Suppose we could, by that absolute power which belongs to imagination, remove from the universe all intelligence, would there remain nothing, or something entirely different from what was considered existence *before* intelligence was removed?

This very general view of the relativeness of knowledge only exists on the supposition that, in forming our notion of knowledge, we start, if I may so express it, with the subject; and in reality, though it does not at first appear so, this general view of relativity is inconsistent with the more particular views. When it is said, Object involves subject, and this is relativity—if by *subject* is meant subject in the same generality which the term *object* here has, there is nothing which with any significance can be called relativity—if by subject is meant particular subject, *then* the statement is not necessarily true. If we mean that the notion of existence involves the thing being understood to exist, I do not see any relativity. By relativity we mean, I suppose, that the thing in question is, in its relation to some thing, different from what it is in itself, or in its relation to some other thing: but the thing being understood to exist in the way just mentioned, makes no sort of difference of this kind. If we mean that 'the notion of existence involves the thing being conceived as existing by an intelligent being with particular faculties of knowledge'—in which case there would be relativity—I deny the truth of the proposition. Of course, in even talking of anything as existent, I am conceiving it by my own faculties of knowledge: but this is no further to the purpose in this question, than to make me understand that I cannot realize, as present to my mind in any way, an object, or existence, in the general sense here spoken of: but there is no reason why I should not conceive there being such. The notion of the *particular* relativity of knowledge implies our forming, as we do form, the notion of the conception of the same existence by different kinds of intelligent beings with different faculties of knowledge, and we say, Each of them has relative knowledge of it. But the meaning of *difference* in the manners of conception depends upon there being some one thing which is thus differently conceived: and this one thing, which is the basis of all the conceptions, we may suppose abstracted from them—none of them being, from their very differences, essential to it—and not particularly conceived at all. To the notion of existence there goes capability of these various kinds of conception, not actually of any one of them, which is what would be relativity. When it is conceived in any of these various ways, there arises particular relativity. If we suppose a general relativity, relativity arising out of the simple fact that existence is understood by intelligence, we destroy all meaning in the *particular* relativity, the point of which is the different conception of the same supposed existence by different intelligences.

This will be easier to understand, if, instead of starting from the subject, we start from the side of the object. We then may freely make the supposition, for of course it is no more, of what I will call an 'objiciend,' which is the object of thought with all such portions of it removed as are relative to the faculties of any particular intelligence. This *objiciend* translates itself into various objects of thought according to the particular kind of intelligence to which it presents itself. It is in *this* that the relativity consists: and the supposition of the non-relative *objiciend* is necessary for the relativity to have meaning. 'A thing' has a double meaning to us, which duplicity, though not of importance in ordinary thought, is of great importance in regard of many questions of philosophy. When we say, we see a tree, it is with more or less feeling that the *colour, e.g.* of the tree would not be what it is, unless our eyes were what they are—with more or less feeling, as metaphysicians some time ago used to express it, that the colour is in the tree or that it is not. By the term 'tree' we mean a something supposed independent of us, which we suppose to have existence for intelligences (supposing there are such) different from our own—though with what kind of appearance, we cannot tell: and yet when we say 'the tree' we mean the object, which we say also is green in virtue of the effect of the light from it on our particular sense. That is to say, we mean by 'the tree,' undistinguished in our mind, what philosophers call the thing in itself, the 'objiciend,' and *also* the phenomenon or thing as it presents itself to us, clothed with its various relations to *our* particular sensiveness,—the *object* of sight as distinguished from the *objiciend* or *thing* which we want to know, and talk of as if we did know, which latter may be called the object of an effort at knowledge, rather than the object of knowledge itself.

The important relativity then is the particular *relativity*, and it appears to me that what is to be said about this is that the human mind is in a manner at issue with itself, or thinks, if we like so to express it, with an undistinguishingness, from which it cannot escape, of two different things, the actual phenomenon before it, and the non-relative fact which presents itself to *its* intelligence *as* this phenomenon: the former involves with it inferior fact, truth, reality, knowledge; the latter the full and desired.

The notions of reality, truth, knowledge, as they are formed, are non-relative, and in my view would not be formed at all, if from the first we had the feeling that we could not get beyond the relative. It is an accompanying feeling of all our sensations and all our thought, that it is good and true, so far as it is good and true, for others as well as for ourselves. What we want to attain, in wishing for knowledge, is something good for all intelligence, not something private, or (if we form the notion of other genera of intelligent beings) generic to the human race. This latter we cherish as *knowledge* in virtue of its being *common* to us and other human beings, *i.e.* in virtue of what there is in it non-relative: but as soon as we begin to look upon it as only a particular manner of thinking, whether it be individual or generic, all its charm as knowledge vanishes. The charm of knowledge is its presumed bringing us face to face with fact, making us in a manner masters of our position, enabling us to exercise our freedom, and without fear to choose our action for ourselves: as soon as our notion of the faithfulness of this knowledge to fact is vitiated, all the charm vanishes. We are no longer free: intelligent beings no longer understand each other.

However I must stop. Non-relative, full, simple, absolute, truth or knowledge is what we mean by truth or knowledge, and we cannot make ourselves mean anything else: but they are ideals, they are what we think of, hope for, struggle after, while what we gain in the effort is relative knowledge, from which as in the case of individuality, we may more and more disentangle the exclusively relative element, and come towards our ideal.

BOOK V.

IDEALISM AND POSITIVISM.

CHAPTER I.

INADEQUACY OF THE POSITIVIST VIEW OF TRUTH AND LIFE.

I WILL now attempt a general summary of the view which I have given above, and describe what seems to me the importance of it.

So far as we make the basis of our thoughts the world of phenomena, that which is most intimate to us,—*ourselves* with our consciousness,—remains alien to our thought, and from the very nature of the one and the other, not comprehendible in it.

The fact that *we know* is prior to, and logically more comprehensive than, the fact that what we know *is*. We assert of, or attribute to, that which we perceive, the existence which we feel in ourselves. Our thought includes its existence, but its existence does not include our thought. When we state that it exists, we state only a part of the fact: when we state that we, existing, know that it exists, we state the whole. And we must consequently be wrong in our view if we state a part of the fact in such a manner as to negative, or reduce to unimportance, or pervert, the whole. What I have called phenomenalism is the giving exclusive attention to the part: what I have called wrong phenomenalism or positivism is the doing so in such a manner as to pervert the whole.

It is therefore of importance, for any general view, that we should consider not only what things are, but what *our knowledge* of them is, means, or implies.

19—2

That we know them implies of course that they can be known: and 'that they can be known' is in my view only another way of describing a fitness or preparedness in them to be known. But if this is so, here is a great and important general fact about them, far more important than any particular fact, implied or presupposed in our very first notion of them. This *knowableness* of them, or preparedness of them for knowledge, is what philosophers have variously expressed by saying that there is *mind* in them; that there is *reason* (not *thinking* reason, but *thought* reason) in them; that if they had not been known from the first, they never could have been known; if they had not been planned, a plan of them, or in them, could never have been discovered, as our knowledge discovers it. Knowing is therefore mind meeting mind; mind analysing, or dissecting, what mind must have compounded; mind sympathizing with mind, as they proceed in their opposite directions.

Again: *knowableness* or order (for they are the same thing) is not something which we unexpectedly find in the universe, any more than *being known* is an *accident*[1] which has happened to the universe, after its continuance for some time without such accident. As the universe must always have been known, so we from the beginning of our knowledge, must have known the universe. As one word of a language implies the whole system of it, so does one particular of knowledge involve thought of the, as yet unparticularized, universe.

Order or knowableness in the universe is then implied by us, or we may say, understood, so far as anything is understood, in the first act of knowledge. And the key to open this order, the clue to follow it by, the alphabet to read it by, is the recognition, continually corrected, of *ourselves* in it. That knowledge comes to us with this character of recognition, is what the ancient philosophy noted, when it spoke of knowledge as the remembrance of a former existence.

The process of correction of this self-recognition divides knowledge into two parts. The corrected knowledge is pheno-

---

[1] Cf. *Exp.* 59.

menalism: but the correction is not condemnation of the former
process, which in reality, always goes on, and is still our way of
knowing, the later or corrected process being *partial* only, and
not of a nature in everything to supersede the other. But
the process of *self-recognition* becomes the process of *mind-
recognition*, which is the important part, and the real character
of it, from the first. Or, if we like rather so to express it, side by
side with the correction of our self-recognition, which generates
phenomenal knowledge, but which still leaves the self-recognition uncorrected for some lines of thought, there occurs an
elevation or generalization of this self-recognition, where it *is*
left existing. The idea of the universe, as consisting of beings
or things like us, and things which we can make or use, becomes
exalted into the idea of the universe as exhibiting mind and
involving purpose, mind such as we exercise in ordering and
arranging things, and purpose such as induces us to construct
or make things.

For my own part, I seem to recognize a higher legitimacy
in the transformed self-recognition, which shows us in the
Universe a Planner or Maker with his ideas and his purposes,
than I recognize in the corrected self-recognition, which shows
us in the universe the concurrences and sequences of a variety
of phenomenal elements, forces, or parts of any kind of
phenomenal nature. There seems to me to be a nature *above*
all this: a nature of which man, in virtue of his consciousness
and knowledge, is partaker, just as, in virtue of his body and
its sensation, he is a portion of the phenomenal nature. And
it is this nature which the one part of his thought points to,
with as much legitimacy as the other to phenomenal nature.

The positivist scheme of thought is really the imagination
of a state of things in which consciousness nowhere exists,
underlying in thought, (and therefore with a natural suggestion
of its preceding in time) a state of things in which it *does*
exist. It makes particular or qualified existence an earlier
idea, or an idea of a higher order, than knowledge or consciousness. I do not mean to imply that there need be anything
irreligious in such a scheme. It is natural to say that a thing
must *be*, and must be *something*, before it can *know*. Thus we

may say that God is a *being*, who (as a quasi-accident) *knows*. But if his *knowing* is in this point of view a quasi-accident, so is his *being*, and all being. In the supposition of existence as in this manner anterior to knowledge, anything being what it is, must be of the nature of accident, for there can be no reason for it.

Let us endeavour as far as we can to grasp what seems to me the true positivist notion, and think about things only that they *are*, without any supposition of reason, either as shown *in* what they are, or (as yet) resulting *from* what they are. Let us suppose the elements of matter, whatever they may be, or, going beyond them, let us suppose something from which what we call matter has become evolved. And let us conceive of ourselves, not in virtue of, or by means of, that consciousness which is our ordinary road to that conception; but as results evolved from these material elements. We have then an order of positivist facts, which we may call matter to begin with, life superadded to this, consciousness superadded again, then perhaps freedom: these all being supposed, not as known to us by our consciousness, but as far as possible independently of consciousness by abstracting from knowledge the *objective* side of it. We have then first something somehow qualified, which we call, *e.g.*, matter: then a quality adding itself to parts of this, which we call life: another to parts again of this living matter, which we call consciousness, and so on.

In all this we must keep carefully out of thought the manner in which things become known to us. Smell, *e.g.* must be treated as a process between portions of matter and nerves of the being which we call ourselves: that it gives us knowledge in regard of the things in which it resides, is what we must not consider, because, so far as we do, we endanger (logically) the independent reality of the thing: if we admit the idea of ourselves as knowing, we cannot help also admitting the notion that this our knowing the thing may constitute the real fact about it; and the purpose of the present or positivist supposition which I am making is to exclude this latter notion.

Of the whole positivist scheme, the great idea is fact or existence: among existing beings there are considered to be some who think or make suppositions about things: truth, in this view, is these suppositions being accordant with fact. It is indeed hardly possible, in this view, to bring out the idea of truth with any clearness: *i.e.* we can hardly hold sufficiently firm the necessary consideration, that the supposition is to be posterior to the fact, or refrain from asking ourselves how the fact can be known to be fact but by supposition, and where we are to go, in the last resort, to find out that the supposition is right. The idea of truth, in the positivist view, has to be aided by various other considerations, besides that which I have given. The *essence* of truth is its conformity with fact, but the *marks* of it are such as its consistency with other truth, its being the common thought of different minds, its being that which we can act upon to an expected result.

I have mentioned the logical error involved in such intellectual philosophy as would start from the notion of an existing order of things of which we form a part, and then would endeavour to investigate the manner in which we come to perceive, or to have an idea of, or to understand, the particulars or objects in this order of things. We cannot superadd the idea of knowledge to that of existence and *then* analyse the knowledge, because if we do so, the idea of knowledge thus analysed disintegrates (logically) the idea of *existence* which we had previously gone upon, and all becomes confusion. Confusion of this kind from which there is no way out is the true meaning of scepticism. It was in this manner that Berkeley and Hume disintegrated the Lockian edifice.

There is an error of the same kind involved in the building any moral philosophy on a positivist basis. The idea of freedom or choice of action will not superadd itself to that of a state of things independent of it, without pulling this latter to pieces and altogether changing the character of it.

Much of Epicureanism and Utilitarianism may be considered a vain attempt to mediate, or to find a halfway standing point, between two schemes of thought which will not thus be brought together.

The idealist or non-positivist scheme is that which starts from what (philosophically) is the full or complete fact or phenomenon, viz. consciousness or knowledge, accompanied with *power* or *freedom*, (whatever, in further analysis, this latter may turn out to be).

According to this, knowledge is not (in its essence) a result of existence, but is an analysing, criticising, judging of it: it looks upon it from above, not from below. The argument of Natural Theology, that all things which exist must have been created, is simply a recognition of the fact, that the mind cannot be got to rest in the notion of particular existence, as the end of its view. 'How comes a thing to be what it is'? is what we cannot help asking: and it is exactly the same mental activity which urges us to the earliest steps of knowledge and which urges us to the last and remotest. Knowledge is really a phase or mode of consciousness and, the object as well as the subject being a part of itself, it is really *mind* that is its object as well as its subject; and existence, the more immediate object, is such, in virtue of its being looked upon as the result of mind or intelligence. Knowledge is the sympathy of intelligence with intelligence, through the medium of qualified or particular existence.

Knowledge and freedom, or choice of action, go closely together, and that *judgment* which is so important a part of knowledge, is of equal importance to freedom. Hence come those ideas, which, along with the idea of truth, enter into the process of knowledge as naturally going on. We cannot really make that distinction between the processes of reasoning and imagination which is often attempted, nor characterize the latter as 'a forward delusive faculty' unless we are agreed to mean by it only such portion of our mental discourse as is really delusive and mistaken.

This sort of opinion about imagination is really founded on the supposition that the positivist scheme of existence is first in idea, knowledge following on that, and then again imagination on that, as a sort of otiose, superfluous, addition to it, or atmosphere surrounding it. In Plato (where the process of knowledge is followed in an opposite direction, and the scheme is idealist) 'good,' or 'that which it is well should be,' is first in idea, then follows knowledge proper, which is of the 'ideas,' or

as we may say, the meanings of things, and then follows such
knowledge as can be had of particular existence, or that fluctu-
ating element in which these ideas are embodied: this is that
which, in Plato, under the name of δόξα, is the superfluous
and the delusive.

It is as unphilosophical and as logically wrong to try to
construct a moral philosophy on the positivist basis, as it was on
the part of the pre-Baconians (in Bacon's view) to conclude
what must be the actual facts and laws of material nature from
their own à priori imaginations as to what would be most
beautiful and harmonious. Positivism, which has its full value
within its own province, is as much injured, and the real fact is
as much distorted, by the former process, as by the latter. If we
have any idea about directing human action, and about one way
of it being better than another, or being what human action
ought to be, we vitiate and falsify our positivist view by determining to find in it some place for this idea, which does not
belong to it and will not harmonize with it. The notion of
duty, or of one thing being better than another, coming into a
scheme of positivism blows it all up.

While therefore idealism must be considered the wider view
and that containing the higher truth, upon which, so far as
direction of action is of consequence to us, we must proceed,
still there is no such contradiction between idealism and a
reasonable positivism, as the language of Plato and as the
encroachments of positivists might lead one to imagine. For
the discovery of what is and has been actual, physical, fact, we
must be faithful to the impressions of our senses and the treatment of these by our logical powers, and no idealism must
interfere here in a province which does not belong to it. The
more our idealism is true and complete, the less will it be
either meddling itself, or allow of other things meddling with it.
Knowledge or consciousness is not itself a physical fact, homo-
geneous with physical facts or forces even of the most refined
kind, such as magnetism or any other. When we speak of the
universe as the sum of existence, and ourselves as a part of it,
we reserve, and we cannot help reserving, the primary consciousness, which presents to us ourselves and our knowledge as

existing more necessarily for ourselves than even the universe exists before us.

The positivist view has the double strength of the *partial* philosophic truth which there is in it, and the entire popular truth, it representing the view to which our intellect evidently impels us. But philosophic and popular truth are both to be found also in such an idea as 'that which is right to be done' or 'that which is beautiful to be looked at': and these are ideas which the positivist, from his point of view, is obliged either to treat as vain sentiment, imagination, or illusion, or else to refer to origins in fact, to which they cannot be referred without destroying their significance. The true idealist point of view will comprehend his, whereas his will not comprehend that.

Again, while on the one hand it is a *part* of our natural impulse, as to knowledge, to attribute to the objects of our knowledge a reality independent of ourselves, or of any one's knowledge of them, on the other hand our natural impulse is not merely to attribute fact and reality to the objects of perception. We want to know also the *reasons* of them, we want to do more than to classify, we want to understand: and we have no notion that in the advance of our knowledge we are after all not really getting beyond extended perception. Positivism consists in the throwing off as extraneous all other considerations except this—What is the fact? The intellectual progress of the human race consists, according to positivists, in its having learnt by degrees to do this. This is well, so long as we are in the region of fact or of the objects of knowledge. But the supposition of *a reason* for things being what they are, is an essential part of the natural effort to know, or process of knowledge. The positivist view that the search for this reason is really only the passage from one fact to a further or antecedent fact, is an abstraction from the more complete view, in the same manner as positivism altogether is an abstraction from the complete view of knowledge. The supposition of a reason for things being what they are, is the same as the supposition of a way in which it is well that they should be, as distinguished from other ways in which they would be less well. Here we come into a wide region of *what might be,* as distinguished from *what is.* And in this region, while *what is* is matter of perception, what is sought, or taken interest in, is that which it is good or well *should be,* and the interest in knowledge is not only in the observation of *what is,* but in the observing its relation to that which it is good or well *should be,* which is *the reason* of it.

The partial or positivist view of the process of knowledge reverses the relative position of imagination and observation, as compared with their position in the complete view of that process. And the consideration how this is so, shows in regard of the positivist view that, like all abstractions, it fails to a certain degree not only in completeness, but in truth. Knowledge is more truly a fixing of vague imagination, than imagination is an extravagation of the mind round about the nucleus, knowledge. Imagination is logically first, knowledge second. As the knowledge of a single word of a language, as a word, implies the idea of language, or as the knowledge of a single organ, as an organ, implies the idea of organization, so the first particular of knowledge implies the idea of a whole or universe of things, which is given us in fact, in every effort of our consciousness. Advance of knowledge is essentially distinction, not aggregation. Each new particular of knowledge is not an addition to, but a newly observed part of, a previously conceived whole. Each notion has its ground or counternotion, the observation of which is quite as important as that of the notion itself[1].

And the notion of our own activity, which is the ground of morals, must be taken in relation to the complete or idealist view of knowledge, not to the other.

[1] *Expl.* 23, 24.

CHAPTER II.

POSITIVISM AS OPPOSED TO RATIONARY PHILOSOPHY IN
REGARD TO KNOWLEDGE. ERROR OF RELATIVISM.

PHILOSOPHY is concerned either with *knowledge*, the object of
which is something in some way existing, or with *action*, which
is the bringing into existence something not yet existent. In
contradistinction to 'positivist,' I use the word 'rationary' in
regard to the former, and the word 'idealist' in regard to the
latter.

By *rationary* philosophy, I mean that portion of philosophy
which deals with those parts, circumstances, or relations of things
(supposing them to be such) which are not cognizable by the
senses, as we ordinarily speak of senses. I am in the habit of
using for these the terms 'cause,' 'reason,' 'meaning,' or others,
as the case may be.

In order to direct our action, however, we must call into
operation thought of a somewhat different kind from any which
enters into our philosophy of knowledge. I do not mean to say
that idealism and rationary philosophy are two really different
things, but there is convenience I think in separating them for
the following reason. When Plato speaks of the idea of the
good, this is what I have called 'an ideal': but when he speaks
of the idea of a chair or a table, (whatever he may mean
besides) he means, the meaning or purpose of them, what they
are for, the subject of thought and of rationary philosophy.
So, when we are thinking what is the proper ideal of our action
and when we are thinking what is the purpose of a chair, we

are in both cases speculating and imagining: there is in both cases a right and a wrong, whether or not we hit the former: and the rightness is in both cases the expression of *fact*: it is upon something that *is*, that depends, as well whether we have taken the ideal rightly, as whether we have hit the right purpose of the chair: we are trying *to know* therefore in the forming the ideal, as well as in the other case, and we are acting upon such knowledge as we can get. But the fact which the ideal imperfectly presents or suggests to us is of a lofty nature quite different from the facts of sense which the thought of our rationary philosophy interprets to us.

Positivism, as an erroneous method and as opposed to rationary philosophy, consists in maintaining that, inasmuch as from the point of view of the universe we are bound to consider that what we want to know is *in* nature, therefore our proper way of gaining knowledge is only what I may call 'adstance' or presence with nature. In studying nature it is important not to confuse with nature (except so far as it is a question of nature itself) the different question, how we come to know nature, or anything. In the knowing and trying to know, we are to follow the road which our mind leads us: when we know the language of nature, we may very fitly describe all knowledge as the interpretation of it, but we have got to learn the language. Positivism, as above, is the failing to attribute sufficient importance to our thoughts *about* nature.

We should not need processes or manners of *thought* for knowledge of particular facts if we were ubiquitous, sempiternous, and omnisensive, *i.e.* if we could be at each moment in all places and of all times, and if we had sensive powers for, that is, if we were consciously affected by, all the different natural forces and chemical agents, as we are by heat and light. This, in fact, is what the *complete* theory of adstance or acquaintance with nature would require. As it is, being confined to one time, and at one time to one place, and having a very partial and limited sensive power, in order to make our one time and place and partial sensive power do for all time and place and all nature, there is required what we call thought—imagination, reasoning, memory, much besides. That is, however we may describe the

fact of knowledge as, on our part, simple adstance or presence
with nature, we cannot conceive the gaining it as such.

What we, with our one time and place and partial sensiveness, are present at, or have experience of, is particular fact
having a history of its own, by which we mean a particular case
of general fact, due to a great variety of circumstances which
have happened in time. This history we can in some degree
follow and investigate, and are thus able partially to make up
for our being creatures of one time. Similarly we can move
about and explore the earth, and in a manner explore
places to which we cannot actually get, as the moon and sun.
Observation and experience of this kind, simple acquaintance
with fact, we very often, in default of better language, call
history also, as natural history. In this way we know a great
many separate things, as it is called historically, or as matter of
fact : *i.e.* they are to us, as to the manner of our knowing them,
what we call *accidents*. When we talk of an accident, we do
not mean that there was no cause or reason for it : we mean
that we know it as a particular isolated fact, by means of
information : a fact in some degree exceptional and striking our
attention : if we speak of it as an *accident* we should mean in a
considerable degree, if as an occurrence, event &c., we should
mean in a small degree exceptional.

Now we being what we are, as I have described, our
acquaintance with nature in the first instance is of this partial
and, in a manner, isolated character; presenting to us a number
of separate occurrences, which we know as quasi-accidents, *i.e.*
as things which have happened, but which so far as we know,
need not have happened. It is their having happened in *this*
manner which is the ground of our noticing them. Now the
positivist, or non-rationary view of the manner of our gaining
our knowledge is that this is in substance *all* the manner of it :
that this manner of knowing what we know as matter of fact,
is *all*, or *the real*, or *the proper*, character of knowledge. Now
I think it will be seen that it is a different thing to say that
knowledge, supposed complete, may be looked at rightly
(though not exclusively) as a presence on our part with nature,
without our taking account *then* of the fact, that not only

II.] ERROR OF RELATIVISM. 303

nature is, but also *we think*; and on the other hand to say, as the mis-positivist method says, that the process of gaining knowledge is only the setting ourselves face to face with nature, and going through a course of successive experience, information, acquisition of historical or matter-of-fact knowledge. Against this the position of rationary philosophy is that the process of gaining knowledge is thinking and imagining, and concurrently with this, observing and verifying. When we describe knowledge as a whole, we may describe it equally correctly either from the side of thought, as thinking and imagining rightly, or from the side of observation, as acquaintance with nature: but when we are describing it, in the *process*, we cannot separate these two, but must describe it as thinking and imagining, and verifying the correctness of our thought by continual observation and exploring.

If we look at the process of knowledge from the first, whether in the individual or in the human race, we shall find it of the double character which I have just described. The history of our intellectual growth is the account how we are brought face to face with one fact of nature after another: but this is only half the process: the same history is also the account how our minds are constantly at work thinking and imagining, and how they find some of their imaginations verified, some not. Knowledge is described with equal accuracy as a perpetual aggregation and acquisition, or as a perpetual analysis and distinction. And these are not *different* processes, but are the same. The notion that we can describe the growth of our knowledge by experience, as it is commonly called, and that this really represents all the fact, is the error of positivism, as the notion that we bring something from our mind to bear upon something which is in the universe, is the error which I have called by the name of 'relativism.' It is well to describe the history of the aggregation of our knowledge, or of our successive acquisitions: but to say that this is all that takes place, or is a sufficient description of the growth of knowledge, is entirely wrong: since the reverse statement is equally true; and it is the two together which present the picture of our mind. In our first look at anything we see the universe, and we never see anything more. All our after knowledge is just as truly an *analysis* of the first thing we know as it is a *building* upon it: that first thing could not have been what it was, unless other things were what they were, and we could not have known as we did, unless we were what we are. When we first open our eyes, there is before us a wide scene in which we distinguish nothing: we begin with confusion: and growth of knowledge is separation and distinction.

I will not go on now about the nature of the growth in knowledge, any further than to say, that every part of knowledge has, not its two *portions*, the mental and objective, which is the error of relativism, but its two *sides*, as all language witnesses. A thing comes into view, and we see it: it looks green, and we see it green. Our seeing it is not our acting upon it, its looking what it does is not its acting upon us, any further than by *us* is meant our corporeal organization, which is itself a part of the objective universe. We *think*, and present to ourselves the object as real; the object *is*, and makes itself known to us in whatever way: these are two descriptions of the same fact, its two sides.

The two errors of positivism and relativism run together in this way. The proposition, 'Two straight lines cannot enclose a space' is said on the one side to be 'an intuitive axiom,' on the other to be 'a truth of experience.' Suppose the latter demonstrated. The interest of the demonstration to the demonstrator lies in this, that our type of truths of experience is taken from particular experiences, in regard of which we have perhaps exercised our imagination and asked ourselves, Is the fact this way or is it that? and then, as a matter of fact or by way of information, we find out that it is *this* way. Truths, as acquired in this way, are called *contingent* (I would call them 'contingential,' *i.e.* having relation to contingency[1]) as contrasted with *necessary*, and it is considered that some truths are of this character, others, possibly, of the other. Consequently, when it is demonstrated that the supposed intuitive axiom is a truth of experience, the impression is given, perhaps felt, that it is demonstrated that all things might have been other than they

[1] *Expl.* 75.

are, that it is only a matter of fact, a kind of chance, that they are as they are; that there is a sort of demand in our mind for something which is true of itself, something necessary, some knowledge gained otherwise than in the way of information or as matter of fact,—a demand which is not satisfied. This is the *point* of positivism. The view which I am trying to give against it is that *all* our knowledge, one part as well as another, is the result of thought and experience in conjunction: we are every moment, by means of the sensive and motive nerves of our body, hitting, knocking ourselves against, one thing after another in nature: but all this (and this is all that our *experience* of itself is) would be fruitless, unless we were *thinking* all the while. As to any particular *part* of knowledge, there may be much thought and little communication or experience: or there may be much of this latter and little thought: this is all the difference between supposedly necessary and contingential truths: there must be thought and experience in both. Only, if supposedly necessary truths are contingential, supposedly contingential ones are necessary.

The demonstrating that two straight lines not inclosing a space is a truth of experience, seems to me something the same as if we were to try to prove, that with one scene before us, and without even stirring from our place, we might, supposing life long enough, think out the problem of the universe. It is exceedingly probable that within that scene there are data enough for it, if only our minds were up to the work. But the reason for our using or needing the word *experience* in philosophy is, because we come to the knowledge of some things in the way of matter of fact or information, of some things by thinking them out—information useless without *some* thought, thinking useless without *some* experience,—but the making the word experience cover all limitation of our otherwise free, but useless imagination, either destroys all point of the word, or else involves error. I accept the above demonstration, as against the saying that an intuitive axiom, such as that relating to two straight lines, belongs to the mind and not to the universe: but reject it so far as it implies that it does not belong to the mind *as well as* to the universe.

There is a double question which we have always to put to ourselves about any subject we are considering, (1) What is the actual, tangible, fact? (2) What is its reason, principle or meaning? That is, we ought to be (and in fact naturally we always are) using our imagination at the same time that we keep ourselves in presence of nature. There is not generally much use in the common psychological analysis of the different mental operations, for this reason, that it is impossible to follow the manner in which almost all these are constantly united in each act of thought or intelligence, and in which the apparently simplest and earliest of such acts involve the most complicated. A truer psychology of the individual may sometimes be found in books which speak of the progress of knowledge in the race than in the ordinary psychological analysis: for Plato's notion is more applicable here than in relation to the moral constitution of his Republic: the fact or process of mental growth is seen clearer and better in the larger unity. We might almost say that every act of thought involves the whole number of what are called the different mental operations or faculties. One of the facts more especially which it is scarcely possible for psychologists to bring out as it exists, is the perpetual activity of *imagination*, which is what gives the real value to perception and educes from it generalization.

I have said that the process of knowledge is twofold, though knowledge itself does not consist of two parts or two elements, or two constituents, but is one, only something which we may look at in two ways. Now of the two processes of gaining knowledge we may look at *either* as the principal, and at the other as subsidiary. Naturally, whatever we look at as the principal, we shall conceive as beginning and ending knowledge, while we look at the other as coming in by the way to shorten or facilitate this. If we define knowledge as acquaintance or presence with nature or reality, we should consider that presence with nature, which we commonly call sensation, as the beginning of knowledge, and we should define complete knowledge to be a quasi-seeing, an 'anschauung,' 'betouchment,' experience of, presence at, acquaintance with, all the universal and continuous reality of nature, in the same manner as now we are brought into contact with various special parts of it by our senses and particular experience. And between this beginning and this end of knowledge there goes, as a sort of artifice, all the thinking and judging process. To help ourselves we make a set of formulas or expressions about things, getting them more and more comprehensive, which we should not need, if our powers of simple, unjudging contemplation or intuition were more complete. Thought comparing, thought judging of relations, is in this view a sort of algebra or currency representing intuition, and convertible on demand into it, having no value in itself, and our attributing to it value in itself is as if a mathematician should value mere formulas, as a miser does his money.

It is upon *this* view that, in a good deal of philosophy, what is called the *understanding*, or the faculty of relations, is considered to stand between two intuitions or intuitive faculties, the lower called, we will say, sensation, the higher called, we will say, Reason. In reality however, exactly as on *this* view of knowledge we may put the formulizing understanding between two intuitions, so on the other view we may put the pictorial imagination between two (what I may call) Reasons. In reality, sensation as distinguished from dreaming, is the having the thought, the making mentally to ourselves the assertion, Such and such a thing *is*. If we give the name 'intuitive' to those judgments which are not the result of previous thought there will be two kinds of such judgments, the lower of sensation, and the higher corresponding (on this view of knowledge) to the higher intuitions of the reason : and then the pictorial imagination, contemplation, preparatory to, or tentative at true judgment, plays exactly the same part between these two kinds of judgment, as the formulizing understanding, judgment preparatory to and tentative at, true contemplation, does between the two kinds of contemplation or proper intuition. So far as we mean by knowledge *right thought*, the three stages of mental state and operation may be distinguished as sensation (or the lower kind of right thought), imagination, Reason (or the higher kind of right thought). So far as we mean by it *acquaintance*

with things, the same three stages are sensation or acquaintance
with lower things, understanding or the faculty of judgment,
Reason or acquaintance with higher things. Our mind proceeds
in the double way, and in reality, imagination is what we may
call the atmosphere of judgment, or that out of which judgment
crystallizes, while exactly in the same way judgments are the
centres of expansive inward sight or contemplation.

It seems to me that neither of these two things is sufficiently
considered by psychologists. It is because we are always more
or less thinking how things *might be*, that the way in which
they *are* strikes us, or that we notice it: thus it is previous or
accompanying *thought* that converts mere *presence* into acquaintance. In the same way when we make a judgment, it is not
something lifeless in the mind, a convenient binding up of past
thought, to be done with: it not only is, but we mean it for,
the centre of an atmosphere of imagination proceeding from it:
our giving a thing a name, or saying it belongs to a kind,
means not only that it has a certain number of properties
which we call its definition, but is in reality a foretelling that it
has endless properties besides, which then we proceed to
imagine or think about.

It will be said that all this represents an exceptional
active-mindedness: that the notion of one thing after another
impressing us, being remembered, being abstracted, &c. sufficiently represents the normal activity of people's minds. As to
this, I believe, that it is impossible to exaggerate the amount
of mental activity which there is in children or wherever the
mind really works, which in adults it sometimes scarcely seems
to do. Since microscopes, we have lost all idea of arriving at
ultimate units of space, and within the magnitude of a grain of
sand we can detect any amount of variety and movement. It
can scarcely be doubted that time is as full of action, as space
of fact and matter, though our will can impress itself only very
coarsely on either, and we have no microscopes for time, as we
have for space and matter. For the earlier mind at least, no
amount of activity seems to me too great to suppose.

Imagination is continually blamed as obtrusive and deceitful
by those upon whom the view of knowledge which most

impresses itself is that it is right thought or judgment, just as
on the other hand the formulizing understanding is blamed as
cold, sterile and hollow by those to whom knowledge seems
most really to be acquaintance with things. It may appear
from the above how little reason there is for blame in either
case.

At the time when Bacon wrote there was no doubt much
reason for calling men from books to nature : but without
books (so far as they represent thought), men might have
known as fact any corner of the world and a host of the processes of nature, and yet have had nothing like what we call
scientific knowledge.   Bacon, like a good lawyer, said, ' Have
evidence for what you say: and learn how to examine evidence:
see what each sort of evidence goes to prove:' accordingly he
tried to catalogue the sorts.   But an inquiry into nature is not
simply a question of evidence.   The wrong, *i.e.* insufficient,
assumption all along is, that curiosity, *i.e.* the thinking impulse,
is a desire of the knowledge of fact as fact.   Curiosity is a
desire to know the reasons of things, and a desire to know
what is the truth of fact when there is a doubt what is.   The
infantile question is ' Why?' and not 'What?' till imagination
has suggested, 'Is it this or that?'   All experiment implies
question, all valuable observation implies previous supposition.

The being satisfied with knowledge of fact (*i.e.* with fragmentary experience) without effort to fill it up and put it
together, or (which seems to me the same thing) without the
strong feeling and belief that we are learning, not separate
things in the way in which we might be informed of one
accident after another, but different portions of *one* thing
which, as such, have a relation together or a meaning,—
this is in substance what I call positivism : and it seems to
me to represent rather the unscientific and unimproving view
of knowledge than the improving one.

The view that fact is the end of our consideration; that
knowledge is a sort of accident afterwards arising in relation
to a part of fact: this seems to me the root of positivism, and[1],
as I have said before, it is to me unutterably dreary.

[1] *Expl.* 15.

The view which I wish to give is this. Thought, or right thought, *i.e.* knowledge, is *one* thing: there is not one kind of knowledge for one set of creatures, and another for another: what variety there is in knowledge is attributable to the various qualities of the known, not to the various faculties of the knowing: there is *one* rightness of thought, and to consider this rightness as relative to the nature of the thinker destroys all notion of truth. Looking at the same thing from the other side: fact or reality is one thing: what is fact for one set of beings is fact for another set: if only they can perceive it, and so far as they perceive it at all, they perceive it as what it is. That is, we may on the one hand suppose the variety of knowledge to arise from the variety of objective fact: in which case, though of course we may admit besides any variety we please of faculties of perception, yet we must consider the knowing power at bottom to be *one*, and these various manners of perception are simply the same kind of thing as if we looked at an object through differently coloured glasses: there are different manners of seeing the thing, but one reality and one truth. There is not one manner of knowledge, one fact, for the man who looks through the red glass, and another for the man who looks through the blue: knowledge in this sense is always absolute, never relative: knowledge, if we look from the side of *fact*, is the coordination of intelligences, so far as we suppose intelligences various, the common part or point of them all.

If, on the other hand, we suppose the variety of knowledge to arise from the various manners of our thinking: if we start from a sort of Berkleian supposition, and consider that God inspires one set of thoughts in one set of beings, another in another set of beings: then (even if we suppose the thought must be *about* something, that there must be an object or a logical subject for it) we must bear in mind that rightness of thought, or truth, does not depend at all upon the thought following any varieties of that subject or object, but (by the supposition) upon the fact that the thought is inspired by God. If we suppose then any object (in *this* sense) or logical subject, —and truth, or rightness of thought, is in the manner in which we think *about* this—it is only a nucleus, a lay figure to be

draped and dressed, and the rightness of this draping and
dressing is dependent, not upon anything in the nucleus, but
upon the original inspiration. The nucleus is not something
unknown, but it is something to which the notion of knowledge is not applicable. To take the image which I used before :
we may consider truth or rightness of thought to consist in
our right appreciation of the colour of the glass through which
we look at an object: then the object is something to be looked
at, and nothing more : it exists for us only to test the glass : we
must not suppose *variety* in *it* : truth or knowledge has nothing
to do with *it* : truth is in the redness or blueness to which, in
our manner of thinking, we must *suppose* a support or groundwork.   Here the *knowledge* is absolute, the relativeness is only
in the form of language : we put our absolute knowledge into
a relative form of expression, because the ordinary manner of
our thought in life, upon which language is framed, is not this,
but the supposition given before: except for this, there would
be no reason for the supposition of a logical subject at all.

It will be seen that the error arises from the supposition of
the independent variation, so to speak, of manners of thinking
on the one side, and qualities of the object on the other : on this
supposition there is really *no* result.   We may *either* suppose
truth to be conformity to fact, *or* we may suppose truth to be
rightness of thought (thinking according to the laws of intelligence, if we like to take *that* as our test of rightness) about
what is the logical *subject* of thought.   What we must *not*
suppose is, that truth is applying one sort of thought (that
according to the laws of our intelligence) to another sort
of thought (that conformable to, because suggested by, fact).

The supposition of knowledge as right *thought* is the
supposition of philosophy and real consciousness, for, as I have
said, thought is all that we can be absolutely certain of.   But
thought presents, or suggests, to us, *fact* : and the supposition
of knowledge as conformity with fact is what we may call the
supposition which we live by.   It is the supposition of language,
and of physical and all ordinary science.   Right positivism (as
a philosophical method) is the holding to this supposition, in
speaking of the nature of knowledge, against the unphilosophical

mixing of it with the other, which I have called 'relativism.'
Wrong positivism is in my view, the considering that in the
progress of knowledge we are only, or ought to be only,
following fact, and are not, or ought not to be, actively speculating, imagining, anticipating, meeting the fragmentariness of
experience by belief in the reason of things and in the
connectedness of all.

CHAPTER III.

I HAVE now to speak of positivism in a different view. We are active beings, and imagination, in the wide sense in which I have used the term, is the director of all our actions. That is, action is the bringing something into being which was not, and rational action is the doing this with pre-imagination of the result in the mind of the agent.

Positivism in respect of thought, or as a philosophical method, is contrasted with what I called rationary philosophy: positivism in view of action is contrasted with idealism.

In each case, positivism stands against imagination, as I have used the word, but imagination, as applied to different purposes.

We have seen that the positivism of which we have spoken, though wrongly opposed to imagination is right as against relativism. In like manner there is something, not fitly perhaps to be called positivism, which is right against the application of relativism to the field of action, which application I will call 'regulativism.'

Positivism says, Man practically always *has* been imagining and idealizing, and no good has come of it. He begins with that, and only late and slowly comes to attention to fact, which is the really important thing. But, thus late, he does learn, doubly : he learns that this attention to fact *is* the important thing, and that he had better quite give up his imagining and idealizing : this first : and then his learning this, as he does,

late in his history is itself a matter of importance, in this way :
being no longer able to make use of imagination and idealism
as guides to action, he has a great fact before him, his own
past history: and this may come in their place as a guide to
action.   Let him do as he is doing, and will do, and must do:
let him follow the logic of facts, work out his destiny, actively
and consciously grow his growth and develope his development, and *this* is his morality.   Let him study what, according
to his nature as shown in his history, he *does* think and feel,
and then let him consider, all the time rejecting imagination
and idealism, that this is how he *ought* to think and feel :
(*I* am not responsible for the logic or consistency): in this
way he will make of morality a positive or inductive science.

Regulativism says, Positivism and fact cannot guide action ;
we must for that, have something of intuitivism (*i.e.* what
I have called imagination and idealism).   But we must be
careful that we keep in mind that this is *only* to guide our
action.   We must not suppose that we have by it any inward
sight of higher fact.   Our knowledge being relative to our
particular faculties and senses, and only true in this relation,
we are in a region of contradictions, as soon as we get out
of what is adapted to these.   We feel certain fragmentary or
isolated principles directing our action, but have no right to
conclude from these to any supposed fact.

It is here that something like positivism, as I have just
now said, might step in and say, An ideal or anything intuitively
seen, if it is to direct action, must represent some fact of that
higher order of facts which can direct action: *e.g.* if we act
in view of a *summum bonum*, we believe that that which we act
for *is* good, in the same way in which we believe the physical
universe exists.   I will examine in a moment the validity of
this: I just mention it to show the relation to each other of
regulativism and, not precisely positivism, but what we may
call the generalized matter-of-fact feeling.

What has made people conceive of morality, or has been
the cause of such a thing entering into their heads, is the belief
(felt, though perhaps indistinctly) in the right and good, *i.e.*
the belief that there is something, whatever it is, which, as

men, they should do, and the belief (another form of the
same) that there is a highest good for man. This, as a fact, has
been the origin of moral thought and philosophy. But then
comes the question, Is this belief justified, or is it a chimera?
When we come to present to ourselves the belief in consciousness, or to philosophize about it, we must have, so to call it,
a belief about the belief. The moral intuitivist has this belief
about the general human belief or supposition of which I have
spoken (the belief, viz. that there is a right and good): he
believes that this right and good represent fact, or in some way
or other are higher fact (this, let it be observed, is the counter-
part in this high region of the view of knowledge in general
from the side of fact, the object, or the universe, of which
I have abundantly spoken); or, if we dismiss all notion of fact,
and still, in this high region, view thought from the side of the
thinker, he believes that in believing in a right and good he
is right: that his belief is justified: that it is what he *ought* to
believe in. If we bear in mind the principles upon which we
have gone all along, it will be perceived that in the two last
accounts I have given of the belief, from the side of fact and
from the side of the thinker, we are saying the same thing
from a different point of view, or on different suppositions: *i.e.*
if we are really right in believing in a right and good, then, so
far as we admit the notion of fact, so far as there is meaning
in the term, such a right and good is *fact*: it is a universe, or
part of a universe, though not the universe of our lower
understanding. The converse is of course more readily seen,
viz., that if there *is* such fact, we are *right* in believing it.

The reason why that which I am here exhibiting is not so
readily seen as its converse, is our tendency to the view which
I have called relativism, which, as applied to thought of the
kind which I am *now* speaking of, becomes regulativism.
Regulativism is, if I may so say, belief in the supposition of a
right and good, *without* belief in any fact corresponding to this
supposition. It puts the mind into this position: simply as
men, we believe that there is a right and a good, *i.e.* something,
if we can find it, which we should do, and something, if we
can find it, which is our highest good: we are right in

this our belief: and yet there is no such thing, at least we
have no business to conclude there is.   The language in which
this is likely to be couched is, these principles (of the right and
good &c.) are proper as regulative of our action, but they are
not proper as directive of our thought.   The mind, it will be
observed, is put *here* in the same position as to *practical*
thought in which relativism puts it as to *speculative*: we do
not know what in that case to think, or in this to do, because
there is supposed a right way of thinking on our part, to which
there is nothing in *fact* to correspond: when we look at
thought from the two sides, of the object and the subject, of
reality and of truth, the lines of view miss meeting: as in a
tunnel begun from the opposite ends and badly engineered, all
comes to perplexity and mystification.   The error seems to me
to consist in the supposition, that rightness of thought can be
anything other than conformity of thought to fact, or, taking
the other course, that *fact* can mean anything else than what
right thought suggests to us.   The two things define each
other: and philosophy seems to me to consist in our understanding that we cannot otherwise define either of them, only
that we must remember that thought lies nearer to us than
any fact beyond ourselves, or, in other words, that the fact of
facts to us is our own thinking.   I see no way of meeting this
error except the supposition which I have made throughout,
viz. that in speaking of knowledge, as distinct from the process
of it, we must not speak of thought and things concurrently,
but of *either* of them, whichever we choose.   Relativism and
regulativism both start from the point of view of thought:
both with great professions of keeping to it, lay down propositions which are true according to it, but which also, according
to it, are not at all paradoxical or surprising: whereas they are
given as paradoxical and surprising, and are *taken* also probably
as such: given, because the philosopher perhaps does not think
it right, perhaps is not able, to keep to his own view from the
side of thought purely: taken, because the hearer is almost
certain to start from the side of fact, and the philosopher is not
above taking pleasure in mystifying him.

    It is important to distinguish relativism and regulativism

from two things which have a tendency to confuse themselves
with them : one, a feeling of the partialness of our knowledge :
the other, the notion of the proper fact being not what our
thought *immediately* suggests.

If, when it is said that we have in our nature principles,
which ought to regulate our action, but which give us no
information as to fact, what is in substance meant is, that any
notion which we have of the right, or the desirable, is something
which, in the exhibition, looks very small indeed, while yet, in
application to action, it may be very fruitful,—I quite agree,
only I call this simply *partialness* of knowledge, not anything
to which there is any reason to give such a name as 'regulative.'
The point of the difference is this : the supposition of *regula-
tiveness* is meant to exclude any utility in our thinking further
about them, and trying in any way to extend our knowledge.
It means, not only that they are difficult to deal with and seem
to tell us little, but that we may know beforehand that no
speculation will be of any use about them. As to whether it
will be so or not, I say nothing : only that there is nothing
in their nature to make us know beforehand that it will not
be so.

Again, if, when it is said that any intuitive feelings of our
nature may be all very well for their purpose and yet give us
no information, what we mean is, that it is exceedingly hard to
apply the notions of information, and fact, in this region of
thought, here too I quite agree. What sort of fact, it may be
asked, *can* correspond to the notion of there being a highest
good for man ? Is not man's having the *idea* that there *is*,
almost the only possible fact that we can conceive about the
case ? I do not hold this myself : I think if we say man is
right in having such an idea, or if we say that it is an idea
which he is right in acting on, we must mean that there is a
state or connexion of things, analogous to the universe of our
lower understanding, in which state or connexion of things our
acting in a particular way is linked with some result in fact,
which may properly be described as the highest good for us.
But let us examine the matter more closely.

One man says, 'I have no promptings to act in the way

which is commonly described as moral, and I am sure that
there is nothing of the kind natural, though there is often, as
the result of education, or in a manner accidental. I see
indeed intellectually a reason why I should act towards *some*
happiness, for otherwise my action would be wasted: it would
be like ploughing the ground for the pleasure of ploughing,
with no intention to sow when the ploughing was done: but
the only happiness which I can myself enjoy is that which,
either mediately or immediately, is my own. I may have
indeed an intellectual disposition to form ideals, and think that
there is one sort of thing which I *should* do rather than
another: but this is an aberration or delusion, which positivism,
or that proper value for matter of fact, which individuals and
human nature alike learn as they get older, teaches me should
be got rid of. My action is therefore entirely unprompted and
undirected by moral ideals: I act according to fact.' This seems
to me to be the groundwork of moral positivism, from which
our acting upon any moral promptings or directions, or in view
of any moral ideals, must stand distinguished.

Another man says, 'I feel that I have moral promptings
such as the first speaker disclaims. But what then? If it is
said to me, Supposing you have such promptings, what reason
is there you should follow them? what shall I say?'

I understand Butler's answer to this to be, 'They are
evidently part of your nature, and if they do not direct your
action they subserve no purpose in it: which cannot be
supposed.' This, though doubtless in a way true, yet as
an answer, rather resembles what disappointed Socrates in
Anaxagoras: it is like giving as a reason for our walking
anywhere that we have got legs.

The real value of this reason I understand to be this:
these promptings in your nature bear witness to you of the
fact, that there is a reason why you should act in a particular
way, and in the way which they direct: if there is such a
reason, you are really in a wider universe of fact than your
simply intellectual faculties tell you of: for the universe of
fact which *these* are concerned with can contain no such
reason. No amount of acquaintance with the material globe

and heavens and the agencies at work in them, can possibly suggest any reason why you should act in this or that manner as regards the happiness of your fellow men. So far then as there exists such reason, there must exist also (in whatever way) *fact* of a different kind from this material fact, and with which this reason is associated, or from which it is derived. Your moral promptings therefore, so far as you admit them, as what should direct your action, are like a new sense (or sensive power) to you in this way, that by means of them you have a notion of the existence of fact, which by your ordinary senses you could have no notion of. This fact then, *being* fact, is something which, once made known to you, your speculative and intellectual powers also may deal with: possibly they may not make much of it, but if it is *fact*, it is true for them as well as for your moral nature, and they are applicable to it.

According to the ordinary division of provinces of thought, I suppose that, if this higher fact is considered only in a very general light and in a practical view, we are in the province of moral philosophy. If the fact is looked at more closely and definitely, and with the earnestness of view which belongs to the attribution of great practical importance to it, it is called natural religion. If we deal with the supposed fact in a purely speculative way, we call the manner of proceeding the higher philosophy, or pure philosophy.

The supposition of, or belief in, this which I call 'higher fact' brings all these three ways of proceeding into relation with each other. On the other hand, the practical application of what I have called regulativism, or the saying that we must not consider moral promptings to introduce us to any higher fact, which we can then speculatively converse with, cuts off the connexion between these three provinces of thought. Its language is, that we must not apply moral considerations to religion, nor judge of it by them: that we must not consider that morality proves religion, or anything like it: that the higher speculations on the nature of truth and existence have nothing to do with religion or morality, nor any bearing on them[1].

[1] The reference is no doubt to Dean Mansel's Bampton Lectures, which the Author has criticised in a separate essay.

Regulativism is not a man's simply confining his thoughts to one only of these provinces: but is the denial of the legitimacy of expansion and comparison of thought (what I should call 'imagination') on the subjects which thought in these provinces deals with.

While, then, positivism denies the existence, even for regulative purposes, of anything belonging to this high region; while in reference to the *process* of knowledge, it attaches exclusive importance to our having had experience of whatever the thing may be, and takes little or no account of the process always going on of supposition, imagination, expansion of thought, mental comparison; regulativism, starting from a different point, comes to the same conclusion as to the fragmentary or accidental character of our knowledge in regard to the higher region of which we have spoken. Positivism, in the lower region, says, Here is this, that, and the other *fact*,—fragments: you may unite them with each other, or each with others, but still you will get nothing more than fragments: the supposition of reasons for them, principles of them, fusing them out of fact into a whole of thought, is what must never be admitted: knowledge is experience, converse with fact, nor must we ever consider it other. In like manner regulativism, in the higher region says, Here is this, that, and the other *idea*: we may describe them in one and another way, but ideas they must remain: we must not suppose them to have any reference, which we can the least follow, to any higher state of facts: even supposing we should allow such higher fact, and conceivably come, through particular occurrences, to the knowledge of one and another point of it, still we must not exercise our *mind* about the ideas or the points of fact, we must not compare, generalize, conclude: we must leave all in fragments, accept the several things, regulate action by them severally, and go no further.

It will be seen thus that regulativism is, in fact, the positivism of the higher regions of thought. Against them both stands the tendency to believe, in the one case, that fact means thought, in the other, that right thought means fact; that we must not say that anything is to be looked at in one of these views only.

What I said as to the difference between regulativism and partialness will be borne in mind. Regulativism prohibits all attempt to enlarge our knowledge in this higher region: the recognition of partialness encourages it.

Leaving regulativism, I will now speak a little about positivism in its relation to idealism.

Action depends upon *what we have*, for the means of it, but upon *what we want*, for the purpose of it.

Besides knowing the circumstances in which we are placed, which, of itself, suggests no action, we feel desires, which do: and so far as we consider ourselves to have a constitution, or to be members of an orderly system of things, such as our intelligence suggests to us in the universe, these desires indicate certain *facts*, viz. wants.

Besides desires, we feel promptings urging us to act or to abstain from action, which promptings are accompanied by a feeling of incumbency or imperativeness. Just as desires indicate the fact of want, so this feeling may be said to indicate the fact of a kind of subjection or subordination.

As I said just now in respect of relativism, the supposition of rightness in thought or feeling, is the same, if we look from another side, as the supposition of *fact* corresponding.

When however we speak of wants as facts, or of the subordination which I last spoke of as a fact, we are using the word *fact* in a wider sense than when we speak of the facts which our ordinary understanding makes us aware of. Speaking generally, the understanding shows us what *is* or what we suppose to be: when we conclude to fact from our desires or promptings, it is not something which *is*, but something which *is not*, something which we wish to be, or think ought to be, that is first in view. But then this suggests further and higher fact as giving the reason why we thus wish, and giving meaning to the thought that a thing *ought to be*: the consideration of this higher fact, varying from simple imagination of it to belief of it, is what I have called idealism.

Positivism, as against idealism, is the notion that all this is chimera. No doubt (it says), we do think, or rather dream, in this manner: but the older and wiser we become the less we do so.

Consequently positivism treats religion first, then philosophy, moral or speculative, or—as when thus thought of it is usually called—metaphysics, as two great dreams of human nature, the first in the main prevailing in the earlier, the second in the later stages of civilization: undoubtedly, it says, they are facts themselves of human history, but it is also a fact of that history that first the one gives place to the other, and then they both cease: and it is proper for us, following fact, to do our best to make them cease, and to cease from them ourselves. This last, it will be observed, is the positivist logic which I neither understand nor recognize.

Against this way of thinking, it appears to me 1st, that it is not historically made out that religion and metaphysical philosophy do cease: 2nd, that in respect of any partial making of it out, we are imperfect judges of the value of this as a fact in view of the whole course of human history; 3rd, that religious and philosophical thought seem to belong to human nature in much the same way that thought applied to physical science does; and last, that whatever the historical fact may be, there remains the question, which I have so many times alluded to, of the validity of the positivist logic, or of the supposition that the fact alone is what is to direct our action. Supposing the nations of Hindustan or Arabia to have had once upon a time some science, and now to have no further mental exercise than such as is furnished them by an unsatisfactory religion, are they to draw conclusions from their history, on the same principles on which we are told to draw the above conclusions from ours?

To me it seems to be a fact that religion and philosophy, if we take large areas and periods, still continue as vigorous as ever, and also that they belong to the mind of each of us, and therefore must continue so: nor have we reason to conclude against their value, from their not being progressive, as physical science is. The progress of physical science, so far as it comes into consideration in relation to religion and philosophy, must be divided into two parts, greater justness of thought, and wider experience. The latter of these, though it is probably what positivists chiefly mean by progress, is a matter really of no merit on the side of physical science as against anything else, but of indifference. It might be that religion and philosophy were susceptible of such widening of experience, or it might not: nothing, as to relative value, can be concluded from it. In our universe of space, not crowded, but apparently infinite, of which the minutest division seems capable of holding any amount of various existence, of course our limbs, and eyes, and mind, might go on travelling and expatiating, that is, experience might go on enlarging, for ever. Religion and philosophy might possibly have value in *this* view: but if they have not, it is not a reason for condemnation of them, when they may have value in other points of view.

Religion and philosophy, however, of course carry their own condemnation in the positivist view, so long as the term idealism is applicable to them: I must a little explain its application.

The positivist condemnation of religion and metaphysics is really a condemnation of imagination in the wide sense in which I have used the term, just as I, by the fact of assigning value to it, have expressed a condemnation of positivism. I have used the term 'imagination' as a starting word, or a starting point, to express all that action of mind which is not perception of what we ordinarily call fact, or what is not *experience*, as the word is often used. It is a matter of language whether we continue to call what we have hitherto called imagination by that name (in which case we must consider that imagination is, to whatever extent, a valuable and important faculty of our mind), or whether we think that imaginations, with value thus attributed to them, should no longer be called by that name, but should rather be called intuitions, beliefs, inward sight or vision, or by whatever other similar name.

I am myself in the habit of using the term imagination with full recognition of the above value. If I seem in this way to be bringing some things nearer together, than some may think they ought to be brought, as conscience and religion on the one side and poetry and worthy moral feelings on the other;

—this is not from any lower notion of the former, but from a higher notion of the latter.

The word imagination goes not unfitly with the word 'idealism'; and 'ideal' and 'idealism' I use always, it will have been seen, in reference to action. I mean by 'ideal' anything which we mentally set before ourselves as the purpose or rule of our action, and (as will have been seen from all that I have said) I do not regard anything as a *proper* ideal for our conduct, a true ideal, except as being fact or part of fact, representing or expressing fact. But then it is not the fact of our ordinary understanding (which can only furnish us *means* for action, not purposes): it is the fact of our imagination, intuition, belief, inward vision, however we like to describe it.

We are here at an undecidable issue, and I suppose so long as the world lasts there will be people who look at the important and most real fact as the fact of our senses, or our understandings in their ordinary application, and others who look upon the important and most real fact as that of imagination, intuition, inward vision. There is no logic to the principles of which we can here appeal. There are different criteria of reality, and what is the reality of the one is the mere phenomenon or illusion of the other.

There is no real boundary between morals and religion; and natural religion, as morally suggested, is only the going on to speculate on this fact, and to bring it into practical application for life, and it may be for devotion. Nor is there any real boundary between religion and the higher philosophy, or I could not just now have used the word 'speculate' as I did: all the three, morals, religion, philosophy, are conversant with the same world of higher fact, and positivism really disallows all.

APHORISMI FINALES.

ONE purpose which I have aimed at in what I have done, has been to bring into a single view various kinds of contemporary philosophical literature—and that English literature—which do not often appear in such conjunction.

It is in a great measure the fact, that anyone who enters into one of these lines of philosophical thought is unable to appreciate, or give any value to, another. They are looked upon as out of relation to each other, or only in the relation of antagonism, involving in it the principles and interests most important to men. Hence a great amount of controversy, both bitter and unfruitful; bitter, because of the principles supposed to be involved; unfruitful, because the parties often scarcely even profess to understand each other, or enter into each other's views; and because they will hardly listen to each other sufficiently to understand in common, on what principles or by what logic the question can be decided.

Nothing is more interesting to me in Bacon than his reiterated abhorrence of the unfruitful controversy in which the scholastic times had abounded, and his earnest effort to make people leave off caring for triumph over opponents, and set themselves to the making, step by step as they could, an intellectual advance. But Dr Whewell has well pointed out that, when such an advance was made, it was in some important particulars made by means of controversy; that in this way men's views were cleared and made more precise, their speculations as to the truth were tested, the chaff separated from what was really valuable. The difference between the one sort of controversy and the other, the wretched dispute and the

profitable discussion, consists in such particulars as these: that
in the one case people do not, in the other they do, respect
their adversaries as seekers, in common with themselves, of
truth; that in the one case they do not, in the other they do,
acknowledge certain principles in common, a reference to which
is to be taken as deciding the controversy; that in the one case
they argue *ad populum*, looking at their adversaries' case from
their own point of view only, under which circumstances it is
likely enough to seem absurd, or even perhaps immoral, and so
to provoke a laugh or indignation; in the other case they argue
as before a judge, and study their adversary's view to find its
strong and its weak points, in order to determine what is the
real truth in the matter.

It is because I have a strong feeling that the best, and it
may be the only, preventive of foolish controversy is good
discussion, that I have taken the various books which I have
spoken of and brought them successively into relation with a
view of my own, as a means both of testing and of illustrating
my own view, and also of showing how they help to the discovery of the truth. Even supposing our view of any one of
these books, or of books like them, is that it is thoroughly false;
such a view is of no value unless we understand the book; and
we cannot understand it without comparing it with others on
the same subject. Of course the book might be not only false,
but worthless: I do not think this is the case with any of the
books which I have noticed or referred to. It is not in regard
of its *authors* that English philosophy seems to me deficient.
What seems to me more deficient is attention and interest on
the part of *readers*. The reason of this, if it is so, is probably
in part because, on any subject not immediately relating to
practical life, there really is less willingness on the part of
readers to give attention, to think out a thing, or to follow an
argument, than there was a century ago. But I think it is due
also in part to the advance in philosophy on the part of the
authors: to its greater breadth, and depth, coupled with the
want of relation between these authors, and their depreciation
of each other. The consequence is, that people are more
puzzled, than they used to be, as to what philosophy is.

Rightly or wrongly, a century ago people had certain principles upon which they went, and so had faith in thought as
likely to lead to a result. At the present time we have various
authors each, I suppose, with a certain number of disciples too
much despising those beyond their own circle, while, on account
of the apparent absence of a common purpose and any common
principles, there is on the part of people beyond these circles
too great a scepticism and neglect of all.

The same is to be said about philosophy, mental and moral,
as a part of education, actual or possible. What is it ? What
is agreed upon it ? What are its principles, and what institutes
could be written about it ? In speaking thus about philosophy
I would not be understood to imply that in the idea of what
are well-established branches of education, say even classics and
mathematics, there is very great agreement, or that such as there
may be is, necessarily, of a very valuable kind. To whatever
extent agreement, as to what constitutes a subject of education
and the manner of teaching it, is the result only of *usage*, it
has advantages, and they are very great ones, but it has also disadvantages. In the absence of usage, philosophical instruction
has to go upon what is reasonable or useful ; and the application
of this test is difficult enough. But for any such instruction to
be even possible, one thing is necessary, viz. that the people
who teach it should understand one another, and should more
or less respect each other's studies or views. In mathematics,
e.g., or classics, with whatever difference of taste or view, there
is common ground upon which all meet : the nature of particular
questions proposed is understood more or less by all who have
pursued the subject. Wherever this sort of common understanding has not been brought about by usage, and yet
education is to be carried on, there is needed that people
should not only think accurately in their own particular way
and line, but should also take some pains to understand the
views of others, and to bring these into relation with their own.
Of course what is thus desirable from the point of view of
instruction of others is equally so in relation to a man's own
mind, if it is to have anything of a liberal character, if he is to
be anything more than a mere specialist, a sort of artizan in

thought, with *one* thing he is capable of doing or thinking of,
and nothing else.

There are various things, both in regard of science and of
education, which make this more difficult just now than it
sometimes has been. To speak of the latter: the strong desire
of thoroughness in education in some respects defeats its own
purpose. We ought ourselves to be liberal-minded, and a main
thing which we have to teach is the being so. But when any
great effort is used, to secure the learning of particular things,
under strong pressure, there cannot but be danger of checking
liveliness of mind, of confining thought in a narrow channel, of
attaching unreasonable importance to technical accuracy, of
want of interest in, and sympathy for, other thought, of looking
upon intellectual pursuits as a business to be attended to with
energy in business hours, rather than as that which gives
interest and meaning to life, of want of opportunity and in-
clination for that measuring of thought with thought at the
same or a higher level, which is real intellectual association.
This is all on the part of the teacher: of disadvantages on the
part of the taught I say nothing here, for indeed on any matter
of education I speak with very little confidence. But what I
mean by liberal-mindedness, as distinguished in some respects
from the characters of mind which I have last mentioned, is
this: an interest in intellectual pursuits, of some one kind, for
one's self; an interest in other intellectual pursuits as intellectual, an interest graduated indeed, some of the pursuits being
nearly allied with our own, some not so; but a sympathetic
interest in all of them, as what others are doing *their* work in,
just as we, mentally at least, should be in *ours*; a care for
accuracy, so far as it is what real knowledge and clearness of
thought will produce, but a superiority to that servile dread of
inaccuracy and mistake, which would keep a man from ever
hazarding a thought or a word beyond the subject which he has
(we might say) professionally studied; a reasonable confidence
in our own knowledge and thought, if only we can justify it to
ourselves as conscientious; a willingness to measure it with
that of others, whether in reading or otherwise; and a candour
in giving full credit to theirs. The opposite to this is the

temper, where there is contempt and jealousy of all subjects but our own, carelessness of thinking because we have no faith either in ourselves or in any results of thought, fear almost of speaking on any subject of real interest for fear of committing ourselves or falling into error, intolerance without *real* (because without grounded) belief in what we are attached to.

Places of learning are, it seems to me, as important in the view of cultivating this spirit by bringing different studies together, as they are for what is directly taught: and it is possible sometimes that the energy of the direct teaching, good in itself, may be indirectly injurious to the spirit above described. And, without going so far as this, the attempt to bring different ways of thinking into relation, so as to form a *branch* of study, so to speak, may be under these circumstances more difficult.

EPILOGUE.

THE notion of *finishing* hardly belongs to these 'rough notes,' which cannot be said to have either beginning or middle, and which, if life be spared, I should wish to take up again. Nor should I like to put forth anything so desultory and fragmentary as much that is here contained, unless I entertained both on the one side the hope that I might be able at a future time to exhibit it in another form more clearly, and on the other side the fear of promising myself in this respect too much, and the desire that in any case what I have thought on these subjects might do something to help the thought of others.

Had the purpose of what I have written had reference to the *intelligence* only, and been what could bear no fruit but that of clearer and juster thought, I should not think it had been at all in vain. In the midst of the difficulty in which one is placed as to what to believe in and to trust to in this world of hollownesses, I do believe in human intelligence: and I do this, I think, very mainly because I recognize in human imagination not a rival of it, but a servant or a helpful sister. I have a belief—of course such a belief can be no more than a sort of moral confidence, and can hardly have intellectual grounds—that the more we can find out in any way about ourselves, our human life and powers, and our real prospects, the better and the happier we shall be: and I wonder, alike at those whose minds are indifferent to thought about such things, at those who are afraid of it and discourage it, and at those who think it hopeless and foolish, and recommend us to satisfy ourselves with 'living by bread alone.'

Supposing then what I have written were good for nothing

but to rectify one or two errors of thought, and to contribute in this way something to truth, I should not think this little: and so anxious am I that it *should* do this, that I am jealous of looking too much forward to any moral or practical result which, if followed up, it may have. My own feeling about this latter is that it is likely to be best consulted by the making as sure as possible of truth. But then I believe in truth as productive of such result, and I think I see the way in which the views which I have given, and which I suppose to be true, are thus productive. I do not mean to deny that this heightens my interest in them: but, as I have said, I believe in intelligence and truth, because they are the most fruitful of all things, and because, if we are single-hearted in our devotion to them, they will not betray us, or show us only what we had better have been ignorant of.

But I think I see several ways in which the view which I have taken is likely to be fruitful in good result, and I will mention them.

1. My aim in trying to clear the ground from the wrong noö-psychology or mis-psychology, is in order that we may have instead of it a good physio-psychology, such as now seems possible. To me however it does not seem that we ever shall have such a thing, unless we can clear our minds from the thought that it will do anything, one way or the other, towards settling the higher questions and difficulties of morality and religion. There are some portions of this physio-psychology to which I feel individually a repugnance, accompanied nevertheless with a full acknowledgment of the importance of them; while on the other hand there are other portions, such as the nature of the intelligence of the inferior animals, and the circumstances and history of the different races of men, in which I cannot but think discoveries of great value could be made. But all physio-psychology seems to me to be vitiated by the want of clearness of view as to its relation to the higher philosophy and to morals. I do not think discoveries will be made in it, even in its own sphere, so long as the singleness of look towards truth in it is hindered by either the fear or the hope on the part of the investigator that man will be proved to be no more than an

animal, or so long as his science is under the suspicion of being likely to prove this. I do not think there will be a good physio-psychology without a good philosophy, and I think the converse is true also. To me, human consciousness and freedom—suggesting to us a personal existence more real than that even of the universe, suggesting moral responsibility, hope of future life, relation to God, or the mind which originated the universe—are things quite unaffectable, *à priori*, by anything which physio-psychology can discover, and which any consideration how the human race has come physically to be what it is, or how it is related to other organized races, has nothing to do with. The study of mind and intelligence from the point of view of consciousness is what I have called 'philosophy.' The study of intelligence, that is animal intelligence (human, *as* animal, included), so far as it can phenomenally be studied, is the main part of physio-psychology. I recognize intense interest in it: for intelligence, even *thus* studied, is more interesting than anything not intelligence: but it will not really come into the place of the other, which *starts*, as I have said, differently.

2. I wish to give what help I can towards our having a good and true view of nature, in which logic and the study of our mind shall have their proper place, without disturbing it or being misapplied. I feel in some respects disposed to think, that if our physical philosophers could enter into each other's studies, so that in some degree physical study could be looked at *as one*, for rudimentary or institutional instruction, this would be the fittest basis of education; not indeed to be rested in as itself sufficient, but because all thought, even philosophical, is so valueless, without some truth and clearness of view as to this[1].

---

[1] The Epilogue ends thus abruptly. The headings which follow, 'Idealism,' 'Religion,' were no doubt intended to be the subjects of future paragraphs.

INDEX TO PARTS I. AND II.

NOTE: *The references in leaded type are to Part II. (the present volume), the others to Part I. (Cambridge, 1865). Where a reference to a chapter is followed by a bracket, the references within the bracket are to the parts of that chapter. Special headings under the index-word cover all the references that are separated only by a single stop (.), i.e. down to the next colon.*

M.

philosophy and natural religion, 319–20 : relation to positivism, **320**)
Reid, T. **92: 93: 94: 117:** quoted (ap. Sir W. Hamilton) 136. 138. 144: **12: 13:** on 'scepticism' about the material world, **86:** on the field of vision, **124:** on consciousness, **161**
Relativism 183 : 228–9 : 236: c. xii.: 303–5 : **312**
Relativity of Knowledge, 62–7 : **Bk. I. c. iv.**: its philosophical and moral bearing distinguished, **268:** not involved in saying that all existence implies a knowing subject, **285:** the important form of, **285–7:** wherein wrong, **310–2**
Religion 232 f. 319. 322. 331
Representation see Presentation
Retroverse of sensation (*a*) = the conscious side, **251–2** : includes the proverse, **252** : its double character of sentience (q.v.) and perception, **252:** more important than the proverse, **256–9** : (*b*) = the physiological conditions, **253**
Revelation 233
Rightness, the feeling of, as distinguishing perception from imagination, 10–11. cf. 28

Scale of sensation and knowledge, 107: 210–3: 217: 223: 241: 250: **30: 105** f. **181**
Scepticism various forms of it in philosophy, **Bk. I. c. viii.** : means really confusion, **295**
Schelling, F. W. J. 190
Science the reason of its former slow progress, 200
Self-consciousness different meanings of, **108–10** : its development from 'immediateness,' **Bk. II. c. iii.** cf. **145–6** : **172** : its relation to perceptiveness, **181**
Self-self 145–6
Sensation phenomenalist view of, 5–8 : ambiguity of the term, 19 : scale of, c. vi. 30 f.: used to include feeling and thought, 106. c. vi.: should hold good for all, if for me, 269–70. cf. 274. **278–80. 282. 287**

Sensationalism Bk. IV. c. i.
Sense the body all one sense, 43. **130** : s. and thought in knowledge at every stage, 213. 216. 257–8. 220–2. **226–7** : distinction between taste-sense and handling-sense, 39
Sensibility distinguished from sensiveness, **185**
Sensive powers 19
Sensiveness not an inferior kind of knowledge, **204–5**
Sentience = the feeling of pleasure and pain, **186. 252**
Sextus Empiricus 263
Sight nature of, 39–47 : presentment and descrial distinguished in, **Bk. I. c. xi.** esp. **115** : relation to touch, **134.** cf. **130–5. 142** : mental experience on recovery of sight, **122** f.
Simplicius 263
Society fundamentalness to an intelligence, overlooked in the 'Philosophy of the Human Mind,' 212–4
Socrates 318
Soul why the term is here avoided, **182. 238**
Space as felt, 26–7. 32–3. 37: considered too largely as 'lighted space,' 22. 28: how far a form given by thought, 108. 111 : and Time, 166: in what sense subjective, 211–2. cf. 239 : in what sense seen, **135–7** : **Bk. II. c. vi.** (the counter-notion of matter, **194:** Kant's pure perception of, **195:** as 'pure phenomenalism,' **197** : the imagination not the notion of, **198:** compared with Time 199– 200)
Spencer, H. 54: 69: 70: **Bk. I. c. ix.** (his Principles of Psychology, **91** : wrong psychology in, 92–8: on the relation of body and mind, **101–3**) : on comparative psychology, **Bk. I. c. x.** : **146**
Stewart, D. on Formal Logic, 153 : quoted and criticised, **12. 13–20.** cf. 26–32: on cause, 19. cf. **101**: on the principle that the mind can only act where it is, 20–1. cf. **102**
Subject and object, confusion in the antithesis, 61–2. **176. 180**

340 · INDEX.

Substance the notion of (esp. in Whewell) 246–51 : and attribute, **47**. 226–7 : is the totality of its qualities, **177**

Substratum unknowable, a figment, **26 foll. 88 foll.**

Symbolism, visual, Berkeley's theory of, **126–30. 134–5. 138. 140–1. 215–6**

Teleology (=the science of the ends of conduct) J. S. Mill on, 199–202

Tests of truth 12. 213 f.

Thing = what we may use or make, 51 : relation to thought, 250 : double meaning in the notion of, **286** : things-in-themselves, 60–2. 65–7. 74–5. 123. 181–2. 187. 244. **246**

Thinghood 106. 110–2 : 123 : =the proper thoughtness of a thing, 188 : 10 : 47 : 177–8

Thinking spatially 108

Thinkingness)(Thoughtness, 140. 82. 163

Thought different theories of, **210** : not divided from sense in knowledge, **220–2**. 226–7 : as process of thinking, 225

Thought-self 146–7

Time the only element common to feeling and phenomenal fact, 24–5 : compared with Space, **199–200**

Touch two elements in, of feeling and handling, 122 : not a special, but the general corporeal sense,**131–5**

Transference special use, 105. 107

Truth phenomenally considered,what, 12–13. cf. **60** : the distinction of empirical and necessary, as belonging only to our manner of arriving at it, 30–2. cf. **304–5** : as conformity with fact, **85** : as transference of fact into thought, **202** : its source in 'immediateness,' 206. 209. 219 : as what is good for all intelligence, **213**. cf. Bk. IV. c. ii. **310–2** : the opinion of

the majority no test of it, **272. 280** : the notion non-relative, **287** : positivist view of, **295**

Ultra-phenomenalism = Positivism, q.v., p. xiii

Understanding and Reason **307–8**

Unity only a supposition, in phenomenalism, 11–2. cf. 45–6. 49–51. 57 : conception of, 113 : as a 'higher intuition' involved in all knowledge, 217–22

Utilitarianism its connection with positivism, **295** : J. S. Mill's, confuses fact and ideal, 202

Vision theory of, Bk. I. c. xii. : three heads of controversy in, **117**

Want as fact and as felt, **190**

Whewell, W. p. xxvii: p. xxxi : misunderstands the relation of the phenomenal and philosophical standpoints, 3 : on primary and secondary qualities, 47 : 57 : 111 : controversy with J. S. Mill on the source of conceptions, 172–3. 211. 219–20. 234–5. 240–1 : c. x. (arrangement of his works, 203 : his logic more 'real' than Mill's, 204–9 : on the fundamental antithesis in knowledge, 213–6. 220. cf. c. xi. **158–9** : on the inconceivability of the contrary, 218 : on cause, 222 : as combining the ideas of Descartes and Bacon, 224–5) : c. xi. (wrong psychology in, 228–33) : c. xiii. (on substance, 246–51 : on the medium in sense-perception, 251–8) : **3** : dualism in, **228**

Will 189

Zoöcosm = the system of kinds, as explicable by natural laws, p. xvii. 253. 105 f.